CITIES
OF GOD

Also by Rodney Stark

The Rise of Christianity: How the Obscure, Marginal
Jesus Movement Became the Dominant Religious
Force in the Western World in a Few Centuries

One True God: Historical Consequences of Monotheism

For the Glory of God: How Monotheism Led to Reformations,
Science, Witch-Hunts, and the End of Slavery
(Winner of the 2004 award of merit for history/biography from *Christianity Today*)

The Victory of Reason: How Christianity Led to
Freedom, Capitalism, and Western Success

CITIES
OF GOD

The Real Story of How Christianity

Became an Urban Movement

and Conquered Rome

Rodney Stark

HarperSanFrancisco
A Division of HarperCollinsPublishers

FIRST EDITION

Library of Congress Cataloging-in-Publication Data is available.
ISBN-10: 0–06–085842–7
ISBN-13: 978–0–06–085842–1

06 07 08 09 10 RRD(H) 10 9 8 7 6 5 4 3 2 1

Contents

—⌇—

List of Maps and Illustrations

—m—

Maps

Illustrations

RECONSTRUCTING HISTORY. The task of the historian is to assemble and interpret the surviving evidence, an often difficult and frustrating quest, as illustrated by the Dead Sea Scrolls. After more than fifty years of effort, parts of them remain irretrievably lost, other parts are indecipherable, and the texts that have been saved still elude our full understanding. But we know a lot more about the context of early Christianity than we did before the scrolls were discovered in the caves at Qumran.

Chapter One

—m—

Missions and Methods

N EW ACCOUNTS of early Christianity are everywhere. A book claiming that Jesus got married, fathered children, and died of old age has sold millions of copies. Bookstores are bursting with 'new,' more 'enlightened' scriptures said to have been wrongly suppressed by the early church fathers. Often referred to as Gnostic gospels, these texts purport to have been written by a variety of biblical characters—Mary Magdalene, St. James, St. John, Shem, and even Didymus Jude Thomas, self-proclaimed twin brother of Christ. Meanwhile, a group calling itself the Jesus Seminar receives national media attention each year as it meets to further reduce the 'authentic' words spoken by Jesus to an increasingly slim compendium of wise sayings.

But is any of this true? How can we know? Presumably, by assembling and evaluating the appropriate evidence. Unfortunately, far too many historians these days don't believe in evidence. They argue that since absolute truth must always elude the historian's grasp, 'evidence' is inevitably nothing but a biased selection of suspect 'facts.' Worse yet, rather than dismissing the entire historical undertaking as impossible, these same people use their disdain for evidence as a license to propose all manner of politicized historical fantasies or appealing fictions on the grounds that these are just as 'true' as any other account. This is absurd nonsense. Reality exists and history actually occurs. The historian's task is to try to discover as accurately as possible what took place. Of course, we can never possess absolute truth, but that still must be the ideal goal that directs historical scholarship. The search for truth and the advance of human knowledge are inseparable: comprehension and civilization are one.

Fortunately, even if the complete truth eludes us, some historical accounts have a far higher probability than others of being true, depending on the available evidence. And it is in pursuit of more and better evidence that I have returned to the history of the early church. The chapters that follow present many revisions and reinterpretations of early Christian history. But the really 'new' contribution is to *test* these conclusions by analyzing quantitative data.

Early Christianity was primarily an urban movement. The original meaning of the word pagan (*paganus*) was "rural person," or more colloquially "country hick." It came to have religious meaning because after Christianity had triumphed in the cities, most of the rural people remained unconverted. Therefore, in the chapters that follow, the thirty-one cities of the empire having populations of at least 30,000 as of the year 100 are the basis for formulating and testing claims about the early church, based on *quantified* measures of various features of these cities. When was a Christian congregation established in each city? Which cities were missionized by Paul? Which were the port cities? Did a city have a substantial Diasporan Jewish community? Where did paganism remain strongest, longest? Where were the Gnostic teachers and movements located? These quantitative measures make it possible to discover, for example, whether the Gnostics were clustered in the more Christian or in the more pagan cities.

It is in this spirit that missions and methods are the principal topics of this opening chapter. Nevertheless, the relatively brief quantitative aspects of this and subsequent chapters are very secondary to, and embedded in, large historical concerns.

Missions and Monotheism

Since earliest days, humans have been exchanging religious ideas and practices. For millennia there was nothing special about the spread of religion; it diffused through intergroup contact in the same way as did new ways to weave or to make pottery. Even with the advent of cities, religion did not become the focus of any special effort to proselytize. From time to time, a priest or two probably pursued new followers, and individuals often recommended a particular god or rite to others. But since no one supposed that there was only one valid religion or only one true God, there were no missionaries.[1] Nor was there really such a thing as conversion.

In a religious context populated by many gods, to accept a new god usually does not involve discarding an old one. As the celebrated Arthur Darby Nock pointed out, within polytheism new gods are merely "supplements rather than alternatives."[2] Nock suggested that the word *conversion* is stretched beyond any useful meaning if it is applied to such relatively trivial actions. Instead, the term should be reserved for *the formation of a new commitment across the boundaries of major religious traditions*. For example, a shift from polytheism to Judaism, to Christianity, or to Islam is a conversion. So is a shift from one of the monotheistic traditions to another, or (rarely) from one of these traditions to polytheism. However, a shift in patronage from one god of a pantheon to another is not conversion, but *reaffiliation*. The same is true of shifts within the boundaries of a monotheistic tradition, as from Methodist to Baptist, from Orthodox to Reformed, or from Sunni to Shi'ite—these too are acts of reaffiliation. In contrast, *missionaries* are those who seek *converts*, who *attempt to get others to shift from one tradition to another*.[3] Some people serve as part-time, 'amateur' missionaries. Others are full-time 'professionals.' But either sort of missionary is produced only within monotheism.

Even so, not just any sort of monotheism produces missionaries, especially the rank-and-file missionaries on which real success depends. For example, once Christianity became safely ensconced as the Roman state church, its missionary activities very rapidly decayed.[4] Likewise, what probably was the first-ever appearance of monotheism—in Egypt during the thirteenth century BCE*— did not produce rank-and-file missionaries, and probably very few sincere professional missionaries either. Pharaoh Amenhotep IV (who adopted the name Akhenaten) attempted to establish worship of an invisible, omnipotent One True God. But he did it by edict and force—by creating a self-sufficient, state-supported religion and by attempting to suppress the other temples. Upon his death, the priests of the discarded gods combined to destroy all vestiges of monotheism—and did so without opposition, because there were few or no converts to resist them.[5] Hence, the world's first missionaries were Jews, and the world's first converts became Jews.

---

*It now is the convention to substitute BCE ("before the common era") for the traditional BC.

Jewish Missions

It recently has become fashionable for many secular Jews, being eager to prohibit all religious proselytizing, to deny that Judaism ever was a missionizing faith.[6] But, as every orthodox Jewish scholar agrees,[7] the historical facts are clear: Judaism was the "first great missionary religion."[8] Maimonides, the famous medieval Jewish scholar, put it plainly: "Moses our teacher was commanded by the Almighty to compel all the inhabitants of the world to accept the commandments."[9] It could hardly have been otherwise. The obligation to missionize is always implicit in monotheism and is explicit in the Old Testament. *Isaiah* (49:6) reads: "*I will give you as a light to the nations, that my salvation may reach to the end of the earth.*" Later in *Isaiah* (66:18–19) God reveals his plan to "*gather all nations and tongues*" and to send missionaries "*to the coastlands far away that have not heard of my fame or seen my glory; and they shall declare my glory among the nations.*" And in *Psalm* 117: "*Praise the LORD, all you nations! Extol him, all you peoples!*"[10]

These and similar verses inspired the renowned third-century-CE* rabbi, Eleazar ben Pedat, to assert that "God sent Israel into Exile among the nations only for the purpose of acquiring converts."[11] Some of Pedat's contemporaries even claimed that "converts are dearer to God than born Jews."[12] Nor was it only rabbis who praised Jewish missions or noted their success. Writing in the first century CE, Josephus reported the very widespread impact of Judaism on the host cultures of the Diaspora: "[T]he multitude of mankind itself have had a great inclination for a long time to follow our religious observances."[13] That same century Philo wrote at length about converts and missions to the Gentiles, even claiming

---

*It now is the convention to use CE ("common era") in place of the traditional AD.

that many converts left Egypt as part of the Exodus.[14] Like Josephus, Philo also described the widespread observance of Jewish customs, and both of them confirmed that it was common for Jews to invite Gentiles to attend services in the synagogues. This was facilitated by the fact that the language of the Diasporan synagogues was not Hebrew, but Greek, and therefore comprehensible not only to everyone residing in Hellenic regions, but also to all educated Romans, since they more frequently spoke Greek than Latin.

As the practice of inviting guests to worship makes clear, Jews in the Diaspora sought converts, and they seem to have been quite successful in doing so.[15] The best estimate is that by the first century, Jews made up from 10 to 15 percent of the population of the Roman Empire, nearly 90 percent of them living in cities outside Palestine.[16] This would have amounted to from six to nine million people. To achieve these numbers, a considerable amount of conversion would have been required. As Adolf von Harnack recognized, "[I]t is utterly impossible to explain the large total of Jews in the Diaspora by the mere fact of the fertility of Jewish families. We must assume ... that a very large number of pagans ... trooped over to Yahweh."[17] Thus, Josephus was probably accurate when he claimed: "All the time they [the Jews] were attracting to their worship a great number of Greeks, making them virtually members of their own community."[18]

Christian sources also acknowledge the existence of many "God-fearers" in the synagogues, as in the case of Lydia and the women at Philippi.[19] Paul began his sermon in the synagogue in Antioch, "*Men of Israel, and you that fear God, listen.*"[20] Later in the sermon he repeated this distinction: "*Brethren, sons of the family of Abraham, and those among you that fear God ...*"[21] The God-fearers were Greeks and Romans like the Roman soldier Cornelius,[22] who had embraced Jewish monotheism, but who remained marginal to Jewish life because they were unwilling to fully embrace Jewish ethnicity—not only adult circumcision, but some other aspects of the Law as well.[23] For the fact was that *religious* conversion wasn't sufficient. Rather than letting other 'nations' extol God, the Jewish leadership demanded that all 'nations' become fully Jewish; there was no room for Egyptian-Jews or Roman-Jews, let alone Germanic- or British-Jews, but only for Jewish-Jews. Given the remarkable success they achieved, this ethnic barrier to conversion probably was the sole reason that the Roman Empire did not embrace the God of Abraham. It was not a mistake that Paul let Christianity repeat.

The Christian Difference

Nearly every aspect of the early Christian church was shaped by the obligation imposed on the disciples by Jesus: "*All authority in heaven and on earth has been given to me. Go therefore and make disciples of all nations, baptizing them in the name of the Father and of the Son and of the Holy Spirit, and teaching them to observe all that I have commanded you.*"[24]

While there are good reasons to suppose that the vast majority of early Christian converts were Jews, the marginal "God-fearers" were among the first to join, once it became clear that Christians didn't have to become ethnic Jews. And there lay the monumental difference between these two great missionizing faiths. Early on, Paul had put it this way: "*Or is God the God of the Jews only? Is he not the God of the Gentiles also? Yes, of the Gentiles also, since God is one; and he will justify the circumcised on the ground of their faith and the uncircumcised through their faith.*"[25] What Christianity offered the world was monotheism stripped of ethnic encumbrances. People of all nations could embrace the One True God while remaining people of all nations.

And so Christians went out to save the world, or at least the 'world' as defined by Rome, and less than three hundred years later they had converted millions of people and enjoyed substantial majorities in the cities. Ever since, historians have asked: How did they do it? How did this tiny messianic sect from the far eastern edge of the empire overwhelm classical paganism and come to rule triumphantly as the state church?

As will be seen, many factors were involved in the triumph of Christianity, but to begin it is necessary to ask: How does missionizing work? How does anyone actually make converts? Some dismiss such a question by calling the success of the Christian mission a miracle. If so, it was a decidedly incomplete miracle, a miracle entirely at odds with Christ's directive in *Matthew* assigning the job of converting the world to all Christians, and a miracle that is quite inconsistent with the doctrine of free will.

Networks and Conversion

For generations it was assumed that religious conversions were the result of doctrinal appeal—that people embraced a new faith because they found its teachings particularly appealing, especially if these teachings seemed to solve serious problems or dissatisfactions that afflicted the new believers. On this, both theologians and social scientists agreed. So much so, that 'everyone' was content to 'discover' how a particular religious movement gained adherents by inspecting its doctrines and then *deducing* who converted to this group on the basis of who most needed what was offered.

It was by this method that it was taken as certain that, in the words of Friedrich Engels, "Christianity was originally a movement of oppressed peoples: it first appeared as the religion of slaves and emancipated slaves, of poor people deprived of all rights, of peoples subjugated or dispersed by Rome"[26] After all, the Bible often directly addresses the poor and downhearted and promises that they will be compensated in heaven, where the *"first shall be last, and the last, first."*[27] Despite this 'evidence,' a consensus has formed among historians of the early church that regardless of biblical assurances to the lower classes, the early Christians were drawn mainly from the ranks of the privileged. E. A. Judge identified the early Christians as recruited mainly from among "a socially pretentious section of the population of big cities,"[28] and Abraham Malherbe concluded that the language used by early Christian writers clearly reflects a literate, educated audience.[29] In his detailed study of the church in Corinth in the first century, Gerd Theissen identified wealthy Christians, including members of the "upper classes."[30] Many other historians of the early church have expressed similar views.[31]

Nevertheless, the method of correlating doctrinal appeals with a target population continued to go unchallenged, because no one ventured out of the library to watch people undergo conversions in order to discover what really was involved. When researchers finally did, what they discovered was that doctrines are of very secondary importance in the initial decision to convert.

In the fall of 1962 two sociologists began an observational study of a small religious group newly arrived in San Francisco from Eugene, Oregon.[32] The group was led by Dr. Young Oon Kim, a Korean woman who had once been a professor of religion at Ewha University in Seoul. She had been sent to America to seek converts to a new religious movement founded in Korea by Rev. Sun M. Moon. Moon had been trained as an electrical engineer, and one day he became convinced that God had chosen him to be the Lord of the Second Advent and to complete Christ's mission on earth by founding a new church that would unite all of the competing denominations and finally convert the entire world. He was quite successful in attracting followers in Korea, and so after a few years he dispatched missionaries to other nations. Dr. Kim and her followers were the very first American members of the Unification Church, often called the "Moonies" by the news media.

Moon's claims were sufficient to place him outside the Christian tradition per se, and thus his followers qualified as converts. The sociologists, as they began to observe the group, carefully studied the Unification Church doctrines, as presented in a scripture written by Rev. Moon called *The Divine Principles*. (It had been translated into English shortly before the sociologists began to study the group.) To their surprise, as they observed several newcomers go through the process of converting, doctrine seemed of little concern to them. Instead, they talked mostly of their growing friendship with other members and of their admiration for Dr. Kim. One put it bluntly: "These are the nicest people I have ever met. What I don't understand is why they are so wound up about this religion." Several months later this person got wound up about the religion too, but still had only sketchy ideas about the group's doctrines. Conversations with other members revealed that they likewise had not been much interested in religion before their conversions. As a late-twenties male told the researchers: "If anybody had said I was going to join up and become a missionary I would have laughed my head off. I had no use for church at all."

After the sociologists watched several more conversions and reconstructed some past events, it became obvious to them that of all the people the Unificationists encountered in their missionary efforts, the only ones who converted were those *whose interpersonal ties to members overbalanced their ties to nonmembers*. This was evident when the first converts gathered in Oregon. Dr. Kim had spent her first year in Oregon visiting various Christian clubs and study groups, attempting to interest people in her message. She gained little attention and no converts. Then, to save money, she rented a basement room in a house at the far edge of town. Her landlady was a young housewife who spent much of her time with the two housewives who lived on either side of her. None of them had children, none of them worked, and all three of them were bored. All were newcomers to Oregon, two of them had troubled marriages, and all three were very flattered by Dr. Kim's interest in them. They also were deeply impressed by her education and by her willingness to discuss serious ideas. Eventually Kim revealed her real mission in the United States, and for the first time she found a willing audience. Soon one of the husbands began to take part in evening sessions, and after a few weeks he brought his closest friend from work to participate. The friend was a single young man who had no other friends or relatives in the community. After a few more weeks these five declared themselves the American branch of the Unification Church, the two unhappy wives left their husbands, and soon the whole group moved to San Francisco, accompanied by several additional converts, all of whom had long-standing ties to group members.

One must, of course, leave room for those rare conversions resulting from mystical experiences such as Paul's on the road to Damascus. But these instances aside, conversion is primarily about bringing one's religious behavior into alignment with that of one's friends and relatives, not about encountering attractive doctrines. Of course, one can easily imagine doctrines so bizarre as to keep most people from joining. But, barring that, conversion is primarily an act of conformity—but so is nonconversion. In the end it is a matter of the relative strength of social ties.

Becoming a Unificationist violated conventional norms defining legitimate religious affiliations and identities, and to join could cost someone his or her friends. In fact, many people spent considerable time around the Unificationists and even spoke highly of *The Divine Principles,* but never joined. In every instance these people had many strong social ties to nonmembers who did not approve of the group. Of those who converted after the group moved to San Francisco, many were newcomers to the city who formed strong ties to members of the group and whose outside attachments were all to people far away who had no notion that there was a conversion in progress. Others were isolates who quickly became deeply involved in their new friendships.

It is important to realize several important things about doctrine and conversion. After conversion has occurred is when most people get more deeply involved in the doctrines of their new group, and most conversionist groups must devote considerable time and effort to the religious education of new converts. Portions of Paul's letters are excellent examples of this activity, for as Nock tells us, the disciples baptized "all who wished to join their number ... [and] there can have been no preliminary training as a condition of admission."[33] Indeed, Philip Jenkins suggested that in the early church, central Christian doctrines, including the crucifixion and resurrection, were "holy truths ... not to be lightly shared, and at least some churches prevented converts to Christianity from hearing the gospels and their mysteries until they had been formally initiated into the new religion, by means of baptism."[34]

Once converts learn what the doctrines are, many decide (or learn) that the real reason they joined was because the doctrines were so convincing and utterly irresistible. But these same people seldom express such views before or during their conversion. In fact, most converts are not especially interested in religion prior to their conversion. More typically they resemble the Unificationist who had "no use for church at all." Converts are rarely atheists, but most are only very weakly attached to any religion. That is, most new religious groups draw their converts mainly from the ranks of the religiously inactive or alienated: the majority of converts to American 'new' religions report that their parents had no religious affiliation.[35] As will be seen, that same principle applied to converts to early Christianity.

By now dozens of close-up studies of conversion have been conducted. All of them confirm that social networks are the basic mechanism through which conversion takes place.[36] To convert someone, you must first become that person's close and trusted friend. But even your best friends will not convert if they already are highly committed to another faith. Clearly, these same principles applied as fully in the first century as in modern times. The portrayal in *Acts* of Paul's missionary career as well as his letters to various congregations all testify to the centrality of friendship and social networks in conversions to Christianity. These same sources also reveal the bitter opposition that Christian missionizing aroused among the most 'religious' Hellenic Jews.

Early Christian Missions

Learning that most conversions are not produced by professional missionaries conveying a new message, but by rank-and-file members who share their faith with their friends and relatives, we discover why 'conversion' involves monotheism. Only monotheism can generate the level of commitment to a particular faith sufficient to mobilize the rank and file to engage in missionizing activities. In fact, even professional missionaries make converts only when, as in the case of Dr. Kim, they have succeeded in building personal bonds of trust and friendship with those they seek to convert. Just as it took Dr. Kim more than a year to build such bonds in Eugene, so too Paul did not rush from place to place leaving a trail of sudden converts. Instead, he spent more than two years building a Christian group in Ephesus, eighteen months in Corinth, and several years in Antioch—and many historians believe his stays in some other places were considerably longer than has been assumed.[37] However, some of Paul's missionary stops did not require him to recruit a congregation, but were visits to groups of local Christians who already were meeting, as was the case even in Antioch.[38]

The principle that conversions spread through social networks is quite consistent with the fact that the earliest followers of Jesus shared many family ties and long-standing associations.[39] And it is consistent with the strategy pursued by the earliest missionaries who decided to target the Jews of the Diaspora. Not only did they share a common culture, but it seems likely that the missionaries were able to utilize many ties of family and friendship between Diasporan communities and Jews in Israel. Put another way, Paul, Barnabus, Timothy, Silas, and all the others who took Christianity to the Roman Empire traveled along social networks that gave them entry to, and credibility within, the Hellenized Jewish communities. The first paragraph of Adolf von Harnack's masterpiece notes that "the synagogues of the Diaspora . . . formed the most important presupposition for the rise and growth of Christian communities throughout the empire. The network of the synagogues furnished the Christian [movement] with centres and courses for its development, and in this way the mission of the new religion, which was undertaken in the name of the God of Abraham and Moses, found a sphere already prepared for itself."[40]

Although the very first Christian converts in the West may have been made by full-time missionaries, the conversion process soon became self-sustaining as new converts accepted the obligation to spread their faith and did so by missionizing their immediate circle of intimates. This offended many pagans and has confused some historians. Pagans saw something sinister in "the personal approaches made by Christians to non-Christians."[41] As for historians, three of the most prominent recent historians of religions in the Roman Empire find it surprising that Christianity continued to grow, since "[a]fter Paul there seems to have been no organized or systematic programme of attracting non-believers."[42] Perhaps it lacked a bureaucratic structure, but personal evangelizing *was* the "programme." Once under way, this program allowed full-time missionaries such as Paul to assume the role of advisers and visiting supervisors of local churches built by, and sustained by, local 'amateurs,' as is fully evident in Paul's letters.

A later chapter will more fully explore the mission to the Hellenized Jews. Here it is sufficient to also note that many of the Jews of the Diaspora were only weakly connected to Judaism, either as a religion or as an ethnicity, and were quite available for conversion to a new religion.

Subjective Methodology: Higher Criticism and Historical Study

During the nineteenth century, many historians, especially in Germany, began to employ various approximations of scientific methods to reconstruct the past "as it really happened," to quote the great Leopold von Ranke. This new approach to history soon showed up in studies of early Christianity, giving special emphasis to efforts to identify Christianity's social setting (*Sitz-im-Leben*) and the religious environment in which Christianity emerged and developed. Eventually, the 'scientific' approach to early church history took many variations (and names), most of them having nothing to do with science, as is evident from the fact that they soon became known as the Higher Criticism, a perspective often associated today with such undertakings as the Jesus Seminar and claims that Gnosticism represents the authentic brand of Christianity.[43] In fact, most of these scholars were (and are) 'scientific' only insofar as they misunderstood this to justify a skeptical or even an antagonistic approach to scripture: they didn't even pretend to fulfill the standards

Post-Modern Relativism

of objectivity that are essential to scientific inquiry. Rather, their highly biased accounts provided apt examples for the anti-scientific tirades from historians of the 'progressive' persuasion, who loudly asserted that any 'true' history is impossible and that therefore, whether wittingly or unconsciously, historians can do nothing other than interpret history to suit their preconceptions.

And it suited many proponents of the Higher Criticism to take the position that unless something reported in the Bible can be completely verified by nonbiblical sources, it must be rejected as mythical—sometimes even extending this rule to deny the historical existence of Jesus.[44] Over the years, *Acts* has been a central focus, and the Higher Criticism soon resembled a competition to determine who could discredit the most passages—a race won by Hans Conzelmann with his absurd claim that, from beginning to end, *Acts* is a made-up story. Paul's missionary voyages never happened! Paul's shipwreck is pure fantasy![45] But, despite the immense influence of personal bias on their historical visions, not even advocates of the Higher Criticism can sustain just *any* claim. For example, in dismissing the *Acts* account of Paul's shipwreck, Conzelmann and others 'proved' that the story must be a fantasy by demonstrating that it has the boat following 'implausible' routes and otherwise goes against common sense. Fortunately for their critics, these historians knew even less about sailing than they did about science. To them the Mediterranean is like an indoor swimming pool and one would, naturally, head directly to one's destination, giving no heed to currents or to the fact that it is impossible to sail directly into the wind. When it subsequently was shown that the *Acts* account is fully in accord with meteorological and nautical conditions and principles,[46] the response was to grudgingly accept the account in *Acts* as accurate, but to claim that it didn't happen to Paul—rather, that the account in *Acts* must have been lifted from another unknown, but nonbiblical source![47]

Examples of such militant anti-scriptural bias among putative Bible scholars fill many long books. They stand revealed as bias because it is not true that each age can write history to suit its current sensibilities and concerns. No doubt many historians attempt to write such histories, and some of them gain fame and credibility. But sooner or later most of them fall victim to incompatible facts (such as winds and weather, as above). Meanwhile, the entire basis for this book is to assemble reliable and pertinent facts and then to demonstrate that they disallow some conventional claims about early Christian history, while encouraging others.

Objective Methodology:
The Scientific Method and Historical Study

Even when historians try to be objective, the introduction of a scientific approach to Christian history often has not been very enlightening, because scientific methods have been very poorly understood and inappropriately applied, not only by historians, but equally by many social scientists who have tried their hands at history.[48] The original sin is to confuse naming with explaining— to mistake concepts for theories.

Concepts and Theories

Scientific *concepts* isolate and identify some aspect of reality; they are names attached to carefully formulated definitions. The term *sect* is a concept. It refers exclusively to religious organizations in a high state of tension with their surrounding society. As a proper scientific concept it is abstract; it exists only in our minds. We can't observe the concept of *sect*. What we can observe are concrete instances of this concept: actual groups of people who fit the definition. It is essential to keep in mind that, because *sect* is an abstract concept, it is *only a name*. To correctly identify some group as a sect does not explain anything about it. It doesn't tell us, for example, why this sect provokes hostility among outsiders. To say it does so *because* it is a sect is circular nonsense—true by definition.

Theories, on the other hand, are explanations. They are statements that link some set of concepts and say why and how they are related. Ordinarily the term *theory* is reserved for highly abstract statements that apply to many specific instances, such as a general theory of sect transformation that explains why and how sects in any society tend to move from higher to lower tension with their surroundings.[49] Historians often usefully apply such a general theory to illuminate a specific instance—to explain how the militant Methodist sect of nineteenth-century America became today's very liberal, low-tension religious denomination.[50] But often, too, historians construct explanations that are rather less general and that are more closely tied to a specific case. For the sake of clarity, such an explanation may be called a *thesis,* or, to use Robert K. Merton's label, a theory of the middle range.[51] An example would be the thesis that the treatment of slaves in the New World was far better in Catholic than in Protestant societies *because* of the greater liberality and intrusiveness of Catholic slave codes.[52] It is a thesis rather than a theory because it is not sufficiently abstract to have very general application, but applies only to a quite limited time and place.

Between the application of general theories and the formation of theses, no historical matter of much interest lacks multiple explanations. However, this proliferation of explanations is indicative of the failure to fulfill the scientific method by means of empirical testing. Not just any abstract statement that says why and how some concepts are related is a *scientific* theory. To qualify as a scientific theory the set of abstract statements must give rise to empirical consequences—to outcomes that are, at least in principle, observable. Put another way, a set of statements does not qualify as a scientific theory or even a scientific thesis unless it predicts or prohibits certain empirical states of affairs. Most scientific research is undertaken to check the predictions of a given explanation and to reject those whose predictions do not jibe with results. Contradictory theories and theses cannot all be true (although all of them could be false). Therefore, when numerous conflicting theories or theses persist, it is certain that they are not being put to adequate empirical tests. That clearly applies to historical studies of the early church. The reason most often given for this state of affairs is that the needed empirical data are long lost in the mists of the past.

Concepts and Indicators

As noted, concepts are abstractions that identify some aspects of reality as forming a class, as being made up of things that are alike—or at least alike for the purposes of theorizing about them. The concept of *mammal* includes all warm-blooded animals that give birth to living young. Zookeepers are quick to point out that there is incredible variety within this biological class: mice, tigers, elephants, apes, dogs, and so on. But these variations within the category of mammal are irrelevant to many biological theories. That is, for many *theoretical purposes,* all mammals are alike! The same is true of sects. Whether a particular group consists of celibate Marcionists or promiscuous Valentinians, sects are alike in that they exist in a high state of tension with their surrounding environment and each raises the same questions about sect formation, growth, or persecution. As these examples of sects reveal, although concepts are abstract ideas that exist only in our minds and are not directly measurable, all scientific concepts have empirical (observable) instances. We cannot see, touch, or smell the concept of mammal, but we can see, touch, and smell many animals that are classified as mammals. Likewise, we cannot see the concept of sect, but we can observe many actual sects.

An *indicator* is any *observable measure of a concept*. Thus, while scientific research is performed to test a theory or a thesis, the actual research necessarily is based entirely on the examination of indicators. Suppose we predict that sect members feel themselves to be much superior to outsiders in terms of possessing religious truth. To test this prediction we need to examine the beliefs of some appropriate group of sect members to see if they manifest feelings of religious superiority. This would be quite easy for a sociologist to do, but it usually is impossible for historians. Just as one cannot interview the dead, historians cannot go out and collect *new* data on anything! They are entirely at the mercy of the past, able to consult only those facts and observations that were gathered back then and have survived. This is an especially acute problem for those who work on the distant past, in eras from which very little data would be available even if it all had survived. For example, the emperors had only rough estimates of the population of Rome; they gathered no statistics on its ethnic or religious makeup, or on the number of slaves, let alone on more sophisticated matters such as divorce rates or the price of food.

This state of affairs is why historians have allowed their explanations to proliferate and why their disputes linger on and on. Fortunately, the available resources are not nearly as slim as has been assumed. Many adequate indicators of key concepts have been overlooked because so few scholars have been properly trained to recognize, or to draw inferences from, less obvious, less direct indicators. For example, scholars have long disputed the level of church participation prevalent among ordinary Europeans several hundred years ago. Theses proposing either high levels or low levels of participation have proliferated, but it seemed they could not be put to the test since no records of church activity ever were kept. Then, while examining seventeenth-century parish account ledgers for some French villages, Jacques Toussaert realized he could measure levels of religious participation by estimating the percentage of villagers who took communion at Easter based on receipts for communion wine.[53] Calculating the maximum number of sips per bottle gave him a quite plausible indicator of the maximum number who *could* have taken part. His results favored the low-attendance thesis. Or, in an instance of central importance to the present study, Adolf von Harnack was able to gauge the "expansion" of Christianity by when and where churches appeared.[54]

The Hypothesis

Theories and theses produce specific predictions about the relationships that will or will not exist among some set of indicators. A prediction about the relationship that exists among indicators is known as a *hypothesis.* Consider the thesis about the treatment of New World slaves and Catholic slave codes. It can be transformed into a testable hypothesis as follows: *Prior to the Civil War, the percentage of free ex-slaves was substantially higher in Catholic Louisiana than in any of the other states in the Protestant Deep South.* Knowing what indicators we should look at and what we expect to find, a brief examination of the census of 1830 will reveal strong support for the hypothesis: the percentage of free blacks was many times higher in Louisiana than in Mississippi, Alabama, Georgia, or other states of the Deep South.[55]

After all the theorizing is done, it is hypotheses that serve as the specific bases for research.

Quantification

The chapters that follow will attempt to place the rise of Christianity within the appropriate social and cultural contexts, but
they will do so in a more fully social scientific way than has ever
been attempted. Although there will be considerable new theorizing and discussion of prominent theses, the chapters attempt to
identify adequate, quantifiable indicators of key concepts and then to
properly test important hypotheses. This approach is in many ways
simply an extension of the *Sitz-im-Leben* approach initiated more
than a century ago, albeit without the skeptical agenda. *Sitz-im-
Leben* can be translated literally as "setting in life" or "life setting,"
and it refers to placing the objects of study—be they texts, communities, or individuals—within their social context. Perhaps the
most fundamental *Sitz-im-Leben* for Christianity was the cities of
the Greco-Roman world of the first several centuries. Of course,
even these ancient cities were not all alike, and some of the fundamental ways in which they differed can be measured and used to
test hypotheses about the rise of Christianity. Hence, one of the
very first things it will be necessary to measure is Christianization.
An adequate indicator can be found in *when* the new faith was able
to establish a significant congregation in each of these cities.
Given this indicator, it is possible to investigate what attributes of
cities influenced whether they were Christianized early or late.

Conclusion

A major purpose of this book is to demonstrate that quantitative
methods can help to resolve many debates about early church history. Even so, the heart of the book is not statistical, but theoretical and substantive. Hypotheses do not simply fall out of the sky;
they ought to be derived from theories and theses; and these, in

turn, must be situated in an adequate historical context if the subsequent hypothesis-testing is to be of intellectual significance. However, given adequate contexts, testing well-formulated hypotheses through quantitative analysis of adequate indicators will put historical studies of the early church on firmer footing—even when the results show that what most historians believe about something is in fact true!

ROMAN TWINS. This fifth-century BCE depiction of Romulus and his twin, Remus, being suckled by a wolf was the universal symbol of the city of Rome, emphasizing that theirs was an urban empire. Although more than 90 percent of Romans lived in rural areas, all imperial power resided in Rome and in the other urban centers.

Chapter Two

—w—

The Urban Empire

ITHIN TWENTY YEARS of the crucifixion, Christianity was
transformed from a faith based in rural Galilee, to an urban
movement reaching far beyond Palestine. In the beginning it was
borne by nameless itinerant preachers and by rank-and-file Christians who shared their faith with relatives and friends. Soon they
were joined by 'professional' missionaries such as Paul and his associates. Thus, while Jesus's ministry was limited primarily to the
rural areas and the outskirts of towns, the Jesus movement quickly
spread to the Greco-Roman cities, especially to those in the eastern,
Hellenic end of the empire.

All ambitious missionary movements are, or soon become, urban.
If the goal is to "make disciples of all nations," missionaries need
to go where there are many potential converts, which is precisely
what Paul did. His missionary journeys took him to major cities

(handwritten margin note: Jerusalem?)

such as Antioch, Corinth, and Athens, with only occasional visits
to smaller communities such as Iconium and Laodicea. No mention is made of him preaching in the countryside.

Paul was not a special case: it was several centuries before the
early church made serious efforts to convert the rural peasantry—
although many were converted by friends and kinfolk returning from
urban sojourns. Fully sharing the views of their non-Christian
neighbors, many early Christians dismissed rural people as subhu-
man brutes. "The peasantry of the countryside were beyond the
pale, a tribe apart, outsiders. Such attitudes underpinned the failure of the urban Christian communities to reach out and spread
the gospel in the countryside. . . . For them the countryside simply
did not exist as a zone for missionary enterprise. After all, there
was nothing in the New Testament about spreading the Word to
the beasts of the field."[1]

Any study of how Christians converted the empire is really a
study of how they Christianized the cities. Consequently, this
chapter is devoted to the Greco-Roman cities. I will begin by examining the nature of cities and of urban life in this era and analyzing the religious situation in the urban empire. I will then identify
a specific set of cities on the basis of population size and provide
brief sketches of each, as these will be the 'cases' on which all of
the subsequent hypothesis-testing will be based.

Urban Life

Greco-Roman cities were small, extremely crowded, filthy beyond imagining, disorderly, filled with strangers, and afflicted with
frequent catastrophes—fires, plagues, conquests, and earthquakes.

Only two major cities in the empire, Rome and Alexandria,
had more than 150,000 inhabitants, and many had fewer than
50,000. But, it wasn't only lack of population that made these

cities 'small'; they covered very small areas and consequently were extremely dense. Consider Antioch. Having a population of about 100,000, it was two miles long and a mile wide, which yields a result of 78.2 persons per acre. Subtract the 40 percent of the city devoted to streets, temples, and public buildings, and the density of the inhabited area rises to 130 per acre—greater than in modern Calcutta. Even so, Antioch was far below the density of Rome, which was somewhere from 200 to 300 persons per acre![2] To get a sense of this density, imagine yourself living on a popular ocean beach.

Great density was reflected in the extremely narrow streets of Greco-Roman cities. Even the famous roads leading out of Rome, such as the Via Appia and Via Latina, were little more than paths, being about 16 feet wide. Within the city, Roman law required that streets be 9.5 feet wide, but many were much narrower than that.[3] The main street of Antioch was admired throughout the empire for its spaciousness—it was 30 feet wide![4]

Unlike dense modern cities such as Manhattan, which are very spread out vertically, Greco-Roman cities had no tall structures—usually no more than three stories. Even so, inhabitants lived in constant danger of having their tenements collapse for lack of adequate beams, to say nothing of the threat of falling down during earthquakes, which were very frequent in the eastern portion of the empire. And if tenements didn't fall down, very often they burned. Although some temples and public buildings were built of stone, most structures were built of wood thinly covered with stucco, and they burned so well that many of these cities were often destroyed by fire and had to be rebuilt repeatedly upon the ashes. Hence, the "dread of fire was an obsession among rich and poor alike."[5] The threat of fire was increased by the fact that the chimney had yet to be invented, so all cooking and heating was done over insecure wood- or charcoal-burning braziers. The result was smoky rooms, but asphyxiation was usually prevented by the lack of window panes, windows being covered only with "hang-ing cloths or skins blown by [the wind.]"[6] Of course, these drafts increased the danger of rapidly spreading fires.

As for sewers, except for several overcited examples of actual underground sewers flushed by running water, sewers in Greco-Roman cities were ditches running down the middle of each nar-row street—ditches into which everything was dumped, including chamber pots at night, often from second- or third-story windows. We know this was a common practice because officials so often condemned it.[7] As for water, it may have come to most cities via the picturesque Roman aqueducts, but once there it was stored in cisterns where it quickly turned "malodorous, unpalatable, and after a time, undrinkable."[8] In any event, except for a few of the wealthy to whose homes water was piped, everyone else had to lug water home in jugs from public fountains. That meant there was little water for scrubbing floors or washing clothes. It was a filthy life. And it stank! No wonder the ancients were so fond of incense.

Not only were these cities struck by deadly plagues, but less dramatic diseases were chronic. Sickness was highly visible on the streets: "Swollen eyes, skin rashes, lost limbs are mentioned over and over again in the sources as part of the urban scene."[9] In a time before photography or fingerprinting, written contracts offered descriptive information about the principal parties involved and "generally include[d] their distinctive disfigurements, mostly scars." In one substantial collection of papyrus contracts examined by Roger Bagnall, *all* of the signers were scarred.[10]

In addition to physical misery, Greco-Roman cities suffered from high levels of social chaos. Because of their very high mor-tality rates, these cities required a large and constant stream of new-comers in order to maintain their populations. As a result, there always were a number of people who were unattached, and many of them eked out a living by victimizing others. Compared with even the most crime-prone modern cities, these cities were over-run with crime. "Night fell over the city like the shadow of a great danger, diffused, sinister, and menacing. Everyone fled to his home, shut himself in, and barricaded the entrance. The shops fell silent, safety chains were drawn behind the leaves of the doors. . . . If the rich had to sally forth, they were accompanied by [armed] slaves who carried torches to protect them on their way."[11] In addition, the constant influx of newcomers resulted in remarkable ethnic diversity in a time that was equally remarkable for its ethnocentrism. Diverse groups did not assimilate, but created and sustained their own separated enclaves—resulting in frequent turf conflicts and sometimes all-out riots and pogroms. At the same time, since (with the exception of Rome) Greco-Roman cities were so small, most people did not suffer from loneliness or alienation, but from the many burdens of living a too-intimate, insufficiently private life—the small town 'claustrophobia' that not long ago was still a principal literary theme.

And finally, disasters. Most of the cities examined later in this chapter were conquered by enemy forces, some of them many times. Antioch, for example, was conquered 11 times during a six-hundred-year span. Conquests sometimes resulted in such complete destruction that cities lay in uninhabited rubble for a time, as in the cases of Carthage, Corinth, and Antioch. In addition, many of these cities were effectively destroyed by earthquakes and fires, and deadly plagues swept through them periodically.

Because life in antiquity abounded in anxiety and misery, suffering played a substantial role in Christianizing the empire, but *not* in the way that has so often been claimed. Many have linked misery and anxiety to Christianization by supposing that in the third century things went from bad to worse, thereby spurring many

to embrace the promise of eternal bliss offered by Christian teachings. In the words of E. R. Dodds, people turned to Christ out of
revulsion "from a world so impoverished intellectually, so insecure
materially, so filled with fear and hatred as the world of the third
century, any path that promised escape must have attracted serious
minds." Dodds's thesis, and all similar deprivation theories of the
rise of Christianity, has two serious deficiencies. First, and most
devastating, there is no evidence that conditions did get any worse
in this era. As Peter Brown put it, too many modern historians
have imposed a "false sense of melodrama" on this critical era.[12] Indeed, as did Dodds, these historians rely heavily on "must have" assertions—people must have felt alienated from city life; they must
have feared their increasingly despotic government; they must have
longed for a life beyond death. But to say something "must
have been" is not evidence. With Brown, I propose that the
Christianization of the empire was not the result of "reactions to
public calamity,"[13] but to *religious influences* per se. That is, religion
did not merely offer psychological antidotes for the misery of life;
it actually made life less miserable!

The power of Christianity lay not in its promise of otherworldly compensations for suffering in this life, as has so often
been proposed. No, the crucial change that took place in the third
century was the rapidly spreading awareness of a faith that delivered potent antidotes to life's miseries here and now! The truly
revolutionary aspect of Christianity lay in moral imperatives such
as *"Love one's neighbor as oneself," "Do unto others as you would have
them do unto you," "It is more blessed to give than to receive,"* and
"When you did it to the least of my brethren, you did it unto me." These
were not just slogans. Members did nurse the sick, even during
epidemics; they did support orphans, widows, the elderly, and the
poor; they did concern themselves with the lot of slaves. In short,
Christians created "a miniature welfare state in an empire which

for the most part lacked social services."[14] It was these *responses* to the long-standing misery of life in antiquity, not the onset of worse conditions, that were the 'material' changes that inspired Christian growth. But these material benefits were entirely spiritual in origin. Support for this view comes from the continuing inability of pagan groups to meet this challenge.

In 362, when Emperor Julian launched a campaign to revive paganism, he recognized that to do so it would be necessary to match Christian "benevolence." In a letter to a prominent pagan priest, Julian wrote: "I think that when the poor happened to be neglected and overlooked by the priests, the impious Galileans observed this and devoted themselves to benevolence.... [They] support not only their poor, but ours as well, everyone can see that our people lack aid from us."[15] But his challenge to the temples to match Christian benevolence asked the impossible. Paganism was utterly incapable of generating the commitment needed to motivate such behavior. Not only were many of its gods and goddesses of dubious character, but they offered nothing that could motivate humans to go beyond self-interested acts of propitiation. Indeed, many pagan temples were essentially 'eating clubs,' where a host furnished an animal to be sacrificed to the gods, after which the beast was cooked and eaten by the host's many invited guests. (Temples employed skilled chefs.) The funds for this came from the host, while the setting—the temple and its priests—was provided mainly by wealthy donors, motivated at least as much by a desire to display their social status as by any religious concerns. And little or nothing was expected of the rank and file—nor could it be.

The Religious Context

To say that the Greco-Roman world was polytheistic is a gross understatement—the Greek poet Hesiod claimed there were 30,000

distinct gods.[16] The precise pantheon of major gods differed somewhat from one city to another, but everywhere urbanites were
confronted with a vast array. In most cities there were temples for
from fifteen to twenty major gods, and additional temples or shrines
for a mass of others.[17] As Roger Brown put it so well, in this era
people "lived in a universe rustling with the presence of many divine beings," and, seen in perspective, even the early Christians
occupied "an ancient, pre-Christian spiritual landscape."[18]

In part, the classical world sustained many gods because each
specialized in a limited range of abilities. But the larger part was
played by the enormous ethnic and cultural diversity of imperial
cities and the extensive amount of trade and travel across the empire—all of which not only spread local gods far and wide, but led
to their recombination and amalgamation. This was well known
in classical times. In his *History,* the Greek historian Herodotus (ca.
484–425 BCE) gave considerable space to comparing gods and rituals and suggesting how they might have spread, based on his personal travels to about fifty different societies. For example:

> *I will never believe that the rites [of Dionysus] in Egypt and those*
> *in Greece can resemble each other by coincidence. . . . The names of*
> *nearly all the gods came from Egypt to Greece . . . but the making*
> *of the Hermes statues with the phallus erect, that they did not learn*
> *from the Egyptians but from the Pelasgians, and it was the Atheni-*
> *ans first of all the Greeks who took over this practice, and from the*
> *Athenians, all the rest.*[19]

Perhaps the most fundamental aspect of Greco-Roman paganism was its inability to sustain itself by contributions from the rank
and file. Most people were involved with too many gods to make
significant contributions to any one of them, nor did they feel sufficient basis for doing so. Instead, the primary source of funding

for paganism came almost entirely from a few very wealthy donors.[20] As the empire expanded and the number of temples multiplied, the financial burden grew increasingly heavy and donations were divided among an ever-larger throng of gods.

As E. R. Dodds recognized, religious life in the empire suffered from excessive pluralism, from "a bewildering mass of alternatives. There were too many cults, too many mysteries, too many philosophies of life to choose from: you could pile one religious insurance on another, yet not feel safe."[21] Moreover, since no god could effectively demand adherence (let alone exclusive commitment), individuals faced the need and the burden to assemble their own divine portfolio,[22] seeking to balance potential services and to spread the risks, as Dodds noted in his reference to religious insurance. Thus, a rich benefactor in Numidia contributed to temples and shrines honoring "Jove Bazosenus . . . Mithra, Minerva, Mars Pater, Fortuna Redux, Hercules, Mercury, Aesculapius, and Salus."[23] Ramsay MacMullen reports a man who simultaneously served as a priest in four temples,[24] while many temples served many gods simultaneously.

Whereas competition within or among monotheistic faiths can result in strengthening each,[25] within polytheism the greater the pluralism the weaker each particular temple was likely to become. Historians continue to puzzle over the fact that beginning in about 260 CE, "inscriptions proclaiming . . . whole-hearted private support to the cults of the traditional gods of the cit[ies] . . . wither[ed] away within a generation."[26] Following Michael Rostovtzeff,[27] many historians have accepted that this was caused by a rapid economic decline of the Greco-Roman cities in this era. This is, of course, what one would expect historians steeped in materialism to conclude. However, a substantial number of subsequent studies, especially those based on specific cities, fail to reveal such economic declines.[28] Indeed, the effects that earlier historians had "taken for the death throes of city life" now are regarded as "the growing pains" of urban evolution.[29] Cities increased in size and in cultural diversity. And it was this diversity that seems the likely culprit in the decline of private donations to the temples. The common vision of a coherent set of a city's gods was being lost, turning civic-mindedness in other directions. In other words, Greco-Roman paganism may have proliferated to the point that it was nearly overwhelming in its variety. This is not to suggest that paganism had thereby lost its credibility. As will be seen at length in Chapter 7, paganism didn't just suddenly succumb to Christian persuasion or even to imperial suppression; vigorous paganism persisted well into the sixth and even the seventh centuries. But the rapid procession of new gods created a cultural fluidity that made it progressively easier for new faiths to gain a foothold: Chapter 4 demonstrates how the influence of Eastern faiths, such as worship of Cybele and of Isis, helped to prepare the way for Christianity.

Now, against this general background, it is time to be more specific about the contexts of the early church.

Cities of the Empire

This book is based on the cities of the Roman Empire. But which ones should be included? One might suggest including all places that were large enough to leave historical traces. However, even in this era when cities were very small, it would be unreasonable to count a place with 1,000 residents as a city, even by the standards of the time.[30] Worse yet, the actual populations of ancient cities are very difficult to determine. Back then, even local officials probably had only crude estimates, although probably not as crude as some used by historians for generations, which accounts for the many extraordinary variations in the figures offered by reputable scholars. Did Rome have a million residents or only 200,000?[31] Were there

8,000 or nearly 24,000 inhabitants of Tiberius?[32] Did Carthage and Antioch each have "over 500,000"[33] residents or only one-fifth that many?[34] As for Pergamum, *Encyclopaedia Britannica* says its population was 200,000, while Tertius Chandler places it at only 40,000.[35] Fortunately, in recent years considerable attention has been paid to reconstructing ancient populations from such things as archaeological evidence. These data are, of course, far from precise, but they are sufficient for our needs.[36] Assuming that 30,000 residents is a reasonable minimum city-size, there were thirty-one cities of that size or larger within the Roman Empire in the year 100 CE. They stretched from London in the west to Nisibis in the east and Oxyrhynchus in the south, as is shown in Map 2-1. Since these thirty-one cities will be the basis for all subsequent analysis, it seems useful to offer a thumbnail sketch of each.

It might be supposed that a study such as this would begin with the city of Jerusalem. However, as of the year 100, Jerusalem had only a small population, having been smashed, burned, and sacked by the Roman army in 70; and it would be almost completely depopulated again when razed by Hadrian in 135. Of course, there will be frequent references to Jerusalem throughout the book, but it does not qualify as one of the cases to be included in the analysis.

The Near East

It does seem appropriate, however, to begin with the imperial cities of the Near East, those closest to Jerusalem.

CAESAREA MARITIMA. Population: 45,000. Located about sixty miles north of Jerusalem, Caesarea was built by Herod the Great, who named it in honor of Caesar Augustus.

Construction began about 22 BCE and was completed twelve years later. As would befit a king's whim, it was a beautiful city made of white marble, in the midst of which, on a hill, stood one of the earliest temples dedicated to the Imperial Cult that elevated some emperors to divinity. This splendid temple contained two large statues of Augustus. But the city's most remarkable feature was the harbor. The site had no natural harbor, not even an inlet, but was a barren beach on a dangerous coast. Herod had a large harbor constructed in 20 fathoms of water by building two moles (or breakwaters) extending 1,600 feet into the sea. The moles were constructed of masonry blocks 50 feet long, 18 feet wide, and 9 feet thick, made of a specially invented concrete that would harden under water. To create a block, a wooden box was floated to the desired position and then sunk. The mortar was poured into the submerged box through a wooden tube with flexible leather joints and left to harden. A gap 60 feet wide between the two moles provided an entrance to the harbor. When completed, the moles were from 150 to 200 feet wide, adequate to stop even very high stormy seas; in addition, they provided space for many warehouses and served as a pier for unloading.[37]

Caesarea figured prominently in early Christian history. Pontius Pilate made Caesarea his headquarters and wintered his legions there. Paul and his companions passed through the port on their return from several missionary journeys, and later Paul was held captive there to await being sent to Rome. The early church father Origen lived there for about twenty years, as did his student Eusebius, the remarkable first church historian who also served as bishop of the city.

DAMASCUS. Population: 45,000. For Christians, the road to Damascus greatly overshadows the city itself. Yet it is one of the oldest cities in the region, mentioned both in *Genesis* (14:15; 15:2) and on clay tablets dating from 2400–2250 BCE found at Ebla. Damascus is located at an oasis sixty miles from the Mediterranean and is surrounded on three sides by desert. In addition to a number of springs, several rivers pass by, providing sufficient water for an abundant agriculture. A number of major caravan routes crossed at Damascus, making it a commercial center. Given its location and lack of any natural defensive features, Damascus was incorporated into one ancient empire after another: Egyptian, Hittite, Aramean, Hebrew, Assyrian, Babylonian, Persian, Seleucid, and finally Roman. Although Damascus served for a time as the capital of the Seleucid Empire (founded by Greeks who had served with Alexander the Great), it soon was eclipsed by Antioch, which was founded by the Seleucids to exploit its far superior strategic location. Pompey conquered Damascus in 64 BCE and incorporated it into Rome's province of Syria. Roman rule allowed rapid expansion of the local Jewish community.[38]

Christianity must have come very early to Damascus, since Paul (Saul) was on his way there to stop Christian missionizing among the Jews when he had his dramatic conversion experience.

ANTIOCH. Population: 100,000. Sometimes called Syrian Antioch, this city was founded around 300 BCE by Seleucid rulers wanting to take advantage of its strategic location on the Orientes River where it cuts through the mountains: "Antioch stands at the focal point for communications with Palestine to the south . . . and with the Euphrates to the east."[39] After Antioch was annexed by Rome in 64 BCE, the emperors regarded it as of such strategic importance that they rebuilt the city and resettled it with veterans each time it was destroyed—by earthquakes, fires, and war.[40] Unfortunately, the city was equally susceptible to internal disasters. Rioting was chronic as various ethnic enclaves attacked one another.

The Diasporan Jewish community in Antioch was old and large, but its first members weren't migrant Jewish merchants, as in many other cities, but Jewish veterans retired from the Seleucid army.[41] In the year 40 CE Emperor Caligula declared himself a god and ordered that his statue grace the temple precincts in Jerusalem. Following Jewish protests against sacrilege, organized mobs burned the synagogues in Antioch and murdered a large number of Jews. A few years later, the Jewish Revolt in Palestine led to even worse riots and more Jewish fatalities.

Meanwhile, some Jews in Antioch became Christians, as did some Gentiles, thus giving urgency to the issue of "uncircumcised" converts. With that issue resolved by a ruling from Paul, what probably was the first Christian church with a substantial Gentile membership came into existence here. In fact, this fortress city was second only to Jerusalem as the most important setting in the early history of Christianity.[42] Paul used Antioch as his home base, and it was from here that he set out on his three missionary journeys. According to *Acts* (11:26), it was in Antioch that the name Christian was coined by city officials needing to distinguish Jesus's followers from Jews and pagans.

APAMEA. Population: 37,000. Located south of Antioch on the route to Damascus, Apamea was long a part of the Seleucid Empire and, along with Antioch, served as its major gateway for trade to the West. In 64 BCE Pompey imposed Roman rule on the area. According to Josephus, as Pompey marched to Damascus he "demolished the citadel that was at Apamea."[43] Subsequently, the city joined in Syria's revolt against the empire and held out for three years against the Romans, finally falling to Cassius in 46 BCE.[44] Even after coming under Roman rule, Apamea remained a very Hellenic city in terms of its culture. Paul probably passed through Apamea on his way back to Antioch at the end of his second missionary journey, but there is no indication that he stopped to visit. However, a Christian congregation was established here by early in the second century.

SALAMIS. Population: 35,000. The principal city of ancient Cyprus, Salamis was on the east coast of the island, north of modern Famagusta. It is not to be confused with the small Greek city also named Salamis, just off the coast of Athens, where the Persian fleet was drawn into the narrow strait and destroyed by the Greeks in 490 BCE. This Salamis on Cyprus was, however, the site of a naval battle of almost equal magnitude when, in 360 BCE, a Greek and Egyptian fleet was sunk by Macedonians.

In peacetime Salamis was, for centuries, a busy port and a major commercial center. Not surprisingly it attracted a Diasporan community of sufficient size and significance to be mentioned in *Acts* (13:5). Like many cities in this region, Salamis was often nearly destroyed by natural and military disasters. Finally, in 648 Salamis was attacked and destroyed by Arabs and has since remained an abandoned ruin.

Mesopotamia

Let us now venture off to the northeast of the cities described above, where two of our cities were located in what was then Mesopotamia.

EDESSA. Population: 75,000. This is one of the most easterly of the larger Roman cities. Over the centuries there probably were many settlements on this site, but Edessa was founded in about 303 BCE by Seleucus I Nicator, who had been one of Alexander the Great's officers. Subsequently, Edessa was ruled by the Parthians, who were vanquished by the Romans. Located on the River Scirtus (a tributary of the Euphrates), the city was subject to repeated devastating floods and frequent earthquakes. A great flood in 201 CE destroyed most of the city, including its Christian church.[45]

Because the ruling prince probably was baptized late in the second century, Edessa may have been the first Christian 'state,' and a substantial body of Christian writings appeared here translated into Syriac (including the Peshitta, a Syriac version of the New Testament). Subsequently, Edessa produced Gnostic literature and the Nestorian Heresy, which proposed that Mary ought to be referred to only as the "Mother of the Christ," not as the "Mother of God," for which its founder had to flee to Persia. Edessa is mentioned in *Revelation* (2–3) as one of the places where Christian communities made an early appearance.

NISIBIS. Population: 67,000. There was a very ancient city on this site, which is located to the northeast of Edessa—some even have associated that city with those referred to in *Genesis*. However, the Nisibis of New Testament times was refounded by Macedonians and was a solidly Hellenic rather than Persian city. Indeed, it stood as a frontier stronghold against eastern incursions, first under the Seleucids and then as part of Rome. In the early days of Roman rule the city was often lost to and retaken from the Parthians. It was strengthened by Trajan, and Septimius Severus made it his headquarters when campaigning in the East. Thus, Nisibis served as "the advanced outpost of the Romans against the East"[46] until it was lost again to the Persians as a result of Julian's abortive fourth-century offensive. Although there was no significant Diasporan Jewish community in Nisibis, it had a Christian church by the second century.

Asia Minor

Let us now turn west to the cities of Asia Minor, in what today is Turkey.

PERGAMUM. Population: 40,000. This Grecian city, sixteen miles from the Aegean Sea, was "easily the most spectacular city of Asia Minor."[47] It began as a fortress situated atop a hill that rose 900 feet above the surrounding plain. In about 330 BCE, the Attalid dynasty added a palace on the hilltop, and then a temple to Athena. Eighty feet down the hill was built a Great Altar of Zeus, and on the other side of the hill a fine theater was located. The Attalids also founded a great library with a reading room about fifty feet square (which has been excavated), said to have included 200,000 volumes of parchment. In fact, when the Egyptians would not export papyrus, parchment (made from treated animal skins) was invented in Pergamum. The word *parchment* derives from the Latin "Pergamena charta," or "paper of Pergamum." During their stay in Pergamum, Mark Anthony gave the library to Cleopatra.[48] Whether she was able to move the library to Egypt to be merged with the great library at Alexandria is not known. If she did, then nearly everything written in classic times, papyrus and parchment, was destroyed during the various disasters that beset the library in Alexandria.

Under Roman rule, which began in 133 BCE, Pergamum served as the capital of 'Asia'—eventually to be replaced by Ephesus. Meanwhile, the city greatly expanded at the bottom of the hill, and many new temples were built. The most significant of these was dedicated to the Imperial Cult. "Here was built the first Asian Temple of the divine Augustus, which for more than forty years was the one centre of the Imperial religion in the whole Province. A second Asian Temple had afterwards been built in Smyrna, and a third at Ephesus; but they were secondary to the original Augustan Temple at Pergamum."[49] In addition, of course, Pergamum was one of the "seven churches of Asia" named in *Revelation* (1:11; 2:12). Christianity arrived here in the first century, perhaps brought by missionaries trained by Paul at nearby Ephesus.

EPHESUS. Population: 51,000. Remarkable feats of engineering kept the harbor at Ephesus from silting up, a chronic problem for all Mediterranean ports at the mouths of rivers because the very small tides are inadequate to scour them out.[50] (Today the city is five miles from the sea.) But even more remarkable engineering was required to construct the Temple of Artemis (Diana) on landfill. Having 128 pillars sixty feet high, it was so huge a structure that it was regarded as one of the "seven wonders of the world." The splendor of the temple is attested by one of the most famous statues from ancient times—that of the goddess Artemis depicted with rows of breasts—which is believed to have come from the temple.

Ephesus enjoyed a lucrative tourist business from pilgrims to the temple, but it profited even more by lending money from the "enormous wealth deposited in the temple itself."[51] According to the Greek philosopher Dio Chrysostom, the temple also served as a bank of deposit; even kings, he said, "deposit there in order that it may be safe, since no one has ever dared to violate that place."[52] Of course that didn't stop Julius Caesar from robbing the temple during the civil war of 49–46 BCE.

When Paul arrived, there already was a functioning Christian congregation, perhaps based on a group that had been committed to John the Baptist and converted to Christ by Aquila and Priscilla. Paul remained for about three years helping to build up the congregation and to train and dispatch missionaries to found congregations in other towns and cities in the area.[53] Various early church fathers, including Irenaeus and Clement, attested that the Apostle John died and was buried in Ephesus,[54] though that fact was not mentioned in *Acts*.

Ephesus was seized by the Romans following their victory over the Seleucids at the Battle of Magnesia and assigned to Pergamum.

About fifty years later the Romans took direct control of the city. Mark Antony and Cleopatra spent the winter of 33–32 BCE in Ephesus.

Nero rebuilt the stadium at Ephesus, but like Caesar he also looted the great temple. Domitian had a large temple constructed in Ephesus and dedicated it to himself as a god. Trajan also built a temple to himself here, and Hadrian claimed that Ephesus was his favorite city and made it the capital of Asia, replacing Pergamum, for which the city built him a temple too. Today the city is one of the finest excavated sites in Turkey.[55]

SARDIS or SARDES. Population: 100,000. It was in Sardis, somewhere around 670 BCE, that the very first metal coins were minted, made of electrum, an alloy of gold and silver. Soon after, the first pure gold and silver coins were struck. In those days, Sardis was part of the Lydian kingdom, and its most famous king was Croesus, celebrated for his immense wealth from the fabulous amounts of gold panned from a nearby stream. Ancient tradition concerning the abundance of gold in Sardis was confirmed in 1968, when archaeologists found nearly three hundred crucibles for refining gold.[56]

As it turned out, Croesus was the last of the Lydian kings, Sardis having been captured by Cyrus the Great of Persia in 546 BCE. Historians disagree as to whether Croesus was executed or spared. The city remained Persian until taken by Alexander the Great. It came under Roman control in 133 BCE. The city was destroyed by an earthquake in 17 CE but was very quickly rebuilt by Emperor Tiberius, whose restoration efforts led to a major outbreak of emperor worship.[57]

The patron deities of the city were Cybele and Artemis. Both seem to have fostered highly sexually charged rites—for example,

Cybele was served by priests who castrated themselves during frenzied celebrations and then wore feminine costumes, makeup, and jewelry.[58] Christianity arrived in the first century.

SMYRNA. Population: 90,000. Smyrna was situated on the coast, thirty-five miles north of Ephesus. It was destroyed and rebuilt several times. When Alexander the Great rebuilt it in the fourth century BCE, the site seems to have been nothing but ruins. Soon Smyrna was known as the "ornament of Asia," and in 195 BCE it became the first city in Asia to "erect a temple for the cult of the city of Rome."[59] Later came temples for both Tiberius and Hadrian. There also was a sizable Diasporan community in Smyrna and a very early and very active Christian community. In 117, when Bishop Ignatius of Antioch dispatched letters during his trek to Rome, one of them went to Bishop Polycarp of Smyrna, who would eventually be martyred in Smyrna's stadium.

BYZANTIUM or CONSTANTINOPLE. Population: 36,000. Destined one day to be the huge, glittering capital of the eastern empire, at the end of the first century Byzantium was a relatively small city, having been founded six centuries earlier by Greeks from Miletus and Megara. Situated at the eastern frontier, the city was "engaged in perpetual warfare with the neighbouring barbarians."[60] In fact, the Persians took the city in 512 BCE. However, it was taken back by the Athenians in 496 BCE. In 343 BCE the city allied itself with Athens, and together their forces defeated Philip II of Macedonia when he tried to capture Byzantium in 340 BCE. The city could not withstand his son, however, and accepted rule by Alexander the Great without resistance. As Grecian power faded, Byzantium came under Roman rule. Then, in 196 CE, Byzantium sided with the usurper Pescennius Niger against Emperor Septimius Severus. As a result, Severus took the city, killed its inhabitants, and reduced Byzantium to ruins. Severus soon realized the strategic importance of this location and had the city rebuilt. It continued to flourish, and its beautiful site led Constantine to make Byzantium his capital city, renaming it after himself at the formal inauguration in 330.

North Africa

From Asia Minor we move to the cities of North Africa.

ALEXANDRIA. Population: 250,000. Founded in 331 BCE by Alexander the Great, it became the capital of Egypt under the Ptolemaic dynasty and developed into "the busiest port in the ancient world,"[61] exporting immense amounts of wheat to feed Rome. Rome's dependence on Egyptian wheat led to Roman rule in 80 BCE, but Roman control greatly increased after Octavian's victory over Mark Anthony and Cleopatra in 30 BCE.

With its huge library and collection of famous scholars, including Euclid, Eratosthenes, and the Jewish philosopher Philo, Alexandria was the intellectual center of the Greco-Roman world. But it was even more important as a religious center. Here a very large Jewish population mingled with an unusually vigorous paganism. It was in Alexandria that the Old Testament was translated into Greek (because the local Jews had mostly lost their Hebrew) and here too that a host of apocryphal books were written.[62] Alexandrian paganism was equally creative, combining Egyptian and Greek gods and rites in innovative ways, and exporting new gods and faiths to the rest of the empire. In the first century, Alexandria's pagans and Jews were confronted by a rapidly growing Christian community. According to tradition, St. Mark is credited with bringing Christianity to the city, and he is believed to have been martyred there in the year 62 for preaching against the worship of

Serapis, a god paired with the goddess Isis and first heard of in Alexandria (see Chapter 4). The story of St. Mark's death is probably mythical, but no doubt it served to inspire subsequent generations of Alexandrian Christians.

MEMPHIS. Population: 50,000. One of Egypt's most ancient cities, Memphis was the first capital of the United Kingdom of Upper and Lower Egypt. Located where the Nile divides on its way to the sea, Memphis was placed on the west bank so that the river served as a defensive barrier against invaders from the east (the desert to the west being devoid of significant enemies). Memphis is the location of the great pyramids and the Sphinx, and in ancient times the city abounded in splendid temples. Many centuries later, when Egypt came under Greek rule, it was in Memphis that Alexander the Great's body was given temporary burial, before being moved to Alexandria. By the time of Roman rule (first century BCE), the city was rather decayed. Today it lies in ruins, thirteen miles south of Cairo.

Memphis is mentioned once in the Old Testament but never in the New, the city having lost much of its importance by that time. However, a Christian church existed in Memphis by the second century, having come up the Nile from Alexandria.[63]

OXYRHYNCHUS. Population: 34,000. Named for a fish of the sturgeon species, which was an object of local worship, this Egyptian city on the western bank of the Nile has been nearly forgotten by history. It rates a brief paragraph in *Encyclopaedia Britannica* only because of the discovery of a huge cache of ancient papyri here at the start of the twentieth century. Included were copies of long-lost classics of Greek literature as well as many Gnostic and apocryphal books. The most significant find probably was a fragment of the *Gospel of John,* dated about 125 CE, which suggests the presence of a Christian congregation in Oxyrhynchus by that date. In all, about 40,000 pieces were unearthed here, including several thousand complete documents. Although, before being overrun by Islam, Oxyrhynchus was an Episcopal See, its fame was as a center of monasticism, with as many as 10,000 resident monks. That undoubtedly is why such an accumulation of buried papyri existed here. The city also attracted and sustained a number of Gnostic writers, whose manuscripts were likewise among those recovered, including three Greek manuscripts of the strange *Gospel of Thomas,* a document that, a century after the discovery of that papyrus, has been touted by an Ivy League professor as a suppressed document that reveals the 'true' Christianity.[64]

Pagal !

The Romans operated a mint in Oxyrhynchus, but today there are only some ruins and a small Egyptian village at this site.[65]

LEPTIS MAGNA or LEPCIS. Population: 49,000. Located on the North African shore, about two-thirds of the way from Alexandria to Carthage, Leptis Magna was founded in about 600 BCE by the Phoenicians. Subsequently, it became part of the Carthaginian Empire, and after the fall of Carthage it was incorporated into Roman Africa. At its height, during the first through third centuries, Leptis Magna was a major port exporting grain and olives from its fertile hinterland. It was a wealthy city, and this was reflected in its architecture: many colonnaded avenues, a magnificent theater and sports field, massive baths, and beautiful temples. As the birthplace of Septimius Severus, who was emperor of Rome from 193 to 211 CE, it enjoyed a period of great imperial favor. During that time there was much refurbishing and additional construction, including the four-way triumphal Arch of Severus, made of the best marble. As Roman strength in Africa waned, Leptis Magna was repeatedly sacked by raiding Libyan tribes and then by the Arabs. What its enemies started, nature finished: soon most of this beautiful city was covered by sand, and it seldom is mentioned in histories of its time. Today it is one of the premiere archaeological sites, with most of the city remaining unexcavated.[66]

CARTHAGE. Population: 100,000. Rome's deadliest enemy was situated on the north coast of Africa. The city was originally founded by Phoenicians, who over many centuries built an empire in Africa and the islands of the Mediterranean to rival that of Rome.

This threat to Roman power led to the Punic Wars. The first of these began in 264 BCE and ended in 241 with a treaty favorable to Rome, but both sides soon violated their agreement: Rome by seizing Sardinia and Corsica, Carthage by invading Spain. The second Punic War broke out in 218 BCE and lasted for seventeen years. After the famous Carthaginian General Hannibal Barca led an elite army of about 40,000 soldiers and a number of elephants on an overland march from Spain, over the Pyrenees, across Gaul, and over the Alps, most of the fighting took place in Italy. For many years, Hannibal won the battles, but he couldn't win the war because Rome kept raising new legions. Finally, Hannibal was forced to withdraw his army to Carthage to head off a Roman invasion. He lost a battle in front of the city, and Carthage surrendered in 201, though many Romans rejected the settlement. For years, Cato the Elder greeted every opening of the Senate with the pronouncement "Carthage must be destroyed." And so it was. The third Punic War was initiated by Rome in 146 BCE and ended in a house-by-house conquest of the city, all of its inhabitants being killed or sold into slavery, every building razed, the city plowed up, and salt sown in the soil.

A century later Julius Caesar formulated plans to refound Carthage, but he was murdered before they could go forward. So, two years later, in 44 BCE, Carthage was refounded by Emperor

Augustus to serve as Rome's administrative center for the region, taking advantage of its strategic location. Augustus sent 3,000 Roman colonists, and they were joined by many people from the immediate area. The city grew very quickly, and Carthage soon regained its position as an important trading center. Christianity arrived early in the second century, probably from Alexandria.

Greece

Three cities in Greece also are included in this set.

ATHENS. Population: 75,000. Although Athens proper was located about five miles from the Mediterranean, the city walls extended all the way to the water and encircled three harbors, which allowed Athens, at its height, to be a major sea power and a busy port. Of course, it was best known as the intellectual capital of ancient Greece. However, by the time of Paul's visit in the first century, "Athens was well past its prime, living on bygone glories, rich in monuments but an intellectual desert compared to what once had been."[67] Athens's human population was less than a third of what it had been in Plato's day, but the population of gods had continued to grow. There were temples everywhere, including one *"to an unknown god."*[68] During his stop in Athens, Paul used this opportunity to inform the local intellectuals of the identity of their unknown god, whom he presented as the One True God of the Jews and Christians. The Athenian philosophers were not receptive, and according to *Acts,* Paul left the city disappointed and convinced that in the future he would not waste time with philosophy, but would stick to the gospel message.[69]

CORINTH. Population: 50,000. Despite its great prominence in early Christian history, Corinth was a "brawling seaport . . . being notorious for its blatant immorality. Much of its population was transitory—sailors, freebooters, adventurers, swindlers of every sort."[70] Corinth's great commercial advantage came from its location on a narrow isthmus, which offered a very substantial short-cut for westbound shipping from most other Greek ports, including Athens and Thessalonica. Rather than making the long voyage around the large Peloponnesian Peninsula, boats were off-loaded at Corinth and their cargoes hauled a few miles overland to the Adriatic, there to be reloaded and sent on. Sometimes the ships themselves were dragged overland and relaunched!

In 146 BCE Corinth served as headquarters for the Achaean League, which rashly challenged Roman rule. The league was quickly defeated by the Roman Consul Lucius Mummis. As a lesson to all, Corinth's citizens were slaughtered or sold into slavery, and the city was burned and reduced to rubble. The Romans then devoted the site to the gods and prohibited any human habitation. But it was too good a site to be abandoned: in 46 BCE Julius Caesar had Corinth rebuilt and settled with a mixture of retired veterans of the legions and thousands of Rome's 'undesirables.' The results were predictable: "It was the most licentious city in all Greece; and the number of merchants who frequented it caused it to be the favorite resort of courtezans. The patron goddess of the city was Aphrodite, who had a splendid temple ... where there were kept more than a thousand sacred female slaves for the service of strangers."[71]

It was here that Paul spent eighteen months and built up a congregation of both Jews and Gentiles. Historians have long attributed his success to the dreadful situation of the city's poor. As recently expressed: "It was primarily among the miserable poor that Paul found a positive response to his preaching."[72] And, as usual, *1 Corinthians* 1:26 was cited as proof: "*[N]ot many of you were wise according to worldly standards, not many were powerful, not many were of noble birth.*" However, as E. A. Judge suggested, substitute the word "some" for the words "not many" and the implications of this verse change dramatically. In a Roman world where the aristocracy "amounted to an infinitesimally small fraction of the total population,"[73] Paul is acknowledging that his small congregation in Corinth included "some" of noble birth and "some" who were powerful. Indeed, scholars now agree that among Paul's members at Corinth was Erastus, "the city treasurer,"[74] and in his remarkable studies of the church at Corinth, Gerd Theissen has identified other members of the "upper classes."[75] This was not unique; all across the empire Christianity was a movement of the more privileged.[76]

THESSALONICA. Population: 35,000. Although located in mainland Greece on a great natural harbor at the head of a large gulf on the Aegean Sea, Thessalonica was nothing but a collection of tiny villages until Alexander the Great's brother-in-law Cassander founded a city there and named it after his wife. The city grew very rapidly, and its economic life continued to prosper under Roman rule, which began in 168 BCE.

As a boom town having a large transient population of sailors, merchants, travelers, and soldiers, Thessalonica developed "a profuse . . . religious life, as foreign cults put down roots alongside the more traditional philosophic schools and indigenous forms of worship."[77] In 1917 a large temple devoted to Isis was excavated, dating from the third century BCE. Other Egyptian gods also were represented in the city, including Anubis.

Paul and his group of missionaries added to this exotic mix when they arrived in Thessalonica about 50 CE or earlier. The Christian mission seems to have been quite successful, but as usual the Christians soon came into conflict with the Diasporan community. To deflect attacks on his host, Jason, Paul withdrew to a nearby town. But because the attacks continued, Paul departed, leaving Silas and Timothy behind to continue the mission.[78] Once back in Corinth, following his visit to Athens, Paul wrote[79] two remarkable letters to the growing church in Thessalonica. He did so to head off the kinds of misunderstandings and conflicts that are inevitable in a new religious community. No one has put this so well and so gracefully as Arthur Darby Nock:

> The letters to the Thessalonians give us a notable picture of the human failings of a new community. There were misunderstandings of the doctrine which had been so recently imparted; there were almost certainly divisions; the leaders on the spot were perhaps a little too anxious to exercise authority and somewhat lacking in tact, while on the other hand, some of the rank and file, in their confidence in the Spirit which they were said to have received, were reluctant to submit to any direction; again, moral problems did not disappear overnight.[80]

To deal with all these problems, Paul had to write a lucid primer of basic Christianity as he understood it, thereby providing a priceless legacy to all subsequent generations.

Italy

Now to Italy (and Sicily).

ROME. Population: 450,000. It seems pointless to devote much prose to the geography or history of the most famous city of ancient times, but something can usefully be reported about its Christianization.

There is no record of missionaries going to Rome. Although both Peter and Paul were executed in Rome, there was a substantial congregation in the city long before either of them arrived. A persuasive clue as to how Christianity arrived in Rome comes at the end of the *Epistle to the Romans* (16:3–16). Despite never yet having been to the capital, Paul greeted a number of old friends in the congregation.[81] This prompted Nock to propose that the "Christian community in Rome seems to have come into being without any missionary act—simply as a result of the migration of men [and women] from Palestine and Syria."[82]

However, these migrants must have engaged in a great deal of rank-and-file missionizing once they reached Rome, since the congregation soon included not only many Romans, but among them some members from the upper strata of Roman society. Historians now accept that Pomponia Graecina, a woman of senatorial class, accused in 57 of practicing a "foreign superstition," was a Christian. Nor, according to Marta Sordi, was she an isolated case: "We know from reliable sources that there were Christians among the aristocracy [in Rome] in the second half of the first century (Ancilius Glabrio and the Christian Flavians) and that it seems probable that the same can be said for the first half of the same century, before Paul's arrival in Rome."[83] Consequently, at the end of the first century, when Ignatius, bishop of Antioch, was arrested and led to Rome for execution in the arena, his special fear was that the Roman Christians would interfere with his desire for martyrdom and obtain his pardon. So he wrote to them: "The truth is, I am afraid it is your love that will do me wrong. For you, of course, it is easy to achieve your object; but for me it is difficult to win my way to God. . . . Grant me no more than that you let my blood be spilled[;] . . . do not interfere. I beg you, do not show me unseasonable kindness."[84] Ignatius's concerns would have been silly had he not known that the Christians in Rome probably could have saved him.

CAPUA. Population: 36,000. Located south of Rome and just north of modern Naples, Capua was situated on an open plain, lacking any natural defensive features. It was the capital of the region known as Campania. In about 300 BCE Capua was linked to Rome by the Via Appia, probably the most important military highway in Italy. It was a very rich city, renowned for luxurious lifestyles, and it also was the home of many gladiatorial schools—Spartacus and his followers were trained there. In fact, as with Spartacus, Capua had a long history of backing losers. During the Punic Wars, Capua defected to Hannibal, and he wintered his army nearby, for which Rome later punished some civic leaders. Then the city became involved with a colonizing scheme led by Brutus. In 69 CE Capua backed Vitellius, whose corrupt and debauched rule as emperor lasted less than a year.

Although it had a small Jewish community, Capua probably did not get a Christian church until the reign of Constantine.

SYRACUSE. Population: 60,000. Located on the southeast coast of Sicily, Syracuse had a magnificent port and a history of intrigue, assassination, revolt, repression, and general bloodiness that was exceptional even for ancient times. Having two harbors, one of them among the largest on the Mediterranean (guarded by two islands), Syracuse was coveted by empire-builders throughout the centuries. Internal conflicts began soon after the city was founded by Corinthians in 734 BCE.[85] Thucydides mentioned the expulsion of a faction in 648 BCE, and in his *Politics* Aristotle mentioned a subsequent, similar event.[86] Around this time Syracuse attempted to sustain democracy and adopted the Athenian practice of "petalism," wherein every man wrote on an olive leaf the name of the most powerful citizen: the one receiving the most votes was banished for five years. But democracy had a very rocky and intermittent existence in Syracuse.

Frequently attacked from the sea by various Greek and Carthaginian erstwhile invaders, the city usually was up to the test, but its domestic rule amounted to serial murder. For example, in 317 BCE a general named Agathocles obtained mob approval for appointment as head of state by slaughtering the six hundred richest citizens. He is remembered as "a good ruler," but eventually he lost his popularity and was murdered by his nephew.[87] The subsequent period of anarchy was ended in 288 BCE by Hicatas, who was killed and replaced by Tinion eight years later. At the start of the Punic Wars Syracuse allied itself with Rome. However, in 216 BCE Hieronymus led the city to support Hannibal, an alliance that was continued even after Hieronymus was murdered by a popular government. Consequently, two years later Claudius Marcellus laid siege to Syracuse and in 212 BCE sacked the city. Syracuse then became the Roman capital of Sicily and remained so until Byzantium took the island.

Local tradition holds that Peter brought Christianity to Syracuse, but historians think it most likely that Christianity did not arrive here until early in the second century.

Gaul

We now move northward to Gaul.

MILAN or MEDIOLANUM. Population: 30,000. Located on the only broad, fertile plain in Italy, near the foot of the Alps, Milan was the capital of Cisalpine Gaul. Before being conquered by the Romans, it was merely a village—as were all Gaulish settlements. It was annexed by Rome in 190 BCE, and its residents were made full citizens of Rome in 49 BCE. Milan rapidly became the largest and most important city in northern Italy, and all of the major roads north crossed here. Thus, it was so strategically located for directing Roman forces against barbarian threats that, beginning with Augustus, Roman emperors spent considerable time in the city. In 303 CE Maximian took up residence in Milan, as did many subsequent emperors. Christianity probably did not establish a congregation here until sometime in the third century.

AUTUN or AUGUSTODUNUM. Population: 40,000. Located in central France (southwest of Dijon), it was founded by its namesake, Emperor Augustus, on the site of a city called Bibracte (after a local goddess) by Caesar in his *Commentaries*. Built as a fortress city encircled by stout masonry walls, Autun was renowned in Roman times for its schools of rhetoric, which educated the sons of nobility from all over Gaul.[88]

Though there seems not to have been an organized Christian congregation in Autun until after the year 200, a marble gravestone found there in 1839 is regarded as one of the important archeological finds concerning the early church. Known as the Inscription of Pectorius, it consists of eleven verses in Greek, which refer to Christianity as "the Fish," and describe the Eucharist while acknowledging "the Redeemer" and the "Lord Savior." Scholars date the gravestone to the third century or early fourth.[89]

LYON or LUGDUNUM. Population: 50,000. Located in southern France at the juncture of the Rhône and the Saône rivers and at the end of several major routes across the Alps, Lyon began as a Roman military colony in 43 BCE. Over time a city grew up around the legion outpost and Emperor Augustus made it the capital of all Gaul, building a number of roads that converged on the city. Consequently, it became a very cosmopolitan city, and the largest in Gaul, drawing merchants and traders from distant places. The city was destroyed by fire during the first century and was restored by Nero, whom the city had supported when Galba challenged Nero's reign.

By early in the second century "the first Christian community of Gaul was established" in Lyon.[90] In 177, during the reign of

Marcus Aurelius, the Christians of Lyon were brutally persecuted. Eusebius devoted many pages to reporting the savagery of both the mob and the governor toward these "martyrs of Gaul."[91]

Then, in 197, Lyon bet on the wrong contestant for emperor, as so often happened to Roman cities. When Albinus was defeated by Septimius Severus, the winner directed his troops to sack the city and had the leading citizens put to death. Severus also destroyed Lyon's aqueducts, hastening the city's decline.

NÎMES or NEMAUSENSIS. Population: 44,000. After Lyon, Nîmes was probably the second richest and most important Roman town in Gaul. Located southwest of Lyon, it was founded by Emperor Augustus on the site of a village that served as the capital of a Gallic tribe that had submitted to Rome in 121 BCE. Augustus named the city Nemausensis after the genie of a sacred fountain.

Augustus not only founded the Roman city and gave it many political privileges, but he also funded a lavish construction program. Most of the resulting structures are still standing: a huge amphitheater with seats for 24,000; a large temple dedicated to Augustus's adopted sons; city walls that include a tower nearly 100 feet high; a magnificent Temple of Diana that was connected to the baths; and a great aqueduct known as the Pont du Gard.

There was no Diasporan community in Nîmes, and Christianity arrived there quite late as well.

Spain

Three Spanish cities are included.

CADIZ or GADIR or GADES. Population: 65,000. This coastal city at the southern tip of Spain, beyond the Pillars of Hercules (the Strait of Gibraltar), was founded by the Phoenicians. "To the Greeks and Romans it was long the westernmost point of the known world."[92] Cadiz has a remarkable location, being surrounded by the sea except for a tiny spit connecting it to the mainland. After the Phoenician era, Cadiz became a major Carthaginian port before surrendering peacefully to Rome at the end of the second Punic War (about 200 BCE). Throughout its history, Cadiz has been a city of seafarers. In fact, the remarkable English historian William Smith suggested that Cadiz usually was "not densely peopled, since a large part of the citizens were always absent at sea."[93] Strabo, the early Greek geographer, reported that the imperial census taken under Augustus revealed that Cadiz had a higher proportion of rich citizens (*equites*) than all but one other Roman city (Patavium), due no doubt to its lucrative trading activities.[94] The city also had a famous oracle and unusually splendid temples, especially those devoted to Saturn and Hercules.

CORDOVA. Population: 45,000. Founded in 152 BCE by Roman colonists, Cordova is situated northeast of Cadiz on the very navigable Guadalquivir River. Cordova was on the wrong side in the war between Julius Caesar and Pompey. Having been defeated repeatedly elsewhere in the empire, the Pompeian forces fled to Spain and assembled thirteen legions. Caesar landed with eight legions and annihilated the Pompeians at Munda in 45 BCE. In the aftermath Caesar took Cordova and killed a large number of its citizens.

The city quickly recovered as newcomers continued to arrive, and Christianity had gained a firm foothold in the city by no later than the second century.

SEVILLE or HISPALIS. Population: 40,000. Originally, this was a Phoenician city valued for its minerals, especially iron, which could be shipped downriver to the coast. The actual site of Seville seems to have moved around a bit as the city went through successive foundings. For a time, Seville was a Carthaginian city. Then came the Punic Wars, and Seville became Roman in 206 BCE when

Scipio Africanus defeated the Carthaginians in the Battle of Ilipa Magna, fought about eight miles to the north. Scipio then settled a number of his veterans here and the city boomed, becoming famous for its many porticoed streets and attractive amphitheater with the capacity to seat 25,000. In 44 BCE Julius Caesar granted Seville the highly sought status of a colony,[95] which later prompted the erroneous tradition that he was founder of the city. Two emperors, Trajan and Hadrian, were born in Seville. Christianity came sometime in the third century, and shortly thereafter Justa and Rufina achieved martyrdom for refusing to bow to an image of the local god Salambó.

Britannia

And finally, across the channel to Britannia.

LONDON or LONDINIUM. Population: 30,000. Supposedly, Julius Caesar imposed Roman rule on a collection of 'semi-savage' British tribes. In truth, these 'barbarians' were sufficiently civilized to use chariots against the legions. Seventeen years after the conquest, Queen Boudicca, head of a British tribe, led a rebellion during which London was sacked and burned. Eventually Hadrian had to build a great wall across the country to hold off rebels from northern strongholds. Still, Roman Britain endured for five centuries, during which London was its commercial and political capital.

Keep in mind, however, that while London technically was a port, it was effectively limited to cross-channel shipping. Except for the last twenty miles or so, the trip to London from Rome was a very long journey by land. Being so remote, London had no early Diasporan community and played virtually no role in church history until perhaps the third century. Later, of course, both British and Irish monks sustained extensive missions to the continent.

Conclusion

Map 2-1 shows all thirty-one cities having a population of 30,000 or more that were part of the Roman Empire in 100 CE. The map shows far more clearly than can be put into words that the urbanites were clustered in the East.

Despite the fact that about 95 percent of its population lived on farms or in tiny rural villages, Rome was an urban empire.[96] As Wayne Meeks explained, "[T]he cities were where the power was ... [and] where changes could occur."[97] The rural "population hovered so barely above subsistence level that no one dared risk change."[98] Thus it was that the overwhelming majority of early Christians were urbanites. Some of these urban Christians lived in cities and towns too small to be included in this set of the thirty-one largest. However, considering that the total urban population of the empire was about three million,[99] the fact that the total population of these thirty-one cities was approximately two million suggests that they housed about two-thirds of the Greco-Romans who lived in towns and cities and probably about the same proportion of all urban Christians. The point is that the focus on the larger cities does not greatly distort our 'slice' of early Christian progress—most of it occurred here.

As is obvious, these cities differed in many ways. Had they not, they would be useless for analysis—all the important indicators being invariant. For it is the differences that matter: Why did only some cities attract Jewish settlements? Why didn't they all welcome Isis? Why did some quickly embrace Christianity while others held out for several centuries? These sorts of questions underlie the entire enterprise. To proceed requires clear definitions and plausible measurements, and the place to start is with the primary concept of all early church history: Christianization.

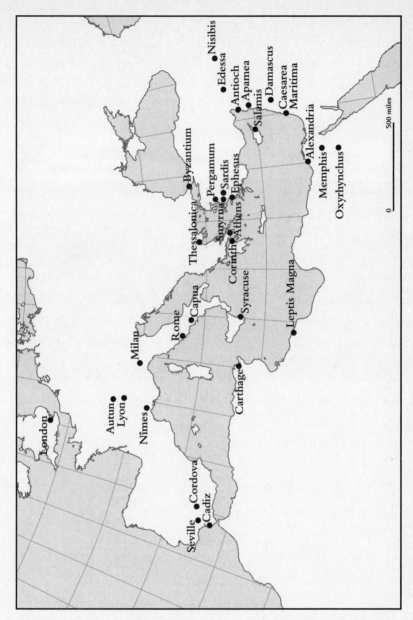

MAP 2-1. All Greco-Roman Cities Having a Population of 30,000 or More

BAPTISM OF CHRIST. Some would say that Christianity began at this mo-
ment when John the Baptist baptized Jesus (as depicted by Joachim Patnir,
ca. 1515).

Chapter Three

—ɯɯ—

Christianization

THE STUDY OF ANCIENT HISTORY suffers badly from a lack of reliable numbers. Most of this is due to the fact that the ancients didn't often gather any numbers, and many numbers they may have gathered did not survive. But some of it is due to a deep-seated disdain for numbers on the part of some historians. As will be discussed in the concluding chapter, too many historians are unfamiliar with techniques of quantification and are vulnerable to innumerate biases. For, despite the dearth of surviving statistics, many needed numbers can be adequately estimated and many seemingly 'qualitative' matters can readily be quantified.

This chapter demonstrates the feasibility of applying quantitative techniques to early church history. First, I will develop an estimated growth curve showing the number of Christians within the empire at various times between the years 40 and 350—a curve

that is validated by known statistics such as increases in the incidence of Christian names on gravestones and on contracts. The
curve clarifies many matters, including how slowly the Christian
movement grew during the first several centuries and then how
rapidly conversions accelerated during the third century—enough
so as to alarm Roman authorities. Against this background, I will
then quantify the Christianization of each of the thirty-one cities,
along with several other important features, including the prevalence of travel and trade, and the relative influence of Hellenic culture in each city. Along the way, I will propose and test a series of
preliminary hypotheses concerning the spread of Christianity.

Converting the Empire

It is agreed that by 350 CE the Christian population of the Roman
Empire had grown very large.[1] As Lucian the Martyr put it early in
the fourth century: "[A]lmost the greater part of the world is now
committed to this truth, even whole cities."[2] This probably was
too optimistic if applied to the empire as a whole (especially to the
rural areas), but there is no disputing that Christians were everywhere and numbered many millions. At issue is how this was
achieved: Was Christianization the result of a relatively *constant rate*
of growth, as social scientists would expect, or was it produced by
a *series of leaps* caused by mass conversions, as many historians and
Bible scholars assume?

Mass conversions are described in *Acts* and are ratified by many
historians. For example, *Acts* 2:37–42 reports a sermon by Peter in
Jerusalem on Pentecost, after which "three thousand souls" came
forward and were baptized. Even so, the result would not have
been three thousand converts, only three thousand wet Jews and
pagans. One sermon, no matter how dynamic, does not prompt
the fundamental shift of identity essential to a religious conversion;

even after these listeners had been baptized, there would have been a great deal still to be done before any of them could have been claimed as a Christian. The same points apply to Eusebius's report that the early Christian missionaries were so empowered by the "divine Spirit" that "at the first hearing whole multitudes in a body eagerly embraced in their souls piety towards the creator of the universe."[3]

Adolf von Harnack confirmed claims of mass conversions on grounds that the growth of the early church was so rapid that "Christianity must have reproduced itself by means of miracles, for the greatest miracle of all would have been the extraordinary extension of the religion apart from any miracles."[4] And even the distinguished Ramsay MacMullen accepted that only "successes en masse"[5] could have produced sufficiently rapid growth to meet the total number achieved by the year 300. Nevertheless, mass conversions seem very unlikely on four primary grounds: theological, sociological, historical, and arithmetic.

Harnack was right that mass conversions would qualify as miracles. And that's precisely the *theological* basis for rejecting their occurrence. God could have created human beings incapable of sin and in no need of Christ's sacrifice. But he didn't. God could have caused all humans to accept Christ. But he didn't. Either act would have violated free will. It was in this spirit that, as scripture reports, Jesus charged his followers to go and "make disciples of all nations." So why would God perform a lot of little conversion miracles? Intervention in human affairs to *compel* even one person, let alone a few thousand people, to embrace Christianity is inconsistent with central Christian doctrines.

Mass conversions also are incompatible with the *sociology* of conversion. First of all, no one who has studied conversion has seen even one 'normal'[6] person join up spontaneously following initial exposure to a group's message. Even people having strong social ties to a group take their time about converting; they usually make their decision only after considerable introspection, playing an active role in "converting themselves."[7] As for conversions taking the form of "mass hysteria," "herd instincts," "mob psychology," "collective madness," or what Freud described as "psychical epidemics, of historical mass convulsions,"[8] the fact is that social scientists have relegated all such terms, and the behavior they postulate, to the dustbin of useless concepts.[9] Fully in keeping with this development is the fact that no one can cite any reliable *historical* cases of mass conversions. Most instances that have been offered as examples have turned out to be revivals, not conversions. When the magnificent eighteenth-century evangelist George Whitefield caused Boston crowds to writhe upon the ground and beg their soul's forgiveness, he was not asking them to change their religious identity, merely to intensify their commitment. The Bostonians had been Christians when Whitefield arrived and were Christians when he left. Of even less relevance are the 'mass conversions' of whole societies to Islam that were produced by treaty or conquest—no change of heart was involved and it often was centuries before most individuals in these societies actually embraced Islam; and when they did so, it was through normal network processes.[10]

Finally, Harnack, MacMullen, and all the rest erred in thinking that the speed at which Christianity spread necessitated mass conversions. As is about to be seen, the Christianization of the empire could easily have been achieved by an *arithmetic* of growth that is entirely compatible with the normal processes of network conversion.

Modeling Overall Growth

What follows is primarily an exercise in the arithmetic of the possible and the plausible. Given realistic assumptions, how large *could* the Christian population of the empire have become within various time limits? Projections of Christian growth require only an estimate of the total number of Christians at some specific time and an assumed rate of subsequent growth. The results can be tested against whatever independent estimates of the Christian population are available for various times.

Although Origen remarked, "Let it be granted that Christians were very few in the beginning,"[11] no one knows how many Christians there were in the early days. Paul claimed that following the resurrection Jesus appeared *"to more than five hundred brethren,"* but it is hard to know whether that was meant as a real number or was a way to say "many."[12] Let us be conservative, and assume there were a thousand active Christians in 40 CE. If so, at what rate would Christianity need to have grown in order for their numbers to have grown as large as many historians estimate it to have been by the beginning of the fourth century? Approximately 3.4 percent per year. Projections based on a starting point of one thousand Christians and this rate of growth are shown below.[13]

Christian Growth Projected at an Annual Rate of 3.4 Percent

Year	Number of Christians	Percent of Population*
40	1,000	—
50	1,397	—
100	7,434	—
150	39,560	0.07
180	107,863	0.18
200	210,516	0.35
250	1,120,246	1.9
300	5,961,290	9.9
312	8,904,032	14.8
350	31,722,489	52.9

*Based on an estimated imperial population of 60 million.[14]

Notice that the growth is very slow in the beginning. By the year 150 there still aren't quite 40,000 Christians, which is in close accord with Robert L. Wilken's estimate that there were "less than fifty thousand Christians" at this time.[15] Even by the year 250 there are only slightly more than one million Christians, or 1.9 percent of the imperial population. This too matches an estimate by a distinguished historian: Robin Lane Fox proposed that Christians made up 2 percent of the population in 250.[16] During the next fifty years, the number shoots up dramatically and by the year 300 reaches slightly fewer than 6 million. This too is consistent with estimates made by many historians.[17] In 312, the year of Constantine's conversion, these projections show nearly 9 million Christians, making up about 15 percent of the population. As will be seen, even as late as the fourth century the overwhelming majority of Christians lived in cities; hence their political importance probably was far greater than their total number might suggest— which no doubt played a role in Constantine's seeking the support of the early church.[18]

When the projection is extended to the year 350, this rate of increase projects that 31.7 million (or about 53 percent of the population) had become Christians. No one would argue that the Christian population was larger than this in 350 and most would argue that it was rather smaller,[19] which would be in keeping with the obvious principle that as the pool of potential recruits diminishes, at some point the rate of growth must slow down as well. But even if there were 31.7 million Christians in 350, these projections show that there need not have been anything miraculous about Christian growth. Rather, many contemporary religious bodies, including the Jehovah's Witnesses, the Mormons, and the Pentecostals, have sustained well-documented growth rates as high as or higher than 3.4 percent a year for many decades. As for objections that there were far more than 1,000 Christians in the year 40,[20] if there were more, then the needed rate of growth would have been substantially lower. For example, had there been 10,000 Christians in the year 40, a rate of growth of only 2.5 percent would have sufficed. Thus, there was plenty of time for Christianity to achieve its growth by way of the conventional network process.

Even though these projections are hypothetical, they so closely match several bodies of actual data that they must be granted considerable credibility. For example, the projections agree very closely with estimates made by Roger S. Bagnall of the percent of Christians in the population from the year 239 though 315 based on an analysis of the percentage of Christian names among those appearing in Egyptian documents.[21] A second basis of comparison is

Figure 3-1: Christian Epigraphs in Rome and Membership Projections

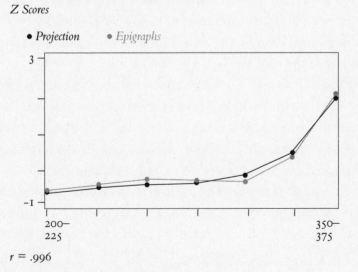

Z Scores

● *Projection*   ● *Epigraphs*

200–
225

350–
375

r = .996

even more compelling. Carlos R. Galvao-Sobrinho[*] has published data on the number of Christian epigraphs appearing on gravestones in the city of Rome, broken down into twenty-five-year groupings.[22] A time series analysis using the Roman data and the projections of the Christian population of the empire, beginning in 200 CE and ending at 375 CE, resulted in an incredibly close match-up. As can be seen in the graphed Z scores shown in Figure 3-1, the two curves are virtually identical and produce an almost perfect correlation of .996.

City-by-City Christianization

Of course, the projections above are for the overall Christianization of the empire. But we know that the new faith spread very unevenly. Christians must have been established in Damascus before 34 CE, since Paul was on his way there to persecute them when he had his mystical conversion. In contrast, there were no Christian congregations in London or Autun until the fourth century. It is this variation from place to place that allows exploration of factors important to the Christianization of the urban empire. To undertake that exploration, it is necessary to 'quantify' Christianization. Fortunately, this task has been accomplished.

Although he wrote a century ago, Adolf von Harnack understood the systematic use of data. Not content to write generalities about the 'expansion' of Christianity, he assembled all available evidence of Christian activity, province by province and city by city. He prepared two lists of places with Christian congregations.[23] The first includes all places that had a Christian community by the end of the first century; the second lists all places that had a Christian

---

[*] I am grateful to Professor Galvao-Sobrinho for graciously providing me with his raw data.

community before 180 CE. Sources for each entry were carefully provided. It is a remarkable achievement and has not been improved upon subsequently: in atlas after atlas, the spread of Christianity is mapped in exact accord with von Harnack.[24] If Christianization is defined as *how soon* Christianity established a congregation, then von Harnack's two lists serve as the basis for quantification in which the thirteen cities having a congregation by 100 CE are scored two; the ten with a congregation by 180 are scored one; and the eight still lacking a congregation in 180 are scored zero. The correct value for each city is provided by Map 3-1.

As mentioned, while the Christian population varied from one city to another, the overwhelming majority of Christians lived in towns and cities, and about two-thirds of them probably lived in these larger thirty-one cities. This allows rough estimates of the Christian population in each of the twenty-three cities that had congregations in 180 CE. That is, we can assign the 107,000 Christians of that year to each city in proportion to the city's total population. That yields an estimate of about 15,000 Christians in Rome, more than 8,000 Alexandria, 3,300 in Antioch, and about 1,100 in tiny Thessalonica. Admittedly, these projections are quite rough, but they do serve to make the point that because the Christian population was concentrated and well organized, it could have had far greater impact on the politics of the empire than the absolute number might suggest. Indeed, by the time of Constantine's conversion Christians probably had achieved majorities in many of these cities.

In any event, with Christianization measured, it is time to address how the conversion of the urban empire was accomplished.

Christianity Goes West

When Christianity first came to their attention, the Romans regarded it as just another eastern faith and Christos as just one more

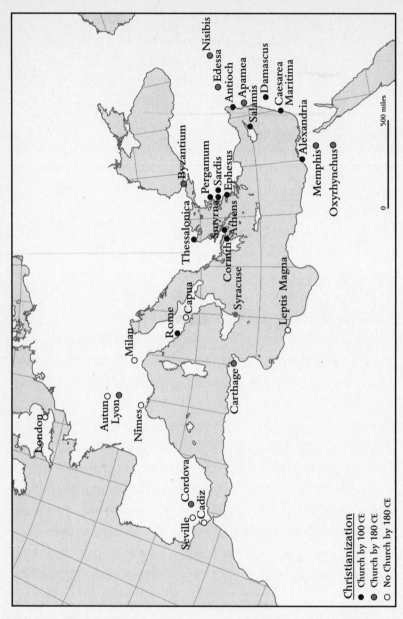

MAP 3-1. Christianization

ROMAN ROAD. To read the many complaints written by classicists about medieval neglect of the 'great' Roman roads, one might suppose that they were akin to modern freeways. This is a stretch of the Appian Way, the most famous and important of all the Roman roads, connecting the cities of Rome and Capua. It is the size of a small country lane—an adequate route for rapidly marching troops north and south, but unsuitable for two-way traffic or large horse-drawn carts.

'oriental' god. Of course, Christianity did originate at the eastern edge of the empire and, like many eastern religions, it too soon went west, probably reaching Rome within a few years of the crucifixion. Although wandering preachers may have been the first Christians to reach Rome, it seems likely that the primary bearers of the new faith were rank-and-file believers who traveled for commercial or personal reasons. This was the typical way in which eastern faiths were transmitted too.

Travel

There was far more travel in classical times than most people now realize. A grave inscription in Phrygia claims that a local merchant had made seventy-two trips to Rome—a one-way journey of more than a thousand miles![25] As Wayne Meeks put it, "[T]he people of the Roman Empire traveled more extensively and easily than any . . . would again until the nineteenth century."[26]

Many have attributed all this coming and going to the extensive network of Roman roads. In fact, the Roman roads were seriously deficient for most travelers, and very unsuited to transporting goods. The notion of *magnificent* Roman roads originated with classicists who either never actually inspected one of the many surviving examples, or were so lacking in practical experience that they failed to notice such obvious shortcomings as the fact that the Roman roads were much "too narrow for large carts"[27] or wagons and in many places were far too steep for anything but foot traffic. In addition, the Romans often did not build bridges, relying on fords that could be crossed on foot but usually were too deep and the banks too steep for carts and wagons.[28]

These inadequacies of the Roman roads existed because, despite being "built and kept up at staggering public expense,"[29] their sole purpose was to permit soldiers to march quickly from one part of the empire to another. Of course, civilian pedestrians used them too, as did animal and human pack trains. But even the soldiers preferred to walk along the side of the roads whenever possible, and that's where nearly all civilian travelers walked or led their beasts. Why? Because the Roman roads were often paved with stone and therefore were hard on legs and feet when dry, and very slippery when wet, making them perilous on steep descents. Add to this the fact that Roman wagons had no brakes and that their front axles did not turn—they had to be skidded around corners.[30] No, it was not primarily roads that made people in this era so mobile. It was boats.

Rome was mainly a waterfront empire surrounding the Mediterranean Sea. Almost a lake, the Mediterranean has very weak tides, is sheltered from storms, and lacks the offshore distances that make sailing far more dangerous on the great oceans. The sailing ships used in this era were quite reliable, capacious, and much faster than any form of land transportation. During favorable weather, large grain transports from Egypt could make the voyage to Rome in less than three weeks.[31] In addition, sailing routes often were much shorter than the best land routes, and they confronted neither hill nor dale. For these reasons, most long-distance travelers went by sea whenever they could, and many of them took their gods with them—"the gods traveled ... in the baggage of the strangers ... [who served] as carriers of cults."[32] These travelers were not missionaries; they spread their gods mainly by example.

In the first century a new element was added. Now, among all these many travelers were some prepared to actively missionize on behalf of the One True Faith; a few of them, like Paul and his associates, were professional missionaries. The great majority of Christian travelers, though, were ordinary members devoted to spreading their faith. How can we assess their efforts other than by the fact that Christianity grew rapidly? Put another way: Can we discover an *indicator* of the incidence of travel?

Since much travel was by sea, travelers were concentrated in *port cities*. Thus, whether or not a city was a port would seem a valid indicator of travel and trade. In light of this, I have scored port cities one and those without ports zero. I scored London zero as well, since although technically it was a port, no one really went there by boat—there was no sea travel from a Mediterranean port to London. Rather, going to Britain required a long journey across Gaul and then a very short boat trip across the channel. Hence, in terms of travel and trade, London was an inland city in this era.

If we use the port variable as an indicator of travel, in combination with the already established measure of Christianization, we are led to:

HYPOTHESIS 3-1: *Port cities tended to be Christianized (that is, to have Christian congregations) sooner than inland cities.*

This hypothesis can be tested by simple cross-tabulation and by correlation coefficients. Both are shown in the Statistical Appendix, as is an explanation of how to read and interpret the data. Here in the text it will be adequate to summarize the results. These show that most port cities (64 percent) had a church by the end of the first century, while far fewer inland cities (24 percent) had a church that soon. Conversely, only 14 percent of port cities still lacked a church in 180, while many inland cities (35 percent) still were without a church by that year (Table 3-1 in the Statistical Appendix). These are very substantial differences. They also achieve a high level of what is known as statistical significance—that is, the odds that a result is real, not the product of chance. In keeping with usual practice, I will accept results here only when the odds are at least twenty to one that they are not the result of chance. When the odds fall below that level, I will dismiss differences as trivial. In the case of port cities being Christianized sooner than inland cities, the odds against this being a difference produced by chance are greater than a hundred to one. The hypothesis is strongly supported: Christianity did become established in port cities sooner than it did inland.

Distance

Ports were not the only factor influencing travel. Distance mattered too. Whether by sea or by land, people were more likely to go to places that were closer. Since Christianity was based in Jerusalem in this era, until forced to move by the Jewish Revolt, initial mission efforts generally originated there. It is a simple matter to measure the distance to each of the 31 cities from Jerusalem (following the most direct route then available, whether by sea or land). Preliminary analysis using the actual distances showed it to be legitimate and appropriate to collapse the mileages into two values: those cities within a thousand miles of Jerusalem and those farther away.

HYPOTHESIS 3-2: *The closer a city was to Jerusalem, the sooner a city had a Christian congregation.*

Most cities (71 percent) within a thousand miles of Jerusalem had a church by the year 100, compared with only one (7 percent) of the fourteen cities farther away. All of the closer cities had a church by 180 while most (57 percent) of the more distant cities did not (Table 3-2). The difference far surpasses the hundred-to-one level of significance, and therefore the hypothesis is very strongly supported.

Admittedly, there is nothing very surprising about the first two results. Most historians of the early church have been aware that migrants "clustered in the ports"[33] and that port cities were where the migrants' gods first became established. And surely no one will be surprised that distance influenced the spread of Christianity. However, this should be interpreted in favor of the quantitative approach, since in these instances the data very clearly show what we all know that they *ought* to show. Had it been otherwise, there would have been strong grounds for abandoning the effort. But because in this instance, and in many examples to come, the data confirm the obvious, we have grounds for placing confidence in the results when less obvious hypotheses are put to the test. As a first step toward more complex matters, the focus shifts from geography to culture.

Hellenism

In the first century far more Jews spoke Greek than Hebrew or Aramaic. Nearly all the Jews in the Diaspora spoke Greek—which was why the Torah was translated into Greek (the Septuagint). Many Jews raised in Palestine were Greek speakers too, including Paul, who "was a Hellenistic Jew who grew up in an environment in which Greek was the everyday language."[34] Indeed, in the New Testament, "even in its oldest layers of tradition, it is taken for granted that Jesus and his disciples spoke Greek in their daily life."[35] This gains support from the fact that Nazareth was located only several miles from Sepphoris, the capital of Galilee and a sophisticated Greek-speaking city.[36] Consequently, scholars have long claimed an affinity between early Christianity and Hellenic culture.[37]

Not only did the first Christians speak Greek, but Christian scripture was initially written in Greek, not in Hebrew or Aramaic. Bible translators have long complained that peculiarities of Greek concepts make it difficult to fully communicate scripture in other languages. In addition, the early church fathers wrote in Greek and the apostles and early evangelists all preached in Greek. Even in Rome, Christian worship probably was conducted only in Greek until well into the second century.[38]

Another link between Hellenism and early Christianity was through the Jews of the Diaspora, who, like the early Christians, also worshipped in Greek. Many of them chafed at the ethnic barrier their religion placed between them and their full participation in Hellenic society—the Law made it difficult for them even to eat with their Gentile associates. As will be discussed at length in the next chapter, when Paul stripped the Jewish prerequisite from Christianity, he not only made the faith open to Gentiles, but offered the Hellenized Jews an attractive religious option, which many of them took.

A third aspect of Hellenic culture that was conducive to Christianization was its easy accommodation of new gods and its conceptions of what the gods were like, in contrast to the religious conservatism of Roman tradition, which is a major reason why so many new faiths from the East did so well in Rome—in fact, Greek gods soon dominated the Roman pantheon (under new Roman names). Many of these Hellenic gods were believed to have begun as mere mortals who attained divinity; hence, aspects of the Christ story had a familiar ring to the Hellenic ear.[39] So did the Christian commitment to a theology rooted in reason and logic.

"What has Athens to do with Jerusalem?" Tertullian asked. The correct answer was not the negative this early church father supposed. In fact, there was remarkable compatibility between Christian doctrines and Greek philosophy. Philo anticipated this compatibility when he analyzed the Pentateuch with the same methods Greek philosophers used to interpret Greek mythology, reading it as "inspired allegories about the cosmos and man's place in it."[40] Philosophical discipline clearly shaped Paul's theological discussions. And by the second century, the early church fathers were making sophisticated use of various Greek philosophers and their schools. In this respect, Justin Martyr was unsurpassed. "For him the gospel and the best elements in Plato and the Stoics are almost identical ways of apprehending the same truth."[41]

For all of these reasons, Christianity should have found a home sooner and more securely in cities having a dominant Hellenic culture than in those where Hellenism was not dominant. It is a simple matter to distinguish the most Hellenic cities as shown in Map 3-2.

HYPOTHESIS 3-3: *Hellenic cities had Christian congregations sooner than did Roman cities.*

Once again the hypothesis is very strongly confirmed. Almost two-thirds of the Hellenic cities had a church by the end of the first century, and no Hellenic city lacked a church by 180. In contrast, two-thirds of the less Hellenic cities still had no church in 180 (Table 3-3).

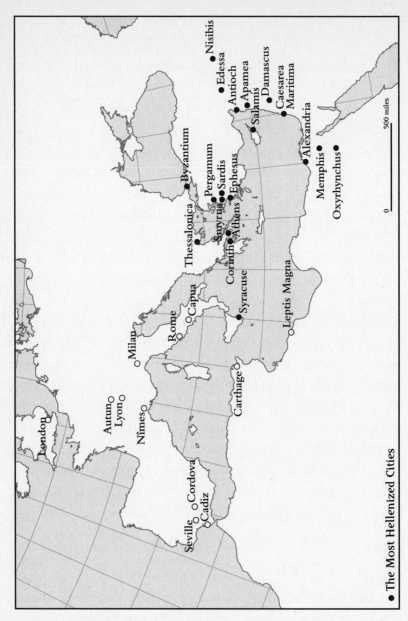

MAP 3-2. The Most Hellenized Cities

City-Size and Nonconformity

For more than a century, social scientists have postulated and explored the effects of city-size on a variety of matters, especially on deviant behavior. In 1975 these efforts were formulated into a subcultural theory of urbanism by Claude S. Fischer. A key proposition is: "The more urban the place, the higher the rates of unconventionality."[42] By "more urban" Fischer merely meant having a larger population. The reasoning behind this proposition is that the larger the population, the easier it is to assemble the "critical mass" needed to form a *deviant subculture*—that is, a group of people who sustain unconventional (deviant) outlooks and/or activities. If, for example, a dozen people are needed to form and sustain a deviant subculture, other things being equal it will be easier to find and recruit a dozen like-minded people out of a population of 10,000 than out of a population of 100. Fischer explicitly included religious groups among unconventional subcultures. Obviously, early Christianity was such a subculture, at odds with the conventional norms governing religious expression in the Greco-Roman world. It follows, therefore, that Christians would have been able to assemble the critical mass needed to form a congregation sooner in larger cities than in smaller ones.

Of course, there weren't many truly large Greco-Roman cities: only two had more than 200,000 people, and only five had 100,000 or more. To attain variation sufficient for analysis, all eight cities having a population of 75,000 or more were classified as larger cities.

HYPOTHESIS 3-4: *Larger cities had Christian congregations sooner than smaller cities.*

The data show a substantial difference: three-fourths of the larger cities had a church by 100 CE, while only a third of smaller cities did so. All of the larger cities had a church by 180 CE, but a third of the smaller cities still did not (Table 3-4). The difference is statistically significant, and thus the hypothesis is supported. (Fischer's proposition will be tested again in later chapters involving other unconventional religious movements.)

An additional statistical procedure can give us greater insight into the data. Thus far the analysis has been limited to two variables—city-size and Christianization, for example. Sometimes, however, social scientists want to explore the effects of two or more variables *simultaneously* on some third variable. For example, it might make sense to see the combined impact of Hellenism *and* city-size on Christianization. The technique involved is known as *regression analysis,* and while the underlying mathematics are complex, the results are easy to understand. (Complete results for the analysis of the impact of Hellenism and city-size on Christianization are shown in Regression 3-1 in the Statistical Appendix.) In this case, regression analysis shows that both Hellenism and city-size have significant, independent effects on Christianization but that the effect of Hellenism is substantially greater than that of city-size.

There was no urgent reason to apply regression analysis here other than to introduce the method. In some later applications, however, it will be important to see if a certain variable has any independent effect in combination with some other variable(s).

Conclusion

As mentioned earlier in the chapter, there is nothing earthshaking about any of these quantitative findings. It is well accepted that Christianity made its earliest appearances in the larger port cities at the eastern end of the empire, where Hellenic culture prevailed.

In that sense, the results are very reassuring. Had the data not supported these hypotheses, that would have been grounds to question the entire approach. Instead, for many scholars the real surprises in this chapter are statistical: the magnitude and the stability of the statistical results strongly testify that a quantitative approach to early church history is possible and plausible. But is it *valuable?* That can be demonstrated only by results that shed light on matters that are in dispute.

TEMPLE OF ISIS. Ruins of a great temple built to Isis on the coast of Egypt. Isis worship came close to being a form of monotheism and served as a very effective forerunner to Christianity.

—ɯ—

Cybele and Isis: 'Oriental' Forerunners

CHRISTIANITY was not the only new religious movement from the East that attracted widespread support in the Greco-Roman world. Nevertheless, even the best and most influential studies of the rise of Christianity give scant attention to the available pagan religious options, perhaps on the assumption that the triumph of Christianity proved that the opposition lacked vigor and plausibility. Not so! Well before the birth of Jesus, two goddess-based 'oriental' religions achieved great power and prominence across the empire: Cybele from Phrygia (central Turkey) and Isis from Egypt.

Cybele and her passionate devotees arrived first. The secret to Cybele's attraction was that she was presented as a far more potent and demanding deity than those forming the traditional Greco-Roman pantheon. Even though the Senate attempted to isolate Cybele and prevent Romans from taking up this faith, her followers proliferated until she had more temples in the city than did any traditional Roman god.[1] However, she fell short of satisfying a growing trend toward monotheism among Greco-Romans. For many people, Isis worship filled this need, being an 'oriental' faith verging on monotheism.

In this chapter I explain why Isiacism—that is, the worship of Isis—could not be transmuted into authentic monotheism and briefly examine why similarities such as those between Isis worship and Christianity do not demonstrate that both religions are 'mythical,' as so often is asserted. Turning to the actual spread of both Cybelene worship and Isiacism, and their role in preparing the way for Christianity, I will derive and test some specific hypotheses. Finally, I will explain why polytheism is never a match for monotheism when people are permitted to choose freely. But first let's look at why 'oriental' religions became so popular in the West.

The Appeal of 'Oriental' Religions

The best analysis of why religions from the East achieved great popular success was written a century ago by Franz Cumont, the great Belgian historian. Cumont argued that 'oriental' religions succeeded because they "gave greater satisfaction." They did so in three ways. First, "they appealed more strongly to the senses," having a far higher content of emotionalism, especially in their worship activities. Second, they appealed directly to the individual rather than to the community, linking faith to the "conscience" and offering converts a path to atonement for their sins. Finally "they satisfied the intellect" by possessing written scriptures and by presenting a more potent and virtuous portrait of the gods.[2] Although the discussion here will focus on pagan 'oriental' faiths, keep in mind that Christianity was, in many respects, an 'oriental' faith as well.

Emotionalism

Traditional Roman religions mainly involved tepid civic ceremonies. They sought to enlist the traditional gods of the city or state to provide protection and prosperity. For the most part this involved public rites conducted by priests and involved little more than some chanting and a sacrifice. Even 'worship' by groups devoted to a specific deity usually amounted to little more than an occasional animal sacrifice followed by a banquet.[3] As Cumont put it: "Perhaps there never was a religion so cold and prosaic as the Roman."[4] Although not quite as restrained, traditional Greek religions also relegated religious emotionalism "to the periphery of religious life."[5]

In contrast, the new 'oriental' faiths stressed celebration, joy, ecstasy, and passion. Music played a leading role in the services of these faiths—not only flutes and horns, but an abundance of group singing and dancing. As for ecstasy, the behavior of participants in the worship of some of these groups seems to have been very like modern Pentecostalism—people going into trancelike states and speaking in unknown tongues. Writing in the second century, the physician Aretaeus of Cappadocia described worshippers of Cybele as entering a state of ecstatic madness. "This madness is divine possession. When they end the state of madness, they are in good spirits, free of sorrow, as if consecrated by initiation to the God."[6] As Cumont summed up: "The Oriental religions touched every chord of sensibility and satisfied the thirst for religious emotion that the austere Roman creed had been unable to quench."[7]

Individualism and Virtue

The 'oriental' religions were not devoted to sanctifying civic life, but were instead directed toward the individual's spiritual life and her or his moral obligations. In contrast, Roman religions imposed a collective standard of guilt: lapses on the part of one or several members of the community, such as failure to properly propitiate the gods, brought punishment to all. Moreover, aside from requiring humans to venerate them properly, the Roman gods seemed to care little about human behavior, moral or immoral. Worse, the Roman gods set bad examples of individual morality: they lied, stole, raped, committed adultery, betrayed, and tortured. Consequently, since "Hermes steals, then there are also Hermes festivals at which stealing is allowed; if the gods rape earthly women, then there are ceremonial occasions on which the most beautiful virgin or even the 'queen' must surrender to a Stronger One."[8] Thus did Roman religion fail to support the moral order. The same applied to Greek religion: the Greeks did not regard morality as god-given, but of human origins—"Greek gods do not give laws."[9]

In contrast, the 'oriental' religions stressed individual morality and offered various means of atonement. Some of these were built into their initiation rites, which stressed purification and the washing away of guilt. Not content to offer atonement through rites alone, the 'oriental' faiths required acts of self-denial and privation, sometimes even physical suffering—actions that gave credibility to doctrines of individual forgiveness. Moreover, *cities* were neither punished nor saved; *individuals* could "wash away the impurities of the soul . . . [and] restore lost purity."[10]

Sophistication and the Intellect

Having noted that the traditional religions of Greece and Rome had degenerated into "a collection of unintelligible rites . . . me-

what Roman & Greek religion couldn't provide, Those societies made up w. ethics, mores, law & philosophy

chanically reproduced ... that were no longer understood or sincerely cherished," Cumont remarked: "Never did a people of advanced culture have a more infantile religion."[11]

Given that their societies were abundant in profound *written* philosophies, it is remarkable that the traditional Greek and Roman religions had no scriptures. "They had no written works which established their tenets and doctrines, or provided explanation of their rituals or moral prescription for their adherents."[12] In contrast, just like Judaism, the 'oriental' faiths were religions of the book, offering extensive written scriptures that "captivated the cultured mind."[13] Moreover, as will be seen, the 'oriental' faiths presented a far more rational portrait of the gods, increasingly trending toward monotheism.

As Cumont summarized: "[T]he Oriental religions acted upon the senses, the intellect and the conscience at the same time, and therefore gained a hold on the entire man. Compared with the ancient creeds, they appear to have offered greater beauty of ritual, greater truth of doctrine and a far superior morality. . . . The worship of the Roman gods was a civic duty, the worship of the foreign gods the expression of personal belief."[14] Until the advent of Christianity, the two most influential, new 'oriental' religions were both devoted to goddesses: Cybele and Isis.

Cybele: The Great Mother (Magna Mater) of the Gods

Cybele's origins are lost in unrecorded history. Many scholars believe she evolved from the generic mother goddess found in many primitive religions.[15] In any event, Cybele seems to have first come into her own in Phrygia, in central Anatolia (modern Turkey). Archaeological evidence from as far back as the eighth century BCE establishes *Matar* (as she was known then) as "the most important cult figure in Phrygia."[16] Unfortunately, thinking leaves neither ruins nor fossils, so almost nothing is known of the mythology surrounding Matar. It was not until she was known as *Kybele* (in Greek) or *Cybele* (in Latin) that her mythology left traces to come down to us. And clearly, much of this mythology was not of Phrygian origin. In Greek and Roman mythology, Cybele is linked to Attis, whose castration, death, and rebirth are central to her story. However, Attis seems to have been unknown in Phrygia, as Matar was usually depicted alone, and any male companions were always depicted as much smaller figures, indicating that they were merely "attendants, not equals."[17]

Turning to the Greco-Roman Cybelene mythology, we read of an unusually handsome Phrygian shepherd named Attis (who in some accounts is of supernatural origins), with whom Cybele fell in love. Unfortunately, the young man became sexually involved with a nymph, and Cybele found out. In a fit of extreme anger Cybele caused Attis to become insane, and in his mad frenzy he castrated himself, lay down under a pine tree, and bled to death.

CYBELE. A votive offering depicting the goddess Cybele (Magna Mater) that was left at one of her temples near Rome by a devotee. These reliefs were pressed out by the thousands and sold to those who wished to seek a favor.

Cybele, sorrowing, caused Attis to be reborn, and he became her companion ever after.

Although Attis never became a major figure, remaining only a member of Cybele's supporting cast, his self-castration became a major feature of Cybelene worship. The most solemn ritual of that worship was the *taurobolium,* wherein a bull was slaughtered on a wooden platform under which lay new initiates, who were then drenched in the bull's blood—all in commemoration of Attis's mutilation. It was believed that the blood washed away each initiate's past, giving each a new life. But perhaps the most remarkable aspect linking the Attis story to Cybelene worship is that all "priests of Cybele were eunuchs; self-castration in ecstasy was part of the process of [their] initiation."[18] This Cybelene mythology and the self-castration of her priests must have developed in Greece, because both were fully developed by the time Cybele reached Rome.

Cybele Arrives in Rome

Just as Christianity gained immense influence by being credited with bringing Constantine victory at the Battle of Milvian Bridge, Cybele (also known to the Romans as Magna Mater, or Great Mother) grew in favor after it appeared that she had helped Rome militarily. She was brought to Rome by order of the Senate in 204 BCE (personified by a hunk of meteorite) because of a prophecy inferred from the Sibylline Books, and confirmed by the oracle at Delphi, that she would deliver victory for Rome over Hannibal. Within months after her arrival in Rome, the prophecy was fulfilled. Soon after, a temple was erected to Cybele on the summit of the Palatine, and the meteorite was set as the face of a silver statue of the goddess. Cybele was worshipped there for more than five hundred years. Every March 27, the silver statue of Cybele was borne by a procession of her priests to a nearby tributary of the Tiber River and bathed, then carried back to the temple.

The Romans soon learned that having Cybele on their side was a very mixed blessing. Cybelene worship was a wild, disruptive affair. "The enthusiastic transports and somber fanaticism of [Cybelene worship] contrasted violently with the calm dignity and respectable reserve of the official religions."[19] Her priests, known as the *galli*, excelled at ecstatic frenzies. Not only did they castrate themselves during their initiation, but subsequently they cross-dressed, wore makeup, frizzed their hair, drenched themselves in perfume, and acted like women. Romans were shocked. Although they were not offended by homosexuality, they found effeminacy disgusting. Yet they could not doubt the power of the goddess: she had ended the Carthaginian threat. They resolved the issue by isolating the religion before it could infect the populace, but permitting the 'barbaric' rites to continue on her behalf. Once a year Cybele was honored by all Romans, and her "priests marched the streets in procession, dressed in motley costumes, loaded with heavy jewelry, and beating tambourines."[20] During the rest of the year the priests were "segregated and inaccessible to the Romans[;] their cultic activities were confined to the temple."[21] Moreover, Roman citizens were prohibited by law from becoming Cybelene priests.

In time, Cybelene worship adjusted to Rome, and Rome adjusted to the Cybelenes. The legend of Attis was minimized, and eventually Romans were allowed to become priests. But having originated as a defender of the state, Cybelene worship remained mainly a state cult, and the major rituals were public—there was little "participation by the population at large."[22] But its hold on the elite, on those most concerned with the preservation of the Roman state, remained strong. As late as the fifth century, as paganism was fading away, many of the Roman upper class still turned to Cybele.

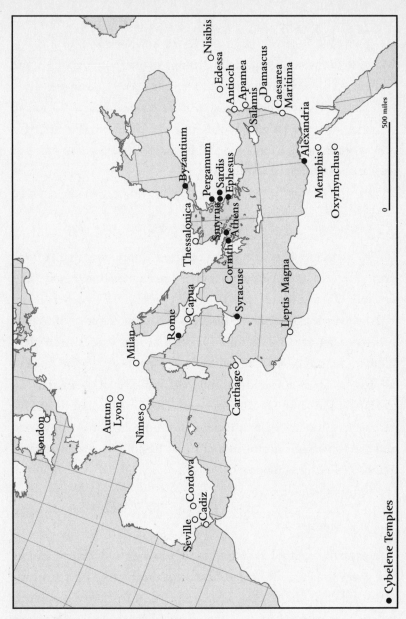

MAP 4-1. Cybelene Temples

Cybelene Worship Across the Empire

Map 4-1 shows which of the thirty-one major cities of the empire
are known to have had a Cybelene temple, based on the fine study
by Lynn E. Roller (1999). As might be expected of an 'oriental'
religion, with the exception of Rome the Cybelene temples were
concentrated in the East. Indeed, because Cybelene worship was
an imported religion, it follows that:

HYPOTHESIS 4-1: *Port cities, with their constant flow of foreigners,
were more likely than inland cities to have Cybelene temples.*

The hypothesis is strongly supported: more than half of the
port cities had a temple, while only 12 percent of the inland cities
had one (Table 4-1).

As we saw earlier, Claude Fischer's subcultural theory of urbanism was supported by data on Christianization. The larger a city's
population, the easier it seems to have been to gather the nucleus
needed to form a Christian congregation. But it seems far less
likely that the same correlation would hold for the spread of Cybelene worship, given that little or no missionizing was involved
and the founding nucleus in a city was based on sojourners from
abroad.[23] Thus the hypothesis:

HYPOTHESIS 4-2: *City-size was not significantly related
to Cybelene worship.*

Although larger cities were more apt to have a Cybelene temple
than were smaller cities, the difference is modest and only margin-
ally significant (Table 4-2). Using regression to clarify the effect,
we see that larger cities were not more likely to have a Cybelene
temple once the effect of port cities was taken into account. Therefore the hypothesis is supported by the data (Regression 4-1).

Later in this chapter we will examine why Isiacism, as an almost monotheistic faith, helped prepare pagans for the Christian message. But 'oriental' faiths in general probably contributed to the spread of Christianity as well, since Christianity manifested those characteristics that, according to Cumont, made 'oriental' faiths attractive: emotionalism, an appeal to individualism and virtue, and sophistication. Hence:

HYPOTHESIS 4-3: *Cities with Cybelene temples had Christian churches sooner than cities without Cybelene temples.*

Eight of the ten cities having Cybelene temples had a church by the end of the first century, while only 24 percent of cities without a temple had a church that early. Slightly more than a third of cities without a temple still had no Christian congregation by the year 180; no city with a temple still had no church at that time. The results are highly significant. The hypothesis is strongly supported (Table 4-3).

But what about ports? With the effect of Cybelene temples controlled by regression, ports no longer have a significant direct effect on Christianization (Regression 4-2). The best interpretation may be that the importation of Cybele fully exploited the receptivity of the port cities, and Christianity did not initially break any new ground in gaining a start.

In any event, it seems clear that Cybele was a significant forerunner to Christianity. Of course, despite her appeal, Cybele was just another divinity among the many. Moreover, a trend toward gods of greater scope had begun in the Greco-Roman world.

Evolution of the Gods

The gods of Greco-Roman paganism were of many sizes, shapes, sexes, and species. Some of them, like Cybele, had many names, while many others shared the same name: "three gods named

Zeus, four named Hephaistos and five [each] named Dionysos, Aphrodite, and Athena."[24] But none was supremely powerful and most were of dubious worth to humans, being unreliable and of doubtful virtue—"charming figures [but] . . . unedifying examples."[25] Eventually, the lack of character of the gods, their great number, and their incapacity drew intellectual scorn. Some people embraced atheism, while others began to conceive of gods having far greater scope.

Bill Clinton

Atheism and Impersonal Essences

There is nothing modern about unbelief. About five hundred years before the birth of Jesus, the Greek poet and philosopher Xenophanes dismissed Homer's portrayal of the gods as immoral nonsense. Given that both Greeks and Romans were prone to punish atheism with death,[26] Xenophanes was careful to acknowledge that "there is one God," before going on to claim that "neither in shape nor in thought [does this God] resemble mortals." As for the abundant gods of Greek polytheism, Xenophanes noted that "men imagine gods to be born and to have raiment and voice and body, like themselves . . . [but these are] fictions of the earlier people." He then pointed out that "oxen, lions, and horses, if they had hands wherewith to grave images, would fashion gods after their own shapes and make them bodies like their own." Xenophanes concluded by flatly asserting agnosticism: "No man has perceived certainty, nor shall anyone perceive it, about the gods . . . for, however perfect what he says may be, yet he does not know it; all things are matters of opinion."[27]

Other classical philosophers, such as Epicurus (341–270 BCE), finessed the issue of atheism by asserting the existence of the gods before dismissing them as utterly irrelevant, maintaining that they played no active role in nature or human affairs—that "there is no

Providence to be feared or divine powers to be feared or hoped for."[28] These views were echoed by Lucretius (ca. 94–55 BCE), who wrote that the gods exist in "complete tranquility, aloof and detached from our affairs[,] . . . exempt from any need of us, indifferent to our merits and immune from our anger."[29] He went on to assert that the gods created nothing, but are a sort of creation of the eternal universe.   *Deism*

Cicero (106–43 BCE) ventured a bit further in his famous *Concerning the Nature of the Gods,* quoting Diogenes that "the prosperity and good fortune of the wicked disprove the might and power of the gods entirely."[30] As for those who credit the gods for good fortune, perhaps by citing the many whose prayers brought them safely to port during a storm, Cicero noted the multitudes who drowned despite their prayers. Sextus Empiricus (perhaps in the first century CE) expanded this argument at some length, concluding that the obvious existence of evil and tragedy proves that if there is a God, he does not "forethink all things." To say he does forethink all things is to say God is "malignant"; to say he does not is to say he is "weak."[31]

Atheism may have attracted some intellectuals, but it could not achieve popular appeal. Nor could the anemic religious ideas proposed by Greco-Roman philosophers and intellectuals, who increasingly favored an extremely abstract conception of a supreme God. Although most classical philosophers taught that the universe is eternal and thus there is no need for a divine creator, many accepted that nevertheless there must have been a first cause, an unmoved mover. Some philosophers characterized this cause or mover as merely a principle representing unknown and possibly unknowable laws of physics—an inactive and unaware 'thing,' at least so far as human activities are concerned. However, since such a principle must be eternal and of a scope corresponding to the universe, many philosophers identified this first cause as God. But even though they employed the word *God* to identify the first mover, many philosophers did not think of it as a conscious entity, as a being, but as an unconscious 'essence.' Some philosophers, including Aristotle, did conceive of this supreme God as a thinking being, albeit one so impersonal that it is never clear what he/she/it might think about, care about, or do. In addition to calling this rather inert divinity God, Plato postulated the existence of a lower divine being he called the Demiurge, who was the personification of reason. Plato proposed that it was the Demiurge, not God, who constructed the world. Even so, Plato viewed the Demiurge as a being having only limited powers, who could only construct the world from already available materials and in accord with an already-given set of ideas. Some historians doubt that Plato really intended the Demiurge to be taken literally as a divine being.[32]

In any event, classical philosophers increasingly leaned toward monotheism in the sense that they limited supreme divinity to one. But, as noted, most did so not by regarding God as a being, but by reducing the divine to an impersonal, remote, *essence* rather like the Asian concept of the Tao, so that the net effect was closer to godlessness than to monotheism. One of the attractions of an impersonal conception of God is that a divine essence bears no responsibility for evil or tragedy. A lost battle cannot be blamed on the Tao, nor can grieving parents wonder why the Tao did not heed their prayers for a dying child. But, of course, that also is the fatal weakness of essences and explains why pure Taoism has never prevailed as a popular religion. Only a few Asian monks and intellectuals ever have been true Taoists. As for popular Taoism, all its temples abound in anthropomorphic gods, as do all the Confucian temples as well. For of what use is a god that does nothing? Where is the comfort in a god that neither hears nor sees? Any statue is every bit as godlike as a divine essence. Hence, much philosophical monotheism was largely irrelevant as a religious factor in antiquity[33] except as it set a tone in favor of embracing a supreme *being*.

And indeed, some classical philosophers did accept the idea that even the supreme God was a being, and dealt with the problem of evil by proposing the existence of two 'gods,' as Plato had done. One of these gods was acknowledged as supreme. Though a conscious being, this ultimate God was so remote as to be irrelevant to daily life. The other, the Demiurge, was a much lower, but very active divinity. It was this lower god, as creator, who was to blame for the existence of evil. In some interpretations, the Demiurge was the equivalent of Satan: a 'fallen' lesser divinity of evil intent. This was, of course, how Judaism and Christianity solved the problem of evil. The concept of one supreme God and an 'evil' creator, having been given a philosophical blessing by Plato and others, predisposed Hellenic intellectuals to accept Christian and Jewish monotheism. But some intellectuals interpreted the thesis of a greater God and a lesser god in a far more radical way. They reasoned that if the Demiurge created the world and everything in it, and if the Demiurge was responsible for evil too, then everything on earth was hopelessly corrupt and ultra-asceticism was the only valid religious option. It was a strange amalgam of philosophy, paganism, Judaism, and Christianity. It appeared in the many forms and varieties that have come to be known collectively as Gnosticism. That development awaits us in Chapters 6 and 7.

Supreme Gods

Many sophisticated Romans were offended by reverence for 'animal' gods or for half-human beasts such as jackal-headed Anubis, falcon-headed Horus, or cat-headed Bast. In reference to Mithra, Emperor Augustus often said he worshipped gods, not bulls; and his sentiments were seconded by Lucian and others.[34] But whatever their taste in gods, many ancients also were deeply troubled by the sheer chaos that existed because of the enormous expansion of the number of gods and the confusion as to their names and functions.

To deal with these matters, around 300 BCE Ptolemy I, a comrade of Alexander the Great and the first Greek ruler of Egypt, commissioned two distinguished priests to impose some order:[35] Manetho was an Egyptian historian[36] with ties to Isiacism, while Timotheus was an Athenian who had settled in Egypt after being involved in the mysteries at Eleusis. Their major innovation was to organize the gods into a hierarchy ruled by a *supreme God:* creator, rule-giver, all-powerful being. Rather than refer to this supreme God as Zeus or by another traditional name, Manetho and Timotheus named him Serapis. Although Serapis was immediately popular in Egypt (especially because his introduction was accompanied by the reopening of the traditional temples that had been shut by the Persians), he "was deliberately created by the Ptolemaic theologians for export abroad. He had powers of assimilation to the leading Gods of Greece and in time won international acceptance."[37]

To acknowledge a supreme God does not constitute actual monotheism so long as the existence of subordinate gods is retained. But to propose that at least one divinity was of great magnitude and rectitude proved to be an immensely popular idea. Soon not only Serapis but a number of other supreme gods were proposed, including Sol Invictus, Jupiter, and Mithras.

Of course, a plausible monotheistic option, portraying God as a conscious, active being, had long been fully available in antiquity. And many took up this option by becoming Jews, while many others went halfway by taking the role of God-fearers. Still others pursued an *almost* monotheistic pagan option, choosing to honor Isis, the Goddess Supreme, the Queen of the Sky, the Mother of the Stars.

Isis Worship: The Almost Monotheism

Isis was widely referred to as "the savior goddess," "or more explicitly 'saviour of the human race.'"[38] As Plutarch explained: "Isis is the female principle in nature, which is the receiver of every act of creation; wherefore she is called 'nurse' and 'receiver of all' by Plato, and by mankind in general 'the goddess of ten thousand names,' because she is changed by reason she receives all shapes and forms."[39]

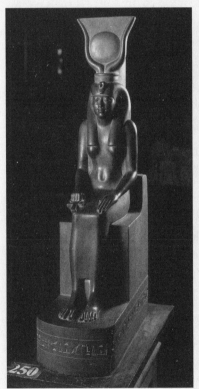

ISIS GOES WEST. The goddess Isis originated in Egypt, and her popularity eventually spread throughout the Roman Empire. As this took place, so did a remarkable change in appearance. The statue on the left is from Egypt. The one on the right is Roman.

The many surviving inscriptions and scriptures in praise of Isis
include such claims as:[40]

It was Isis "who separated earth from heaven, showed the
stars their courses, ordained the path of sun and moon."

Isis is "sole ruler of eternity"; she notes that "all call me the
highest goddess, greatest of all the gods in heaven," and
"nothing happens apart from me."

Isis is "ruler of the world . . . greatest of the gods, the . . .
ruler of heavenly things and immeasurable. . . . [She is] the
ruler of all forever."

In *The Golden Ass,* a work of fiction written in the second century, Apuleius offered this hymn to Isis: "The gods above worship
you; the gods below reverence you; you turn the earth and give
light to the sun, you rule the world. . . . The stars respond to you,
the seasons return, the gods rejoice, the elements give service. By
your will the winds blow, the clouds give nourishment, seeds
sprout, fruits grow. . . . My voice lacks the strength to express what
I think of your majesty, nor would a thousand mouths or tongues
continuing to speak forever."[41]

Not bad for a female divinity who had spent several thousand
years as no more than a respected Egyptian goddess. The original
Isis myth is typical of its Egyptian origin. As was frequently the
case among Egyptians, commoners as well as royalty,[42] Isis was believed to have married her twin brother, Osiris. Their initial mat-
ing took place within the womb of their mother, Nut, goddess of
the sky. Osiris and Isis had a brother Seth and a sister Nephthys,
and they too married. Seth turned out to be evil and jealous, and
eventually he murdered Osiris, tore his body into fourteen pieces,

and flung them all over the earth. A mourning Isis searched far and wide for the pieces of her beloved Osiris's corpse. Having found everything but his penis, she carefully reassembled his body, placed him in a tomb, and then raised him from the dead. Subsequently, Osiris became the judge of the dead.

At this point Isis became pregnant with Horus. In some accounts she was impregnated rather miraculously by Osiris after his resurrection (sans penis). In others, she was impregnated by a flash of lightning. After Horus was born, he too became the target of Seth's jealousy, and Isis was forced to flee into the marshes with her son to prevent him from being murdered. When Horus grew up he defeated Seth—a detail reminiscent of Moses having been hidden in the bulrushes and living to defeat the pharaoh. As for Isis, she ruled on for centuries as the goddess in charge of the annual inundations of the Nile, as a healer, and as a patron of lovers and married couples.

But Isis experienced a sudden rise to supremacy when Manetho and Timotheus, in their ranking of the gods, paired her with Serapis. As temples to Serapis proliferated, a section always was devoted to Isis. Probably in part as a reflection of the popularity of Cybele, Isis emerged as far more important than Serapis when the duo made their way westward, and many temples devoted exclusively to her were built. Eventually she had almost twice as many temples in the city of Rome as did Cybele, and almost three times as many as Jupiter, the leading traditional Roman god.[43]

Although Isis sometimes was referred to as the "one True and Living God,"[44] she could not rise above the station of supreme God because the existence of a whole pantheon of other gods, including her offspring, could not be denied within the context of paganism. Moreover, hers was entirely an otherworldly tale, in contrast to the manifest historicity of Judaism and Christianity. Or, as Cyril Bailey put it: "On the one side were the legendary figures, unhistorical and mere puppets in a story[;] ... on the other side there were indeed historical personages."[45] God was believed to have revealed himself to mortal Jews, and the Old Testament tells the history of a real people as it occurred on this earth. In similar fashion, the New Testament reports the thoughts and actions of real people in real places. Jesus was an actual man raised in Nazareth. He preached to real people, walked the hills of a real land, and died a real death. It was to a worldly tomb that he was taken and from which he is believed to have arisen: the resurrection of Jesus was not situated in another world. Both the Old and the New Testaments abound in geographical and historical details, although, as Larry Hurtado pointed out, readers of the "Gospels may have become so accustomed to these things that they have to pause to note the sheer abundance of local color ... an impressive body of information about the geography and sociocultural features of Roman Judea."[46] In contrast, Isis's 'biography' took place entirely within the invisible world of the gods. No human ever clasped her hand or joined her at table. Isis simply could not be freed from the fundamental shortcomings of mythology.

Even so, there are significant correspondences between the Isis story and Christianity. Isis's birth (with Osiris) was greeted by heavenly displays.[47] Her conception of Horus without intercourse, as well as her frequent depiction as the loving mother nursing her child, has led to many comparisons with the Virgin Mary.[48] Of course, it was not Isis who was resurrected. Instead, she was credited with the powers of a supreme God by resurrecting Osiris. But resurrection came to play such a powerful role in her story that eventually she was celebrated as the savior who could help humans triumph over death,[49] at least to the extent of gaining a fuller life in the underworld.

Much the same can be said for the Cybelene myths. The idea of being washed in blood was not only of central importance (recall the *taurobolium*), but for less affluent devotees a lamb was substituted for the bull, and worshippers were thereby "washed in the blood of the lamb." In commemoration of the death of Attis, March 24 was designated the Day of Blood, a day devoted to fasting and mourning, and the next day was designated the Festival of Joy, noting the rebirth of Attis. This two-day event became one of the great festivals of Rome.[50] The correspondence with Good Friday and Easter has often been noted.

On Similarity and Secularity

Having noted similarities between Isiacism, Cybelene worship, and Christianity, it seems appropriate to pause briefly to discuss whether such resemblances, and the many others involving pagan gods, discredit Christianity.

For centuries, comparative religion has been a bastion of atheism.[51] The "first [serious] work of comparative religion" was composed in 1593 by Jean Bodin, a former Carmelite monk, who argued that by virtue of the competing claims to truth made by the many faiths found around the world, "all are refuted by all."[52] A century later Pierre Bayle published his *Dictionaire historique et critique,* in which he focused on the sexual irregularities among Greco-Roman gods and goddesses as a safe way to attack all religion, being confident that his readers would see the many obvious parallels with Christianity. During the eighteenth century many skeptics disguised their attacks on religion as critiques of paganism or of the many primitive faiths being discovered by western explorers. This aspect of comparative religion may have reached its peak with James Frazer's many volumes of *The Golden Bough* (1890–1915). Frazer compiled an enormous set of examples in order to argue that tales of crucifixion and resurrection are standards of world mythology. He claimed to have established that there is nothing original whatever in the Christian tradition—or in any religious tradition, for that matter. All is generic, especially if one's criteria are as elastic as Frazer's.

But if Frazer's was the most extensive effort to advance secularity by demonstrating similarities among religions, it surely was not the last. These days scholarly neo-pagans are especially hostile toward any hint that Christianity had anything new, let alone better, to offer.[53] Indeed, it is their usual claim that Christianity can hardly have been inspired since it offers only a rather stale mixture of conventional pagan ideas and myths. Their point seems to be that one either embraces all of the gods or none.

Of course, from the beginning Christian theologians have been fully aware of similarities between the Christ story and pagan mythology. And it did not disturb them to admit that elements of God's final revelation had seeped into human awareness to help prepare the way. Moreover, the familiarity of the Christ story was entirely consistent with the long-standing Christian premise that God's revelations are *always limited to the current capacity of humans to comprehend*. For example, in the fourth century St. John Chrysostom noted that even the seraphim do not see God as he is. Instead, they see "a condescension accommodated to their nature. What is this condescension? It is when God appears and makes himself known, not as he is, but in the way one incapable of beholding him is able to look upon him. In this way God reveals himself proportionately to the weakness of those who behold him."[54]

In similar fashion, St. Gregory of Nyssa wrote in the fourth century that God is so "far above our nature and inaccessible to all approach" that he, in effect, speaks to us in baby talk, thereby giving "to our human nature what it is capable of receiving."[55] St. Thomas Aquinas agreed: "The things of God should be revealed to mankind only in proportion to their capacity; otherwise, they might despise what was beyond their grasp. . . . It was, therefore, better for the divine mysteries to be conveyed to an uncultured people as it were veiled."[56] So too, John Calvin flatly asserted that God "reveals himself to us according to our rudeness and infirmity."[57] If scriptural comparisons—as between the two testaments, for example—seem to suggest that God is changeable or inconsistent, that is merely because "he accommodated diverse forms to different ages, as he knew would be expedient for each[;] . . . he has accommodated himself to men's capacity, which is varied and changeable."[58]

Thus, if the Christ story seems steeped in pagan conventions, this does not necessarily show these elements to be false. Rather, their very conventionality can be interpreted as having been the most effective way for God to communicate within the limits of Greco-Roman comprehension. These were 'proofs' of Christ's divinity that pagans could most easily recognize. Cyril Bailey expressed this very well. At the time Christianity arose, he said, "Men were looking in certain directions and couched their religious aspirations and beliefs in certain terms. Christianity spoke the language which they understood and set its theology and its ritual in the forms which to its own generation seemed natural[;] . . . the Gospel [could not] have won its way if it had not found an echo in the religious searchings and even the religious beliefs of the time."[59] After all, an incomprehensible faith would surely have required miraculous conversions.

Hence, the similarities between Christianity and paganism can be explained in terms of human limitations—that is, as instances of divine condescension. At the very least, the claim that similarity necessitates secularity is far less convincing than has been supposed by ardent atheists or the theologically uninformed.

All this having been said, back to Isis as the trailblazer.

Measuring the Spread of Isiacism

A remarkable archaeological as well as textual legacy makes it possible to measure the spread of Isiacism with some accuracy. However, it is necessary to impose some restrictions. Although Isis had begun to spread quite rapidly by the third century BCE, she continued to gain in popularity and to prompt the construction of new temples well into the Christian era. If, however, we want to focus on Isiacism as a trailblazer that facilitated the rise of Christianity, it seems appropriate to cease coding new sites by the year 100 CE. That is the date of selection of the thirty-one cities used in this study, and thus new Isis temples beyond that date are of less significance as *fore*runners. This limit posed a problem as I compiled data, since not all of the sources are adequately dated, nor do they all agree. However, by cross-checking various sources I was able to produce the coding shown in Map 4-2.[60]

Isis Goes West

Having benefited from being paired with Serapis, Isis gained substantial followings throughout the Grecian world ruled by Alexander's heirs. Then it was her turn to go westward into the Roman world, transported by Greek merchants and sailors.

To adequately report this westward journey it is necessary to anticipate discussion in Chapter 7 of misguided current notions about pagan 'tolerance.' As Jonathan Kirsch explained: "Nowhere in the ancient world was the open-mindedness [of paganism] more apparent than in imperial Rome."[61] In support, Kirsch quoted Ramsay MacMullen to the effect that paganism was "no more than a spongy mass of tolerance and tradition."[62] If that was true, then why all the intolerance of Cybele? And, lest that be

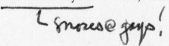

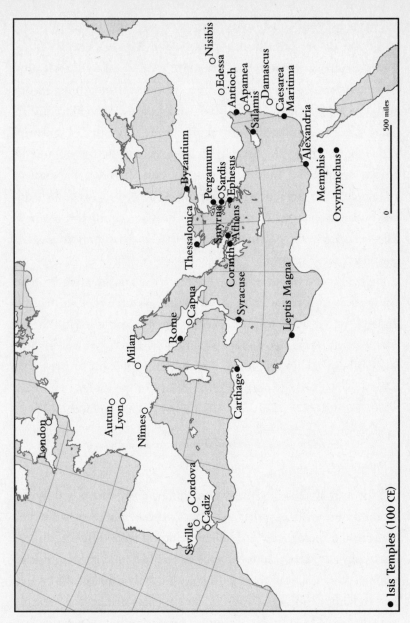

MAP 4-2. Isis Temples (100 CE)

thought to have been a unique case, perhaps provoked by the self-castration of her priesthood, why did the Roman Senate outlaw Isis worship in 58 BCE?[63] If paganism was so tolerant, why did Roman consuls around the empire respond to this ruling by destroying Isiac altars as "disgusting and pointless superstitions"?[64] Why was Isiacism "vigorously repressed by Augustus,"[65] and why did Tiberius have the Isiac temple in Rome destroyed and its priests crucified?[66] Indeed, it was Caligula, hardly a paragon of tolerance, who first allowed a temple dedicated to Isis to be built on Rome's Campus Martius, and it was not until the reign of Caracella early in the third century that an Isiac temple was allowed on the Capitoline.[67]

So when Isis went west, she encountered considerable Roman opposition to foreign cults, especially those of Egyptian origins. Indeed, well after political intolerance of Isis had ceased, Roman intellectuals continued to rage against all things Egyptian, including (and especially) religion.[68] Consequently, it is no surprise that Map 4-2 displays a marked eastern tilt: in Europe there are no Isiac sites west of Rome. This suggests a quite obvious hypothesis:

HYPOTHESIS 4-4: *The more Hellenized a city was, the more likely it was to be receptive to Isiacism.*

Not only was Isis of Egyptian origin, she was promoted by the Greek court in Alexandria—a court whose sphere of influence was limited mainly to the Hellenic cultural area. This is fully reflected by the data. Three-fourths of the Hellenic cities had Isiac temples as of the year 100 CE. In contrast, only three of the twelve less Hellenic (and hence more Roman) cities had an Isiac temple at that time. The difference is large and significant (Table 4-4).

A faith that radiated from Egypt was unlikely to have traveled far by foot. Alexandria, as the busiest port of the era, favored sea traffic. This too is the basis of a rather likely hypothesis:

HYPOTHESIS 4-5: *Port cities, with their constant flow of foreigners, were more receptive to Isiacism than inland cities.*

Once again the hypothesis is very strongly confirmed. Nearly all of the port cities had Isiac temples, while two-thirds of the inland cities did not (Table 4-5).

It seems useful to examine the independent and the joint effects of these two variables though regression. Each of the two variables has a strong independent effect. Together they account for 36 percent of the variation in the presence of Isiac temples (Regression 4-3).

Claude Fischer's subcultural theory of urbanism was supported by data on Christianization. The larger the population, we saw, the easier it seems to have been to gather the nucleus needed to form a Christian congregation. But the correlation did not hold for Cybele, and it seems unlikely that it would hold for the spread of Isiacism, since little or no missionizing was involved in the spread of Isis worship. Of course, many residents of various cities were drawn to an Isiac temple once it was up and running, but judging by inscriptions, the founding nucleus in a city was based on sojourners from abroad.[69] Thus another hypothesis:

HYPOTHESIS 4-6: *City-size was not significantly related to Isiacism.*

Although larger cities were more apt to have an Isiac temple than were smaller cities, say the data, the difference is very modest and not significant. The hypothesis is supported (Table 4-6).

Cultural Continuity and the Advance of Isiacism

The principle of cultural continuity holds that when making a religious choice, people will tend to conserve their religious 'capital.'

That means that even those who abandon their original religious heritage will prefer a relatively familiar faith. As an example, in modern Africa Mormon success is far more rapid in Christian than in Islamic nations. Christians who become Mormons retain their entire Christian culture, simply adding on to it. But Muslims, in becoming Mormons, must abandon a good deal of their original religious culture. The principle of cultural continuity can be rendered less precisely in a form that may be more agreeable to those not initiated into the social scientific temple as follows: people tend to find comfort in the familiar, even (and perhaps especially) when they are venturing into novelty.

Chapter 5 will demonstrate that cultural continuity favored Christianity vis-à-vis the Jews of the Diaspora. Along with much that was familiar to Jews, Christianity brought a vital, transformative new faith. But no matter how successful and long-lasting the mission to the Jews may have been, in the long run it was the mission to the Gentiles that was decisive. Put another way, even though there were at least six million Jews in the empire, what counted most as the Christian numbers mounted was not cultural continuity with *Judaism,* but cultural continuity with *paganism*! And it was here that Isiacism played a most significant role. Not only had many Greco-Romans participated in Isiacism, but by early in the Christian era most of them must have been familiar with the following key elements of her faith: even if Isiacism was not fully realized monotheism, at least it asserted the existence of a supreme creator-God; devotees of Isis accepted the idea of resurrection and something closely akin to an immaculate conception; and Isiacism promised a form of life after death far more attractive than had been typical of prior paganism. In all these ways Isiacism prepared the way for Christianity by making many elements of Christianity comfortably familiar to pagans.

This leads to:

HYPOTHESIS 4-7: *Cities with Isiac temples had Christian churches sooner than cities without Isiac temples.*

The hypothesis is confirmed overwhelmingly by the data. Nearly two-thirds of cities having an Isiac temple had a Christian church by 100 CE, and all of them did by 180 CE. In contrast, only two of fourteen cities without an Isiac temple had a church by 100 CE, and half still lacked a church in 180 CE (Table 4-7).

One might argue that this is a spurious correlation produced by the simple fact that both Isiacism and Christianity traveled the same sea routes west, but regression shows that this is not so. In fact, as with Cybelene worship, with Isiacism controlled ports have no independent effect on Christianization, while the independent effect of Isiacism is robust. This can be interpreted as a sequence: that travelers brought Isiacism to port cities, which in turn was such a potent factor in the rise of Christianity that it left no independent port effect (Regression 4-3).

HYPOTHESIS 4-8: *Cities having a temple to Cybele were more likely than those without also to have an Isiac temple.*

This hypothesis is strongly supported: cities tended to have worshippers of both Isis and Cybele or neither (Table 4-8). Thus it is appropriate to see the joint and independent effects of these two variables on Christianization (Regression 4-4). These results strongly attest to the independent effects of both Cybele and Isis on the rise of Christianity, although the effect of Isis is greater, as might be expected.

When Doctrine Matters

It is true, as noted earlier, that doctrine does not play the primary role in attracting converts, but we must not forget that doctrine determines whether or not the term *conversion* even applies to a shift in religious orientation. Not only does monotheism require an exclusive commitment; only monotheism generates missionizing activities on the part of its ordinary followers—and monotheism is a matter of doctrine. Because it is based on acceptance of One True God, monotheism generates strong, competitive organizations of people prepared to act on behalf of their faith, unlike those attached to a multitude of gods, or even those attached to one god from among a pantheon. The key to these differences in motivation and commitment lies in the far greater value and credibility of exchanges with a God of maximum scope, power, virtue, and dependability, as opposed to small gods whose intentions often are not benign. It was this comparison that fueled the early success of Isiacism and that, by the same token, caused the supreme Goddess to vacate her position to Christianity.

The fundamental element in all human involvement with divinity is exchange. Even small, local gods having very limited powers are a plausible source of many things humans greatly desire: they may grant benefits or withhold misfortunes. To obtain these advantages humans seek to learn what will please the gods and offer whatever that may be in hopes of gain. And, just as often occurs when humans engage in exchanges with one another,[70] humans frequently develop strong emotional attachments to divine trading partners; they often worship the gods out of love and respect, not merely for instrumental reasons.

It is a matter of self-evident economics, confirmed by millennia of religious practice, that the greater the number of gods, the lower will be the cost of exchanging with any one of them. 'God-shopping' is typical in polytheistic systems. In pursuit of rewards, people try various gods and make the specified offerings, repeating their patronage as justified by results and sometimes taking angry measures when a god fails to deliver. (In Taiwan people sometimes beat the statue of a god with sticks when their lottery tickets do not win.)[71] But such fleeting exchange relations do not apply when there is only one God, so long as that God is a *conscious, virtuous being*. In that case, people will accept an *extended exchange relationship*—that is, they will make continuing exchanges with such a God over a substantial length of time, usually until death. It is these long-term exchanges that make monotheism so irresistible and powerful.

One True God who knows and cares can inspire lifelong commitment and devotion. Consequently, such a God can require sustained, active participation in organized religious activities and can stimulate, even require, missionizing efforts to the unconverted. This capacity to unite and motivate people explains why Jews and Christians could overcome periodic efforts by tyrants to stamp them out of existence, most recently in the Soviet bloc and in China. It also explains why polytheistic faiths cannot withstand monotheistic missionizing. The evidence on this point is not merely historical, but current. A recent study in Singapore found that the overwhelming majority of college students from Buddhist families or those committed to various Chinese folk religions had converted to Islam or Christianity, while conversion from these monotheisms to Buddhism or to folk religions was essentially unknown.[72] In Japan, where polytheism still prevails, Soka Gakkai, a variant Buddhism that demands exclusive commitment, grew from fewer than six thousand households in 1951 to more than eight million in 1995. In Africa, traditional polytheism is vanishing in the face of very rapid Christianization as well as a substantial, but slower, rate of conversion to Islam. The current progress of Christian growth in China is astounding, especially in the face of continuing government interference; very credible sources estimate that there are anywhere from 50 to 100 million Christians now in China, nearly all of this growth having come subsequent to the imposition of Communist rule.

By the same token, only One True God can provide an adequate religious basis for the moral order. Divine essences such as the Tao do not command us to love one another. The "first mover" does not forbid us to covet another's spouse. Paul Tillich's conception of God as the "ground of our being" is not a being and therefore is incapable of having, let alone expressing, moral concerns. As for the little "beings" who populate pagan pantheons, they seem to concern themselves only with their own welfare and to ignore what people do to and for one another. Only monotheism serves as a basis for morality, for compelling and significant "thou shalts" and "thou shalt nots." This certainly is not to suggest that pagan societies lack morality, but to acknowledge that their moral orders are not justified on religious grounds. The link between monotheism and morality has been well demonstrated by research based on modern societies as well as by anthropological reports on premodern groups.[73]

In all this, the key is doctrine. Monotheism prevails because it offers a God worth dying for—indeed, a God who promises everlasting life. And that's why Christianity triumphed and why, even in the midst of a profoundly Christian world, Judaism has endured.[74]

Conclusion

The historical record strongly supports the idea that Cybelene worship and Isiacism served as important stepping-stones to Christianity by shaping pagan culture in ways that made the Christ story more familiar and credible. This thesis also is strongly supported by the statistical results showing that both these pagan faiths had strong independent effects on Christianizing the urban empire. In many ways, both Isiacism and Cybelene worship had more in common with the essential Christian message than did a whole raft of later religious writers and movements, often lumped together under the label of Gnosticism. But, of course, neither had nearly as much in common with Christianity as did Judaism.

MISSIONIZING. St. Paul's missions have inspired many paintings such as this one by Eustache Le Sueur, which shows him preaching at Ephesus. But how successful was Paul? And if his mission was to the Gentiles, why did he seem to spend most of his time among Jews?

—ɯɯ—

Paul and the Mission to the Hellenized Jews

MANY HISTORIANS seem to assume that the Christian mission to the Jews was a failure and that only a rapid influx of Gentile converts saved Christianity from obscurity. But that's not true. Christianity not only began as a Jewish movement, it continued to be dominated by Jews for a considerable period; in fact, it's possible that very substantial rates of Jewish conversion lasted until well into the fourth century.[1] That issue will be considered at the end of the chapter. The more fundamental question concerning early Christianity is: *Why* was the mission to the Jews initially so successful? It also seems pertinent to ask: If Paul's mission was mainly to the Gentiles, why did he seem to direct most of his attention to the Hellenized Jews of the Diaspora?

To pursue these questions, our first task is to 'measure' the Diaspora by determining whether or not there was a significant Jewish enclave in each of the thirty-one cities. Then we need to examine the religious and cultural circumstances of the Diasporan Jews, to show why they were an ideal target for Christian missionaries, including Paul. Against this background, we will then explore some linkages between Christianity and the Jewish Diaspora using statistical methods, giving special attention to the role played by Paul.

The Jewish Diaspora

The Jewish Diaspora was not unique; ethnic enclaves were common in the Greco-Roman cities. Greek neighborhoods probably existed even in all of the non-Hellenic cities, and colonies of Syrians, Cretans, Phoenicians, Cypriots, Persians, Egyptians, and many others were widespread. Like the Jews, all of these "sojourners" (as they were called in official documents, even after generations of residence)[2] remained quite attached to their homeland, and "every people, or fragment of a people, thrown into a foreign land continued to worship its ancestral gods."[3] The difference was that most of the sojourners were willing to worship local gods too, including the gods of each particular city and the deified emperors of the Imperial Cult, and to participate in "the frequent festivals and sacrifices,"[4] while devout Jews were not. This very clearly set the Jews apart and often stimulated anti-Semitism.[5] But, unlike the Christians, people in the Jewish Diasporan communities usually were exempt from these pagan obligations, having successfully appealed to the authorities that their unwillingness to worship any other gods was inherent in their traditional faith—tradition being the whole basis for religious legitimacy in the eyes of Roman authorities. Indeed, that is why conversion so unsettled Roman authorities: it involved renouncing the faith of one's ancestors.

In any event, Jews had long been congregating in cities outside Palestine, and this trend accelerated when it was encouraged by Alexander the Great and his heirs—hence the term Hellenic Diaspora, often used to distinguish the relocations of this time from earlier resettlements of Jews (such as their time in Egypt or the Babylonian Captivity). Too much probably has been made of the Diasporan communities as consisting primarily of traders and merchants. Many Diasporan Jews followed more humble callings, including many craftsmen[6]—as in the case of Paul and some of his associates. In fact, some Diasporan communities consisted mainly of mercenary soldiers, as was true of the Elephantine community in Egypt; and others had been formed initially by discharged Jewish veterans after their mercenary service, as in the case of the Antioch community. Nevertheless, trade and commerce were of primary importance to the founding of most Diasporan communities, and to sustaining them.

It would be useful to be able to distinguish various Diasporan communities in terms of such details, but it is a sufficient challenge to determine the relative size of these communities. The major problem in accomplishing that task is that the Diaspora continued to grow and spread throughout the early Christian era, and most sources have reported on Diasporan communities as of the year 200 or 300, rather than the year 100. For example, when Byzantium became known as Constantinople in the fourth century, the city had a very large Jewish community, but back in the year 100, when it was still called by its earlier name, it had relatively few Jewish residents. Eventually, however, I was able to assemble the needed data, starting with a map of known Diasporan synagogues[7] and aided by several recent atlases[8] and histories.[9] I assigned cities with a significant Jewish community in 100 CE a score of one. Those with relatively fewer Jewish residents were scored zero. Map 5-1 shows how each city was scored.

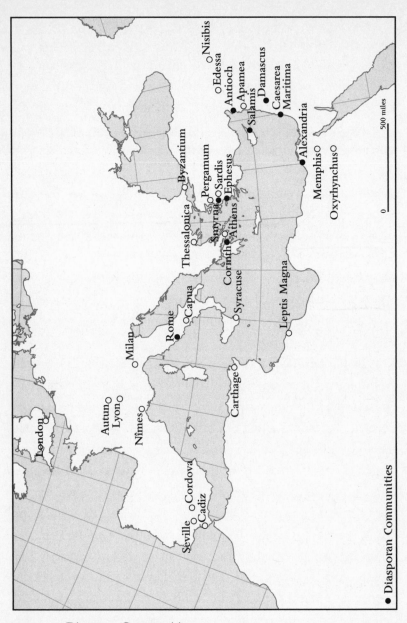

MAP 5-1. Diasporan Communities

Several quite obvious hypotheses will demonstrate the credibility of this measure:

HYPOTHESIS 5-1: *The closer a city was to Jerusalem, the more likely that city was to have a significant Diasporan Jewish community.*

Of cities within a thousand miles of Jerusalem, about half had a large Diasporan community, while only 7 percent of those further away had a sizable Jewish community. The difference is very statistically significant, and the hypothesis is supported (Table 5-1).

HYPOTHESIS 5-2: *Diasporan Jewish communities tended to be located in port cities.*

In this era when trade and travel were dominated by water transportation, it is not surprising that Diasporan communities were clustered in the port cities—half of which had such communities, compared with only 12 percent of the inland cities. The difference is significant, and the hypothesis is supported (Table 5-2).

It also seems worthwhile to use regression analysis to examine the independent and the joint effects of these two variables upon the formation of the Diaspora. The regression results show that both variables have an equally strong independent effect (Regression 5-1).

In the previous chapter we discovered that neither Cybelene worship nor Isiacism did better in larger cities, because neither was dependent on recruiting a founding nucleus within a city; rather, they were carried by sojourners. Diasporan Jewish communities, having likewise been founded by sojourners, should not have been related to city-size either.

HYPOTHESIS 5-3: *City-size was not significantly related to the presence of Diasporan Jewish communities.*

Again, larger cities were more likely to have a large Diasporan community; but as hypothesized, the difference was *not* significant (Table 5-3). It should be noted that these findings in no way challenge Fischer's subcultural theory of urbanism. His concern was with local recruitment to deviant religious movements, not with the arrival of congregations from outside.

Marginality and Accommodation

The portrayal in *Acts* of the religiousness of the Diasporan Jews is one-sided, depicting them as very pious and easily aroused against Christian preaching. This is to be expected, since the focus is on those Diasporan Jews who remained active in the synagogues, which is where Christians usually launched their mission efforts. Even so, the accounts in *Acts* provide several contrary hints about the religious situation in the Diaspora. Surely the Jews who frequented the synagogues represented the most pious members of their community. Yet Christians often were able to preach their clearly heretical message in the synagogues for a considerable time before any effective opposition arose. In addition, Paul, Barnabus, and the others managed to make some converts even from among those they met in the synagogues! In contrast, modern new religions quickly learn that it is futile to frequent religious settings in pursuit of converts. Recall that Dr. Kim wasted a year going from one church study group to another, and similar efforts by other Unification Church missionaries proved equally futile. The fact that the early Christians did find converts in the synagogues suggests that even there they found Diasporan Jews who were not firmly committed to Judaism, being of at least mixed mind about religious matters. As for the Jews outside the synagogues, among them religious apathy and confusion were rife. Had it not been for their lingering Judaism, many (possibly most) would have been fully assimilated. In fact, many did fully shed their connections to Judaism.[10]

Even most of the Jews of the Diaspora who did not assimilate were remarkably Hellenized. As noted, they spoke Greek and thought in Greek—Philo referred to Greek as "our language."[11] Most had taken Greek names, and "intermarriage was frequent."[12] All but a very few had so entirely lost their Hebrew that they worshipped in Greek and the Torah had to be translated into Greek. Many Diasporan Jews, probably the majority of them, had abandoned some provisions of the Law well before the arrival of Christianity. For example, the prohibition against eating with non-Jews probably was widely ignored.[13] It seems equally likely that many took part in feasts and festivals having pagan significance, since tolerance of paganism had crept into even their scripture. In the Greek of the Septuagint, *Exodus* 22:27[14] was not translated as "You shall not revile God" but as "You shall not revile the gods." Calvin Roetzel is surely right that this was an open declaration of tolerance, utterly "alien to Hebrew Scriptures."[15] Equally dramatic evidence of a tolerant attitude toward paganism comes from the fact that the Diasporan Jews "did not even hesitate to [adopt] names derived from those of Greek deities, such as Apollonius, Heracleides and Dionysus," or those of Egyptian gods—Horus was especially popular among the Diasporan Jews.[16] Further proof of pagan inroads into Diasporan Judaism comes from the Jewish shrine in Elephantine in Egypt, where not only was Yahweh worshipped, but so were two goddesses who were said to be Yahweh's consorts—Anath the goddess of war and Eshem the goddess of the sun.[17] Accommodation of paganism also is reflected in the fact that Paul found it necessary to admonish his Corinthian congregation to *shun the worship of idols[;] . . . what pagans sacrifice they offer to demons and not to God. I do not want you to be partners to demons.*[18]

But if they no longer were very Jewish, neither were they Greek. Instead, they were trapped in marginality, their Hellenism compromising their Judaism, and the latter preventing their full embrace of the former. Caught between two worlds, they found it degrading to live among Greeks and yet to remain "enclosed in a spiritual Ghetto and be reckoned among the 'barbarians.'" Many longed for "a compromise, a synthesis, which would permit a Jew to remain a Jew" and still be able to claim full entry into "the elect society of the Greeks."[19]

For all these reasons it is not at all clear who benefited most from Paul's victory vis-à-vis the admission of Gentiles without the requirement that they become Jews. For many Hellenized Jews, a monotheism with deep Jewish roots, but without the Law, would have been extremely attractive.

Cultural Continuity

Although social networks play the critical role in conversion, doctrine matters too, as we saw earlier—just not in the way that usually has been supposed. It is not so much a matter of what the doctrine promises to do for people as it is the *investment* of time, effort, and emotions that bodies of doctrine and the religious culture that surrounds them represent. That is, any religion requires an adherent to master a lot of culture: to know the words and actions required by various rituals or worship activities; to be familiar with certain doctrines, stories, music, symbols; perhaps even to know some jokes. Over time people become increasingly attached to their religious culture. Someone might say, for example, "It just wouldn't be Christmas for me without an angel at the top of the tree." Expressed as a social scientific concept: *religious capital* consists of the degree of mastery of and attachment to a particular religious culture.[20]

It follows that, other things being equal, *people will attempt to conserve their religious capital.* This proposition has many implications. For one thing, people will tend not to change religions, and *the greater their religious capital, the less likely they are to change.* There is a large research literature showing that converts overwhelmingly are recruited from the ranks of those having a very weak commitment to any other religion. In the United States, the group most likely to convert to a new religious movement consists of people raised in an irreligious or nonreligious home.[21] In addition, people are more likely to change faiths to the extent that they are presented with an option *that allows them to conserve much of their religious capital.* This explains why, in a Christian culture, people are more apt to convert to Mormonism than to Hinduism. To become a Mormon, a person of Christian background need discard none of his or her religious capital (including Christmas tree decorations), but only add to it. In contrast, to become Hindus, Christians must discard all of their religious capital and start over.

Applied to new religious groups, this becomes the principle of *cultural continuity.* Other things being equal, *a new religion is more likely to grow to the degree that it sustains continuity with the religious culture of those being missionized.*

For all that many Diasporan Jews may have dabbled in paganism, rarely did they go all the way and convert. Those who did would have needed to undergo a great deal of religious reeducation and to discard their Jewish religious capital. In fact, it is likely that Jews who did become pagans had only modest amounts of Jewish religious capital at risk, probably having been raised by parents whose Judaism was nominal at best.

In contrast with paganism, Christianity offered Diasporan Jews a chance to preserve virtually all of their religious capital, needing only to add to it, since Christianity preserved the entire Old Testament heritage. Although it made observance of many portions of the Jewish Law unnecessary, Christianity did not impose a new set of laws to be mastered. In addition, services in Christian congregations were very closely modeled on those of the synagogue, and in early days also were conducted in Greek; thus, a Hellenized Jew would have felt right at home. Finally, Christianity carefully stressed how its central message of salvation was the fulfillment of the messianic promises of orthodox Judaism.

All of this is, of course, quite familiar. Less familiar is the cultural continuity Christianity presented to the Hellenic religious capital possessed by many Diasporan Jews. As discussed in Chapter 4, Christianity was explicitly compatible with Greek philosophy— with its form, with its celebration of reason, and with much of its content. Indeed, this compatibility had been foreshadowed by prior accommodations of Hellenized Judaism. For example, Philo and others had adopted allegorical interpretations of the Law in order to "reduce the dissonance between the Jewish scriptures and philosophical religion."[22] As W. H. C. Frend put it, Philo attempted to interpret the Law "exclusively through the mirror of Greek philosophy."[23]

Furthermore, the Christ story has elements that were far more familiar and acceptable to pagans and to Hellenized Jews than to traditional Jews. The union of gods and mortal women was a common theme in pagan mythology. Astonishing signs and portents upon the birth of a divine son were to be expected. For such an offspring of the gods to have a tragic destiny was not unusual. Nor was a horrible death followed by ascension into divinity. As was seen in Chapter 4, a remarkable number of these elements occurred in the religious culture surrounding Isis worship, another quite successful eastern faith that helped prepare the pagan world for Christianity. Although this aspect of cultural continuity was vital to the conversion of pagan Gentiles, for Hellenized Jews it offered them, in effect, *double* continuity, allowing them to retain most of their Jewish *and* their Hellenic religious capital.

Christian missionaries quickly grasped that the Hellenized Jews of the Diaspora were especially receptive to Christianity, far more so than the Jews in Palestine.

Paul and the Diaspora

Clearly, Christians had been spreading their faith in the West for some time before Paul took up that task. Following his mystical conversion in about the year 35, Paul then seems to have devoted more than a decade to missionary efforts in the East, in Syria and Cilicia, with what results we do not know. But when Paul turned westward and began his missionary work at Antioch in the year 48 or 49, there already was an active congregation in that city,[24] as was the case in Rome and some other communities in the West as well.[25] These congregations need not have involved more than a few people. Indeed, Paul's inclusion of greetings to lengthy lists of individuals in various letters to congregations need not be taken as evidence that these congregations were large. Dr. Kim wrote letters to her Unification 'congregations' in various American cities that also began with special greetings to specific persons and then "to all the others who embrace the truth in [name of city]." But her individual greetings included all actual members in that city, and the "others" referred to anyone currently being missionized.

In any event, Paul quickly developed a standard approach to his mission. First of all, he typically began a visit to a new community by holding "privately organized meetings under the patronage of eminent persons . . . who provided him with . . . an audience composed of their dependents."[26] Second, Paul did not travel alone, but often took a retinue of as many as forty followers with him, sufficient to constitute an initial 'congregation,'[27] which made it possible to hold credible worship services and to welcome and form bonds with newcomers. (This same approach is currently being used very successfully by the Vineyard Fellowship, an evangelical

Protestant group that spreads when a dozen or so members decide to move to a new community and start a new congregation.) Among Paul's entourage there undoubtedly were scribes, as was typical in that day before typewriters, printing presses, or copy machines. (Most of the prolific early church fathers had remarkably large staffs to write down and copy their words.)[28] We even know the name of one of Paul's scribes, since he revealed himself at the end of *Romans* (16:22), where, after Paul's long list of individual greetings, he added "I Tertius, the writer of this letter, greet you in the Lord." Third, upon arrival, Paul would "gather any Christians already living in the city,"[29] attaching them to his 'imported' congregation, and then use their social networks as the basis for further recruitment. Finally, once the congregation was a going concern and had adequately trained local leaders, Paul moved on, but he maintained close contact through messengers and letters, and sometimes by making return visits. As Helmut Koester summed up: "Paul's missionary work, therefore, should not be thought of as the humble efforts of a lonely missionary. Rather, it was a well-planned, large-scale organization."[30]

Although much has been made of Paul's breakthrough in missionizing Gentiles, far too little has been made of the impact of his subsequent demand that Jewish Christians cease observing the Law. This had no consequences for Gentiles, but it would have had immense appeal to Hellenized Jews who wished to be free of the Law's social limitations. And for all the emphasis on Paul's mission being aimed at Gentiles, in fact nearly all of his efforts took place within Diasporan Jewish communities. Except for Luke, of course, most of his entourage was Jewish. He was welcomed by Jews. He preached in Jewish homes and in the synagogues. And most of those greeted in his letters seem to have been Jews. In addition, if Paul really was devoting his efforts to the Gentiles, why did he continue to receive so many severe beatings (at least eight, plus a stoning) from Jews?[31] Surely he would have been ignored by Diasporan Jewish leaders had he kept to Gentile circles.

Paul himself admitted that it was much easier to convert Diasporan Jews than Gentiles, noting that efforts to convert the latter forced him to work "harder than any of [the other apostles]."[32] Irenaeus expanded on this matter at some length, displaying a clear grasp of the principle of cultural continuity. "[Paul] did labour more than those who preached [to the Jews]. For they [who missionized the Jews] were assisted by the Scriptures, which the Lord confirmed and fulfilled, in coming such as He had been announced." But in preaching to the Gentiles there was "a foreign erudition" to be overcome, "and a new doctrine to be received, namely that the gods of the nations were not gods at all, but even the idols of demons; and that there is one God."[33] For Jews, Christianity added to their religious capital; for Gentiles, Christianity required them to replace their capital. This raises the possibility that, despite the emphasis on missionizing the Gentiles, Paul's efforts actually more often brought in Jewish converts. True enough, Paul's rejection of the Law created an even more profound gap between Christianity and orthodox Judaism. But, as a practical matter, devoutly orthodox Jews were not going to convert to Christianity anyway. Which is why Palestine was not a rewarding mission area. Rather, as Nock explained, it was Hellenized Jews "who had lost their traditional piety . . . [who] were receptive of new convictions."[34] Or, as W. M. Ramsay put it in his classic study, where Greek culture prevailed, "there Paul by preference goes."[35]

Together, these considerations lead to several hypotheses concerning Paul's mission. We can test these hypotheses, since it is possible to identify those cities known to have been missionized by Paul: Antioch, Athens, Caesarea Maritima, Corinth, Damascus, Ephesus, Salamis, and Thessalonica. (Rome and Syracuse are not included here, since Paul did not visit these cities until taken there under arrest.)

The first hypothesis concerning Paul's missions is quite evident:

HYPOTHESIS 5-4: *Paul concentrated on the more Hellenized cities.*

Paul visited only 8 of the 31 cities, but of these none was among the less Hellenized group (Table 5-4). That is, only Hellenic cities were missionized by Paul (Hellenism thereby being a necessary factor), even though many Hellenic cities were not missionized by Paul (Hellenism thereby not being a sufficient factor to have drawn Paul).

The second hypothesis about Paul is also obvious, since much of his travel was by boat:

HYPOTHESIS 5-5: *Paul tended to missionize port cities.*

Once again the data support the common view. Nearly half of the port cities were missionized by Paul, but he visited only 12 percent of the inland cities (Table 5-5).

Finally, it seems obvious that Paul primarily went to cities with substantial Diasporan communities.

HYPOTHESIS 5-6: *Paul tended to missionize cities with substantial Jewish Diasporan communities.*

Here too the obvious is true. Two-thirds of the cities with a significant Diasporan Jewish community were missionized by Paul, while he visited only two of the cities lacking a Diasporan community (Table 5-6).

The question arises, just how successful were Paul's missions? Unfortunately, the answer is biased by several important factors. First, the existence of a Christian community, or at least some people ready to receive him, often determined where Paul went. Second, it is somewhat circular to say that cities visited by Paul had early Christian congregations, since accounts of Paul's mission journeys provide a substantial part of our knowledge of where Christian congregations existed during the first century. Thus, it would be remarkable if it were not true that:

HYPOTHESIS 5-7: *Cities missionized by Paul had churches sooner than cities Paul did not visit.*

Although it could hardly have been otherwise, it is reassuring that this is a very strong relationship: all of the cities Paul missionized had a church by the end of the first century (Table 5-7). Of course, Paul concentrated on cities with Diasporan communities, and that's where all Christian missionary efforts were initially directed—Christianity began, after all, as a Jewish movement.

The Diaspora and Christianization

It wasn't, in the first instance, cultural continuity that led Christian mission efforts to the Hellenized Jews of the Diaspora. It was social networks. For missionaries headed out from Jerusalem, the pressing first questions were, Where should we go? Who would receive us? The answer seemed obvious. All across the Greco-Roman world were relatively well-to-do communities of people to whom the missionaries had ties—people who were relatives (even if very distant), or friends of friends. Indeed, at least until the destruction of the temple in 70 CE the Diasporan communities were accustomed to visits by religious teachers from Jerusalem. So that's where the early Christian missionaries went. Keep in mind, too, that there were far more Jews in the Diaspora than were needed to provide *every* Christian convert until the fourth century, and no one would suppose that Gentile conversion played an insignificant role until then. Finally, if most of the very early Gentile converts were God-fearers, they too could best be found through the synagogues. For all these reasons:

HYPOTHESIS 5-8: *Cities with a significant Diasporan community were Christianized sooner than other cities.*

The data supporting this hypothesis reveal a truly impressive statistical relationship. All of the cities with Diasporan communities had a church by the end of the first century, while only 18 percent of the cities without such a community had a church that early—in fact, a third of them still lacked a church by 180. The emphasis on the Hellenized Jews of the Diaspora as providing the basis of early Christianity is fully justified (Table 5-8).

But what about Paul? Did his missions have an independent effect on Christianization? Or was it that he went where the pickings were best and, in fact, where all the Christian missionaries went—as is suggested by Paul's constant conflicts with interloping competitors? An answer to this question requires regression analysis (Regression 5-2).

Looking at the data, we see that Paul's missionizing had no significant, independent effect on Christianization, while the importance of Diasporan communities was quite significant. These results strongly suggest that Paul's impact on the spread of Christianity was incidental to the general receptivity of the Diasporan communities to Christian missionizing. This is not to detract from Paul's immense importance to the early church. He did, after all, write much of the New Testament, and the second part of *Acts* is mainly devoted to him. But perhaps his personal role as a missionary has been overplayed, partly because of his towering theological importance and partly because we know about it in such detail. It should be remembered that Paul was only one of *many* traveling professional missionaries,[36] to say nothing of all the rank-and-file missionaries who circulated from city to city. Indeed, Paul may have been far more important as a trainer, organizer, and motivator of missionaries than as an actual founder of congregations.

Next, the factor of Hellenization must be considered, since it

That's news!

seems to have been of critical importance in setting the religious context not only of the Diasporan Jewish communities, but of the Gentile communities as well. Recall from Chapter 3 that the more Hellenized the city, the sooner it was Christianized. Of the less Hellenic cities, only one had a church by the year 100, compared with about two-thirds of the very Hellenic cities. Conversely, none of the very Hellenic cities still lacked a church by 180 CE, while about two-thirds of the less Hellenic cities were still without a church. But perhaps this too is simply an artifact, in that the very Hellenic cities also tended to have large Diasporan communities. The regression results are these: *both* Hellenism and the Diaspora had strong, significant, independent effects on Christianization (Regression 5-3).

Regression 5-4 puts all the pieces together, revealing that there is no longer any trace of a Paul effect! Perhaps this should not be a surprise. Although the New Testament often describes Paul's mission as aimed at Gentiles, what scripture mostly reports him doing is missionizing to Hellenized Jews. Nor was Paul the only missionary at work, as his constant complaints about 'other' Christian missionaries make clear; and it was obvious to all that the Hellenized Jews were the prime candidates for conversion to Christ. Keep in mind that while all eight of these cities visited by Paul had a church by 100 CE, some of them already had a Christian congregation before Paul arrived, and five cities he didn't visit had churches by 100 CE too. Clearly, then, the other Christian missionaries had been very busy and effective.

Of course, Judaism was not the only forerunner of Christianity. In the previous chapter we saw that both Isis and Cybelene worship prepared the way for successful Christian missionizing. However, both of these 'oriental' faiths also tended to be located in cities having large Diasporan communities as well. Did all three make independent contributions to Christianization? The regression results strongly attest to the independent effects of both Judaism and

Isiacism on the rise of Christianity (Regression 5-5). The same is true for Cybelene worship, although it is no surprise that the Diasporan effects are greater (Regression 5-6). After all, Christianity did begin as a Jewish sect. But the 'oriental' faiths also served to prepare the way.

The Cessation of Jewish Conversion

Virtually everyone believes that the mission to the Jews soon failed. Some suppose that an impervious barrier to Jewish conversion was erected during the Jewish Revolt of 66–74, when many Diasporan Jews supported the rebels and Christians did not. Others accept that substantial Jewish conversion continued until the Bar-Kokhba Revolt in 132–135, which further alienated the church and the synagogue. But from then on, it is assumed that Jewish conversion was at an end. Perhaps so, but this conclusion seems contrary to a considerable variety of evidence and inference.

The first objection to the claim that the mission to the Hellenized Jews ended in failure early on is that the fundamental circumstances that led to its early success did not change. Granted, Diasporan Jews suffered various degrees of persecution in reaction to the nationalist uprisings in Palestine—but that would not seem to have lessened the appeal of Christianity. Indeed, it might well have made the Diasporan Jews, many of whom greatly resented (and feared) being implicated in zealous Palestinian politics, even more concerned to shed their marginal status.

Of even greater significance is the abundant evidence of continuing Jewish influence within Christianity. Consider that, with the exception of *Acts,* the New Testament was written by Jews. Moreover, many of the early heretical movements, such as Marcionism, as well as the bulk of writings identified as Gnostic, were remarkably anti-Jewish. These attacks, as well as the ease with which they were rejected as heretical, support an inference of continuing

— too partisan an outlook!

strong Jewish influence. Turning to a later period, what are we to make of all the concern over Judaizing expressed by various Christian leaders as late as the fifth century? Historians agree that in that era large numbers of Christians showed such an affinity for Jewish culture that it could be characterized as "a widespread infatuation with Judaism."[37] It seems unlikely that this was but a lingering attraction[38]—not if it had really been several centuries after Jewish conversion had ceased. On the other hand, this is precisely what one would expect to find in Christian communities containing many members of relatively recent Jewish origin, who retained ties of family and association with non-Christian Jews, and who therefore *still retained* a distinctly Jewish aspect to their Christianity. Moreover, this is consistent with repeated Roman prohibitions against mixed marriages between Christians and Jews, one such statute being promulgated as late as 388 CE.[39] Governments seldom bother prohibiting things that are not taking place.

Consequently, what may have been at issue was not the *Judaizing* of Christianity, but that in many places—especially in the eastern end of the empire—a substantial Jewish Christianity *persisted.* And if that was the case, there is no reason to suppose that Jewish Christians had lost the ability to attract new converts from their network of Hellenized families and friends. Hence, rather than seeing the evidence as indicative of a sudden outbreak of Judaizing, we can more plausibly interpret it as proof that Jewish conversion had never stopped. When John Chrysostom railed against Christians frequenting the synagogue, he addressed his remarks to an audience that knew whether he spoke the truth, so we can assume this was actually going on. The most reasonable interpretation of Chrysostom's polemic is that it aimed to separate a church and synagogue that were still greatly intertwined—and this at the start of the fifth century!

Probably the most fundamental assumption concerning the 'failure' of the mission to the Jews is that, because after the triumph of Christianity there remained a substantial Diasporan Jewish population actively sustaining synagogues, the Jews *must have* rejected the Christian mission efforts. But that overlooks that there were millions of Diasporan Jews—far more than enough to have provided large numbers of Christians while still sustaining synagogues. If the projections that there were only about a million Christians by the year 250 are close to correct, then only about *one* out of every *five* or even *nine* Diasporan Jews need have converted to fill that total without any Gentile conversions at all—and of course there were many Gentile converts.

Population data lend further support to the assumption of a very large number of Jewish converts. As noted, the Diasporan Jews constituted at least 10 percent of the total population of the empire, and perhaps as much as 15 percent. Medieval historians estimate that Jews made up only 1 percent of the population of Latin Europe in about the tenth century.[40] Granted, some of that percentage decline was caused by the Islamic conquest of areas having substantial Jewish populations. Nevertheless, the figures also suggest a considerable decline in the Diasporan population during that millennium, which is consistent with there having been a substantial rate of conversion. Nor was the survival of strong synagogues inconsistent with that supposition. Indeed, by peeling away all of the tepid, Hellenized Jews, conversion to Christianity would have left an increasingly orthodox, highly committed Jewish community, a community ideally constituted to sustain obdurate resistance to Christianization.

Finally, a wealth of archaeological findings in Italy (especially in Rome and Venosa) show that "Jewish and Christian burials reflect an interdependent and closely related community of Jews and Christians in which clear marks of demarcation were blurred until the third and fourth centuries CE."[41] Similarly, excavations in Capernaum on the shores of the Sea of Galilee reveal "a Jewish synagogue and a Jewish-Christian house church on opposite sides of the street. . . . Following the strata and the structures, both communities apparently lived in harmony until the seventh century."[42]

It also is worth noting that Origen mentioned having taken part in a theological debate with Jews before 'umpires' sometime during the first half of the third century.[43] This seems inconsistent with the assumption that church and synagogue had long been separated. Equally inconsistent is evidence that as late as the fourth century Christian theologians consulted "rabbis about the interpretation of difficult Scriptural verses."[44]

Of course, Jewish conversion might have ceased in the latter half of the first century, or by the middle of the second. But the grounds for believing that it did are far weaker than has been assumed. Unfortunately, our data on cities can shed no light on this significant issue other than the enormous correlation between the Diasporan communities and Christianization.

Conclusion

As in previous chapters, many of the statistical findings above merely confirm things 'everybody' knows about the Christianization of the empire. That not only should inspire confidence in quantitative methods and in the quality of the available data, but should encourage very serious consideration of findings that do not support the conventional wisdom, as in the case of Paul. Despite the tradition that his was mainly a mission to the Gentiles, and that that factor allowed the Christian church to burst beyond its Jewish origins, the weight of scripture deals with Paul's mission to the Jews of the Hellenic Diaspora. In that sense, our finding that Paul's missionary visits had no independent impact on Christianization once statistical controls are made for the Hellenic and the Diasporan effects is very scriptural even while it is very nontraditional.

HIDDEN MANUSCRIPTS. Here are the thirteen bound volumes of manuscripts found buried in an earthenware jar at Nag Hammadi in Egypt in 1945. Their discovery has produced endless controversy over what books *should* have become part of the New Testament.

Gnosticism and Heresy

THESE DAYS Gnosticism is the center of much interest, confusion, and faulty analysis. The term has long been applied to a number of esoteric ancient manuscripts, some of which claim to reveal a secret Christianity that is very different from the faith that appears in the New Testament. In addition, a variety of dissident religious movements, the first dating from as early as the second century, also have often been referred to as Gnostic.

I will take up both these aspects of Gnosticism in this chapter. First and foremost, however, I will examine the proposal made by Michael Allen Williams in the subtitle of his remarkable study *Rethinking "Gnosticism": An Argument for Dismantling a Dubious Category*. As Williams so carefully documented, when the many manuscripts and movements usually categorized as Gnosticism are examined closely, various clusters of characteristics can be identified, but the only element *common to all* is that each is remarkably heretical, which is how they were quite properly judged by their contemporaries—not just "one heresy but a swarming ant-heap of heresies," as the distinguished Simone Pétrement explained.[1]

Purely as a matter of faith, one is free to prefer Gnostic interpretations and to avow that they give us access to secret knowledge concerning a more authentic Christianity, as several popular authors recently have done.[2] But one is not free to claim that the early church fathers rejected these writings for nefarious reasons. The conflicts between many of these manuscripts and the New Testament are so monumental that no thinking person could embrace both. Consider that some Gnostic 'scriptures' equate the Jewish God with Satan! Should those who defended conventional Christian teachings stand condemned of bigotry for *not* siding with such views? In addition, many of the Gnostic scriptures are obvious forgeries, easily recognized as such by the early church fathers, just as they ought to be today,[3] in that whoever wrote them tried to deceive readers into believing they were the work of famous figures of first-generation Christianity—Peter, James, Mary Magdalene, Pilate, or Thomas, for example—or someone claiming extraordinary status, such as being the twin brother of Christ.

Whether the Gnostic teachers were 'right' or 'wrong,' that they were heretics vis-à-vis conventional Christianity cannot be disputed. Hence, the major portion of this chapter is devoted to heresies, and readers should imagine single quotation marks around the terms 'Gnostic' and 'Gnosticism' to indicate that they are being used very provisionally. However, by the end of the chapter, after we have empirically explored variations among these many heresies, it will become clear that there is a coherent subset of cases that deserves a collective identification.

This chapter begins by assessing Gnosticism as a category and then deals with a common confusion among manuscripts, schools, and movements. Many Gnostic manuscripts have been treated at various times in history, including the present, as if they had inspired social movements. But in many instances no trace of any such movement exists, and the most likely interpretation is that the manuscript was written by someone having few if any followers—so few, in fact, that we haven't the slightest idea of who wrote the manuscript, when, or where. In other instances, prominent Gnostic writers are known to have gathered only small 'schools' of devotees, some of which met in secret and none of which bore any resemblance to even a small popular movement. After we have quantified a set of such schools, we will test several significant hypotheses concerning them. Then we will shift our attention to heretical movements that did attract popular support: Marcionism, Valentinianism, Montanism, and Manichaeism. These too we will quantify in terms of where each attracted supporters in order to test a variety of hypotheses concerning each, paying particular attention to correlations among heretical movements.

Gnosticism: A Dubious Category?

The word *Gnosticism* comes from a Greek word meaning "one who knows," and what such a person knows is called *gnōsis*,[4] which "does not refer to understanding of truths about the human and natural world that can be reached through reason. It refers to 'revealed knowledge' available only to those who have received secret teachings of a heavenly revealer."[5]

The term *Gnostic* was applied by Irenaeus about 180 CE to the writings and followers of Valentinus.[6] Several years later, Tertullian applied the word to groups other than the Valentinians.[7] The name came into more frequent use by scholars during the eighteenth century, slowly gaining acceptance, and it has enjoyed great popularity since an international colloquium on Gnosticism was held in Messina, Italy, in 1966. In their "Final Document" members of the colloquium formally defined the term *Gnosticism* as claims to "knowledge of the divine mysteries reserved for an elite."[8] Many of

the writers and groups taken to be Gnostic did "understand themselves to be the elite 'chosen people' who, in distinction from the
'worldly-minded,' were able to perceive" sophisticated matters and
were in accord with the "goal of gnostic teaching . . . that with the
help of insight (*gnōsis*), the elect could be freed from the fetters of
this world."[9] This particular form of Gnosticism resembled what
are known today as initiation cults.[10] But not all putative Gnosticism involved secret elites; some inspired mass movements. So,
knowing that secret elitism was not a criterion sufficient to embrace the full body of writings and organizations they wished to
call Gnostic, the colloquium added many features to their definition and in doing so made it progressively less useful.

The stimulus for this international gathering of scholars was the
discovery at Nag Hammadi in Egypt in 1945 of fifty-three fourth-
century-CE manuscripts (forty-eight of them different). This trove
of ancient texts had been carefully buried in a large earthenware
jar. In all there were thirteen volumes bound in red leather, each
volume containing multiple manuscripts. Some of these have no
"Christian character whatever, a point established by the presence
of part of Plato's *Republic*."[11] However, at least forty of these manuscripts were subsequently labeled as Gnostic, many of them being
complete copies of works known previously only by name. Others
had been known only by excerpts included in attacks on them by
early Christian opponents, beginning with Irenaeus, Bishop of
Lyon, whose *Adversus haereses* (*Against Heresies*) appeared in about
180 CE. Perhaps surprisingly, when these actual Gnostic texts were
compared with the synopses and excerpts included in the writings
of their conventional opponents, they were in remarkably close accord. Jean Doresse, one of the earliest to study the manuscripts
found at Nag Hammadi, noted that comparisons of the actual text
of the *Secret Book of John* with excerpts quoted by Irenaeus show
that the good bishop followed the Gnostic text essentially "word
for word."[12] This came as a very great surprise to most modern

scholars, who had made it an article of faith that, of course, the church fathers had greatly misrepresented the 'heretics,' the better to discredit them. Instead, the church fathers had quoted them accurately, perhaps because they thought that "the views they were quoting were so contorted and ludicrous that the heretics were best condemned out of their own mouths."[13] Even so, the charge that the early church fathers greatly distorted the Gnostic texts lives on among their modern advocates. Marvin Meyer, for example, wrote in 2005 that their "accounts are biased and apparently distort many features of the gnostic religion."[14]

By the time of the conference at Messina, these newly found materials had all been translated from Coptic and published in several modern Western languages, and in 1977 splendid English translations of the entire set were published under the editorship of James M. Robinson. Aside from being at substantial variance with the New Testament, these Gnostic works contain no themes or theses common to all. But certain elements are common to many, and we turn to those now.

Chief among the common themes is the idea of two gods, taken from Greek philosophy and carried to a radical extreme: a supreme good God who is very remote from the world, and a less powerful, evil Demiurge who created a completely worthless, evil world and who torments humanity.

Radical Dualism

As discussed in Chapter 4, except for monotheisms based on impersonal divine essences such as the Tao, all monotheisms are dualistic to some extent. This provides them with a solution to the problem of evil. If there is but one God, creator of everything and in charge of everything, why is there evil in the world? It follows that God, being the source of all things, is the source of all evil. What is to be made of such a being? The traditional Jewish,

Evil is the absence of God "in all things but sin"

Christian, and Muslim solution to this thorny issue is to accept the existence of lesser supernatural beings who are the source of evil—who for various reasons and within various limits brought evil into the world. Satan and his demons are fallen angels who tempt humans to sin, but whose powers are puny compared with God; and therefore these fallen ones will eventually be defeated— in God's good time.

For many Gnostic writers this was much too accommodating and failed to acknowledge that the world is evil to the core, that nothing in this life has any redeeming features. Influenced by Plato's ideas about a remote supreme God who allowed a lesser god, the Demiurge, to create the world, some Gnostic writers spun out extremely dualistic accounts of the universe.

To summarize these views, the best source to consult is *The Secret Book According to John* (or *The Apocryphon of John*). In part this is because this Gnostic manuscript has survived in four copies (three of them from Nag Hammadi), which suggests that it was widely circulated. Moreover, because it is a complete document dating from around the fourth century, no one can dismiss it as a biased summary written by the conventional Christian enemies of Gnosticism. Finally, to the extent that there is a core Gnostic work, this is it—Michel Tardieu has called it "the gnostic Bible *par excellence*."[15]

The manuscript identifies its author as the Apostle John, based on a postresurrection appearance by Christ, who instructed John about "*the mysteries which are hidden in silence*."[16] The revelation begins with the supreme mystery, the nature of God, who is identified as the "*invisible spirit*," so "*superior to deity*" that it "*is not fitting to think of it as divine*." Eventually, when God thought about his own perfection, that resulted in the existence of an independent entity known as First Thought, or Barbelo. Barbelo also is the Mother and hence the consort of God the Father, and this resulted in a self-generated Child. This trinity then produced a whole entourage of divine entities known as "aeons." For some immense time all went well: "[T]he scene portrayed in this divine realm is one of complete order, peace, and reverence."[17] But the calm didn't last. One of the divine entities went bad—the one named Wisdom. Without permission from God, Wisdom did her own creative imagining, bringing forth a child. It was a grotesque monster: "*serpentine, with a lion's face, and with its eyes gleaming like flashes of lightning.*" To hide her folly, Wisdom "*surrounded it with a luminous cloud. And she put a throne in the midst of the cloud, so that no being might see it except for the holy spirit . . . and she called its name Ialtabaoth.*"

Now things get interesting. Ialtabaoth doesn't merely look like a monster; he is one. "Completely self-willed, he steals spiritual power from his mother and runs off and sets about creating a world he can control as he pleases."[18] He is none other than the God of *Genesis,* who creates "a gang of angelic henchmen, rulers ("archons") who are to help him control the realm of darkness, and he goes about setting up his rule in the classic style of a petty tyrant," as Michael Williams so aptly summarized.[19] Having created the earth and given it inhabitants, Ialtabaoth began to assert, "*For my part, I am a jealous God. And there is no other god apart from me.*" The book now relates a revised version of the whole Adam and Eve, Garden of Eden saga. Once having thrown Adam and Eve out of the Garden, Ialtabaoth instilled a desire for sexual intercourse in humans and then seduced Eve to produce Cain and Abel, the former with the face of a bear, the latter with that of a cat. Adam then fathered Seth, who, unlike Cain and Abel, possessed the spirit of God. Seth and his descendents were regarded as an affront by Ialtabaoth and his henchmen, so he tried to kill them all with the flood. Having been thwarted by Noah, next Ialtabaoth sent evil angels disguised as men; they took women for their brides and generated a polluted humankind.

At this point the secret book offers a "poem of deliverance," wherein Jesus explains that he came to free humanity from the chains of Ialtabaoth. However, Jesus does not end his revelations by encouraging John to go forth and convert the world. Not at all: *"For my part, I have told you all things, so that you might write them down and transmit them secretly to those who are like you in spirit."*

The core message of *The Secret Book of John* and of many other Gnostic teachings is that the earth is held in thrall by an evil God. But since many other Gnostic teachings propose no such thing, it fails as a definitional criterion.

Anti-Judaism

According to many Gnostic texts, the evil God is the God of the Jews, and his Chosen People were so designated for good reason—in that they worship and proselytize on behalf of this evil creature. Although some Gnostic texts do not condemn the God of the Old Testament as evil and are very favorable to Jews,[20] most of them display what Hans Jonas described as "a kind of metaphysical anti-Semitism."[21] They "portray the Old Testament God as vain, ignorant, envious, and jealous—a malicious Creator who uses every means at his disposal to keep humanity from attaining true perfection."[22]

In *The Testimony of Truth,* another of the manuscripts recovered at Nag Hammadi, a section begins by recounting the story of Adam and Eve eating from the tree of knowledge as told in *Genesis.* Having reached the point where God found out that Adam and Eve had eaten of the tree, God said:

> *"Behold, Adam has become like one of us, knowing evil from good."*
> *Then he said, "Let us cast him out of Paradise lest he take from the*
> *tree of life and eat and live forever." But of what sort is this God?*
> *First (he) maliciously refused Adam from eating of the tree of*
> *knowledge. And secondly he said, "Adam, where are you?" [This]*
> *God does not have foreknowledge; (otherwise) would he not know*

from the beginning? (And) afterwards he said, "Let us cast him (out) of this place, lest he eat of the tree of life and live forever." Surely he has shown himself to be a malicious grudger.

At this point the *Testimony* shifts from an exclusive focus on the God of the Old Testament to those who worship him.

For great is the blindness of those who read, and they do not know him [for what he is]. And he said, "I am a jealous God; I will bring the sins of the fathers upon the children until three (and) four generations." And he said, "I will make their heart thick, and I will cause their mind to become blind, that they might not know nor comprehend the things that are said." But these things he said to those who believe in him (and) serve him!

These passages are not exceptional. Many Gnostic texts abound in antagonism toward the God of the Jews—and some do not.

Sexuality

Christianity may be somewhat ambivalent about sexual expression, but, being very pro-natal, it values marital sexuality. Not only did Paul admit, "*It is better to marry than to burn,*" but he also counseled married couples not to practice chastity, but to fully extend to one another their "conjugal rights."[23] In contrast with many Gnostic texts, Paul seems a virtual libertine.[24]

For most early heretics, sexual intercourse was to be absolutely avoided: it provided the wicked angels (archons) with the means to continue to mislead and torment humans, in that sex was assumed to be an act of utter defilement. In *The Sophia* (or *Wisdom*) *of Jesus Christ* (found at Nag Hammadi), following his resurrection the Savior appears to "*his twelve disciples and seven women [who] continued to be his followers*" and informed them that, among other

…be released from the grip of forgetfulness con-
…m if they do not engage in *"the unclean rubbing"* of
…ercourse.[25] *The Paraphrase of Shem* condemns intercourse
…*"defiled rubbing."*[26] *The Gospel of Philip*, another work recovered
at Nag Hammadi, gets right to the point: *"There are two trees growing in paradise. One bears animals, the other bears men. Adam ate from the
tree which bore animals. He became an animal and he brought forth animals."*[27] Or, as it says in *The Book of Thomas*:

> *Woe unto you who love the sexual intercourse that belongs to
> femininity and its foul cohabitation.*
> *And woe unto you who are gripped by the authorities of
> your bodies; for they will afflict you.*
> *Woe unto you who are gripped by the agencies of wicked
> demons.*

Consequently, many heretical texts advocate absolute celibacy and
rate it as especially virtuous to not bring children into the world.

This persistent element in Gnostic writings, especially as reflected in the commitment to radical abstinence by major heretical
movements such as the Marcionists and Manichaeians, may have
been a major factor in the failure of such movements. Although
the conventional Christian church accorded special sanctity to
those who observed celibacy, it fully embraced those who lived in
marital bliss. Nock put this well: "Christianity did indeed go a
long way with those in whose eyes sexual life was unclean; it gave
satisfaction to the many who were fascinated by asceticism, but it
repressed those elements within itself which overstressed that
point of view, and it never set its face against the compatibility of
normal life with the full practice of religion."[28]

Of course, some heretics also accepted sexuality, at least within
marriage. Moreover, a few seem to have gone far in the other di-
rection, taking the view that their access to secret wisdom liber-

ated them from all need for sexual restraint. As Robert M. Grant summed up: "Gnostic ethics ran the gamut from compulsive promiscuity to extreme asceticism."[29] Several somewhat obscure Gnostic groups believed that the sexual morality of the Old Testament was but a control mechanism by which the archons enslaved humanity, and those groups therefore advocated unrestricted sexuality as a means of bursting these evil bonds. It was charged against the Valentinians that they approved of adultery. In the words of Bishop Irenaeus:

> *Wherefore also it comes to pass, that the "most perfect" among them [Valentinians] addict themselves without fear to all those kinds of forbidden deeds. . . . [Some] yield themselves up to the lusts of the flesh with the utmost greediness, maintaining that carnal things should be allowed to the carnal nature, while spiritual things are provided for the spiritual. Some of them, moreover, are in the habit of defiling those women who have been taught the above doctrine, as has frequently been confessed by those women who have been led astray by certain of them, on their returning to the Church of God, and acknowledging this along with the rest of their errors. Others . . . seduce [women] from their husbands. . . . [Others] pretend to live in all modesty with [women] as with sisters, [but] have in course of time been revealed in their true colors, when the sister has been found with child by her pretended brother.*

Two centuries later, Epiphanius of Salamis claimed firsthand knowledge of libertine practices among members of a Gnostic sect, stating that as a young man he had been seduced by members of this group during a ritualized orgy and that "they curse anyone who is abstinent."[30]

Most of those Gnostics who denounced sexuality did so as means to thwart the evil Demiurge, not on grounds of right and wrong. The concept of virtue is incompatible with the idea that

ll that is in it is totally and inherently evil, being
f a diabolical deity. On these grounds, the great
.tury Neoplatonist philosopher Plotinus condemned the
Gnostic schools in his famous *Enneads* (2.9.15): "Their doctrine[,]
. . . by blaming the Lord of providence and providence itself, holds
in contempt all . . . virtue . . . [and] puts temperance to ridicule, so
that nothing good may be discovered in this world. . . . It is revealing that they conduct no inquiry at all about virtue and that the
treatment of such things is wholly absent from their teachings. . . .
Without true virtue, God remains an empty word."

Of course, abstinence was not the only plausible response to the
denial of virtue; on logical grounds alone, libertinism was an
equally valid conclusion. As for the truth of charges that some
Gnostics were libertines, one should note the many instances in
which modern elitist, esoteric groups have opted for promiscuity—
for example, the many Hermetic and Wiccan groups.

Heresy

Elaine Pagels stresses that the Gnostic writers "did not regard themselves as 'heretics.'"[31] Of course not. But the issue of heresy is
hardly a matter of self-designation. Let us assume that these writers
(including the forgers) sincerely believed that they possessed the
truth and that the conventional Christians had it all wrong, while
the conventional Christians were equally sure that theirs was the
true Christianity. Within the confines of faith, the charge of heresy
can be resolved objectively only on the basis of which side more accurately transmitted the original teachings of Jesus. That decision
must come down to sources. The New Testament gospels claim to
be based on the recollections of those who knew Jesus and heard
his words. The four gospel narratives abound in correct historical
and geographical details, and nearly everything takes place on this

earth and involves people who very probably existed. As Philip Jenkins put it: "[O]rthodox Christians at least believed that Jesus had lived and died in a real historical setting, and that it was possible to describe these events in objective terms. For Gnostics, by contrast, Christ was not so much a historical personage as a reality within the believer."[32] Hence, the typical Gnostic work, like *The Secret Book of John,* gives its origins as the author's visions and mystical revelations, which are set in another reality and include almost no historical or geographical content. As Pheme Perkins explained, "Gnostics reject gods and religious traditions that are tied to this cosmos in any way at all! Thus, Gnostic mythology often seems devoid of ties to place or time."[33] In this way, Gnostic scriptures far more resemble pagan mythology than the New Testament, in that 'events' so often occur in an immaterial, otherworldly, 'enchanted' setting. In fact, many Gnostic works are an exotic amalgam of paganism, Greek philosophy, Christianity, and Judaism.

In keeping with their intuitive methods and their lack of worldly referents, various Gnostic writers stressed that *originality* was the test of true inspiration. Irenaeus put it wryly: "[E]very one of them generates something new, day by day, according to his ability; for no one is deemed 'perfect' who does not develop among them some mighty fictions."[34] Elaine Pagels has taken a rather more favorable view of the matter: "Like circles of artists today, Gnostics considered original creative invention to be the mark of anyone who becomes spiritually alive. Each one, like students of a painter or writer, expected to express his own perceptions by revising and transforming what he was taught. Whoever merely repeated his teacher's words was considered immature."[35] Pagels went on to contrast this 'creative spirituality' with what she seemed to regard as the rather constipated orthodoxy of Bishop Irenaeus, who thought it both bizarre and wicked to propose that "mighty fictions" were a superior guide to history and truth.

Bam!! Elaine !

Had the Gnostics prevailed, they presumably would be viewed today rather more in the manner that Pagels and other 'Ivy League' Gnostics would wish, assuming that such a thing as Christianity still existed. But the Gnostics did not prevail, because they did not present nearly so plausible a faith, nor did they seem to understand how to create sturdy organizations. Instead, most of them did and taught their own 'thing.' To sum up, the Gnostic gospels were rejected for good reason: they constitute idiosyncratic, often lurid personal visions reported by scholarly mystics, ambitious pretenders, and various outsiders who found their life's calling in dissent. Whatever else might be said about them, surely they were heretics. As N. T. Wright put it, they "represent . . . a form of spirituality which, while still claiming the name of Jesus, has left behind the very things that made Jesus who he was, and that made the early Christians what they were."[36]

Even so, these writers and groups weren't Gnostics, unless we deprive that word of any useful meaning. Some were radical dualists; some weren't. Some were extremely anti-Jewish; some were very pro-Jewish. Some were remarkably ascetic; some were libertine. Some regarded their beliefs as arcane secrets to be revealed only slowly to a small elite initiated into the inner circle; some led mass movements. Because of these gross inconsistencies (and many others),[37] it seems wise to shelve the term *Gnostic* except when dealing with traditional discussions of these movements and materials. Instead, let us use the one concept that fits them all—"early heresies"—as we look at early heretical manuscripts, schools, and major movements.

Early Heretical Manuscripts

It too often is assumed that manuscripts imply social movements. Thus, the existence of a Gnostic manuscript often is taken to mean that it served as the gospel of a heretical movement. But that simply doesn't follow. Today's New Age bookstores are filled with publications that represent nothing more than one writer's opinions. The same seems plausible in the case of many of the surviving heretical manuscripts. They are works entirely without provenance or context. We don't know who wrote them, where, or (within several centuries) when. Nor is there the slightest surviving hint that most of these strange works were associated with a social movement—there is no necessary reason even to suppose that it was an organized heretical group that buried the manuscripts at Nag Hammadi. Consequently, these works can be studied only as literature. It is not idle to examine the ideas in these works or to compare them to other works of the era. But even the existence of similarities does not establish that any one of them influenced other works; it could as well mean that the author of the work in question was influenced by others. In the end, it is impossible even to say who read many of these anonymous manuscripts, except that the works quoted by Irenaeus, Hippolytus, and Epiphanius obviously had circulated sufficiently to arouse opposition, and the books buried at Nag Hammadi presumably had been read by someone.

Of course, some surviving heretical manuscripts were written by known historical figures. While some of these people also led major heretical movements, others modeled themselves on classical philosophers and were content to found a 'school' consisting of a small group of disciples, among whom the "authoritative teaching was transmitted, interpreted, and kept secret. There must have been regular meetings of some sort."[38]

Early Heretical Schools

Very little is known about the "School of *St. Thomas*"[39] other than that it was probably located in Edessa. Beyond that, what survives are manuscripts that clearly were not written by their central character: St. Didymus Jude Thomas, Apostle of the East, and self-proclaimed twin brother of Jesus. The Thomas literature lacks some 'typical' elements of Gnosticism. For example, although these works stress that the spiritual world is within the individual, they do not posit an inferior, evil creator-deity. However, most of the Thomas works appear to be very strange fantasies, although some interpreters propose that there is profound meaning concealed "behind a figurative fairy tale or folktale."[40] However, the most famous of the Thomas works, *The Gospel According to Thomas,* has no story at all. It consists entirely of 114 sayings attributed to Jesus, beginning:

1) These are the obscure (or hidden) sayings that the living Jesus uttered and which Didymus Jude Thomas [his twin] wrote down. And he said, "Whoever finds meaning in these sayings will not taste death."[41]

Some of the sayings appear in the New Testament. Some do not. Some seem to be of Gnostic origin. Some are remarkably obscure. Some seem quite inferior, straining for profundity, compared with those of New Testament origin. Since the entire work can be printed on a few pages, it seems remarkable that Elaine Pagels would have written a book-length celebration of the liberating ideas she finds in this "secret gospel" without providing her readers with all 114 sayings, even if only in a brief appendix. In fact, she very seldom quoted from Thomas—perhaps so that she could emphasize the joys of seekerhood and mock the constraints of creeds without having to interpret 'sayings' such as these:

As to freedom from constraints:

27) Jesus said: "If you do not abstain from the world you will not find the kingdom. If you do not make the sabbath a sabbath you will not behold the father."

As to elitism:

49) Jesus said: "Blessed are those who are solitary and superior, for you will find the kingdom; for since you come from it you shall return to it."

As to feminism:

114) Simon Peter said to them: "Mary should leave us, for females are not worthy of life." Jesus said, "See, I am going to attract her to make her male so that she too might become a living spirit that resembles you males. For every female (element) that makes itself male will enter the kingdom of heaven."

In fairness, Pagels did include this last saying (114) in her earlier (1979) book on the Gnostic gospels.

Those most favorable to the Gnostics assign a very early date to *Thomas,* but most historians date it from the middle to late second century, when the New Testament canon was already formed. This later date is encouraged by the fact that no mention is made of it by Irenaeus; the first known reference to it is by Hippolytus, who wrote between 222 and 235 CE. In addition to probably having begun in Edessa, the St. Thomas school seems to have stimulated several 'branch campuses,' in Alexandria, Memphis, and Oxyrhynchus.[42]

Historians agree that *Saturninus* (often Satornil or Satorninos) was a real heretical teacher who founded a school in Antioch around the end of the first century. But that's all that is known about him. As to his views, no manuscript has survived, but his teachings, as summarized by Irenaeus, included all of the 'classic' elements of Gnosticism. To quote from Irenaeus:

Saturninus . . . set forth one father unknown to all, who made angels, archangels, powers, and potentates. The world, again, and all

things therein, were made by a certain company of seven angels.
Man, too, was the workmanship of angels. . . . He [Saturninus] also
laid it down as a truth, that the Saviour was without birth, without
body . . . that the God of the Jews was one of the angels; and, on
this account, because all the powers wished to annihilate his father,
Christ came to destroy the God of the Jews. . . . They [the followers
of Saturninus] declare also, that marriage and generation are from
Satan. . . . Saturninus represents as being himself an angel, the
enemy of the creators of the world, but especially of the God of the
Jews.

Since these all are frequently expressed Gnostic tenets supported by actual surviving texts, there is no reason to doubt the
accuracy of Irenaeus's summary. If only the good bishop had also
included some biographical information on Saturninus.

Slightly more is know about *Basilides*, who founded a very influential heretical school in Alexandria during the second century.
It was he who 'discovered' that there had been no crucifixion or
resurrection of Jesus. Again Irenaeus:

[Basilides claimed that Jesus] did not himself suffer death, but
Simon, a certain man of Cyrene, being compelled, bore the cross in
his stead; so that the latter being transfigured by him, that he might
be thought to be Jesus, was crucified through ignorance and error,
while Jesus himself received the form of Simon, and, standing by,
laughed at him.

No one now disputes Irenaeus's summary, although many seem to
prefer Basilides' versions to those in the New Testament. As to influence, Basilides' school in Alexandria "was apparently still active
in the mid–fourth century."[43]

Valentinus opened a heretical school in Alexandria before moving it to Rome. Born in the Nile Delta about the year 100 CE, Valentinus was educated in Alexandria, quite possibly as a student of Basilides.[44] He is believed also to have been greatly influenced by the writings of the Hellenized Jewish philosopher Philo and to "have been exposed to the mystical Thomas tradition that originated in Mesopotamia and was popular in Egypt in Valentinus's time."[45] He moved to Rome around 140 CE, where he soon became a serious candidate for the office of bishop of Rome (before being expelled from the Christian church for heresy).

Valentinus was very much the academic intellectual, and his "movement had the character of a philosophical school, or network of schools, rather than a distinct religious sect." What he and his students aspired to achieve was "to raise Christian theology to the level of pagan philosophical studies"; in fact, "the very purpose of the school was speculation." They justified their speculations as based "on the authority of a secretly transmitted academic tradition, whose origin they traced back to St. Paul."[46]

What Valentinus actually taught is open to some dispute, since most of the views attributed to him were actually expressed by his outstanding student Ptolemy. There is no reason to suppose that the student departed greatly from his master, however, and therefore it seems reasonable to associate Valentinus with at least some of the radical speculations presented in Ptolemy's own teachings. Consequently, many scholars "see in Valentinus' teachings the apex of gnosticism, the greatest and most influential of the gnostic schools."[47] Not only do many later Gnostic texts clearly reveal Valentinian influences, but his students carried on his work by establishing several branch campuses (one in Carthage) and by organizing a major heretical movement, as will be seen. What made Valentinus so successful, and such a threat to conventional Christianity, was his effort to reconcile the New Testament with classic

elements of Gnosticism by applying "a peculiar allegorical interpretation of those commonly accepted texts,"[48] thereby discovering hidden and deeper levels of meaning consistent with those
revealed to Gnostic visionaries. Put another way, what Valentinus
and his students did was 'discover' proofs in support of Gnostic interpretations hidden in the conventional gospels.

These four heretical schools, then—the schools of Valentinus,
Basilides, Saturninus, and St. Thomas—were the best known. In
addition, both Cerdo and Heracleon probably had schools in
Rome, as did Marcus in Byzantium.[49] Several others, including
Isidore, Justin, Concessus, and Marcarius,[50] may have led schools
too, but we know nothing of these 'writers' except their names.
Some scholars place Gnostics in Corinth on the basis of passages
in *1* and *2 Corinthians,*[51] and this may be so. But even if Paul's local
opposition in Corinth did come from some extremely early Gnostics, there is nothing to suggest that they constituted a 'school.'

Map 6-1 shows cities thought to have had heretical schools
prior to 300 CE. By scoring all eight cities having a school as one
and the others as zero, we transform the location of heretical schools
into a variable.

Travel

We have seen that Christianity and Isiacism spread across regular
trade and travel routes, gaining supporters in port cities sooner
than elsewhere. But Robert M. Grant has argued that the reason
early heretical schools exhibited such "remarkable diversities in
doctrine" is because they did not *spread* nearly so much as they
were independently constructed by various 'teachers' who shared
only "a common Gnostic attitude."[52] This leads to:

HYPOTHESIS 6-1: *Port cities were no more likely than inland
cities to have heretical schools.*

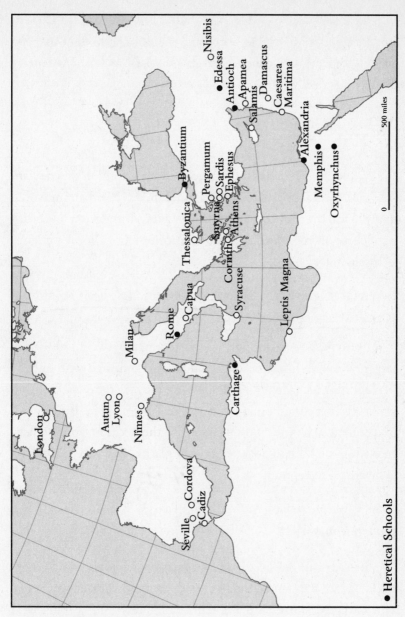

MAP 6-1. Heretical Schools

The data show that Grant was quite right (Table 6-1). There is no relationship between ports and heretical schools—as with other intellectual pursuits, heretical scholarship was a sedentary activity.

City-Size

Heretical schools surely fit Claude Fischer's definition of a deviant subculture, meaning that his subcultural theory of urbanism would apply. Moreover, since schools did not travel, their existence depended upon rounding up a sufficient number of local students. Consequently:

> HYPOTHESIS 6-2: *Larger cities were more likely than smaller cities to have heretical schools.*

This hypothesis is strongly supported: nearly two-thirds of the larger cities did shelter heretical schools, as compared with only 13 percent of the smaller cities (Table 6-2). However, this relationship probably isn't just about population size per se. The larger cities also tended to be the cultural centers of their region, and intellectuals always have congregated in such places. The heretical teachers were no exception.   *U city !*

Jewish Roots?

We turn now to one of the great controversies concerning Gnosticism. Until the start of the twentieth century, scholars were content to regard Gnosticism as a Christian heresy—in keeping with the judgments of the early church fathers. Then, in keeping with the impulse to novelty prompted by the fact that the rapid road to academic status is innovation, Moritz Friedlander traced the origins of Gnosticism to Jewish roots and claimed that Christianity

haha !

and Gnosticism were parallel offshoots of first-century Hellenic Judaism.[53] This view soon gained a great deal of support, culminating in Birger Pearson's assertion: "Gnosticism is not, in its origins, a 'Christian' heresy, but . . . it is in fact a 'Jewish' heresy."[54] As for the intense anti-Judaism of much of this literature, it was said to reflect the antagonism of bitterly rebellious ex-Jews against the faith of their fathers.

But it is not only its widespread "metaphysical anti-Semitism" that gives pause to accepting the claim that Gnosticism originated in Judaism. There also is the fact that, with only several exceptions, the Gnostic writings are greatly concerned with new stories about and new interpretations of Christ. Other than giving great attention to *Genesis,* most Gnostic books focus on New Testament matters: about what Jesus really said, his true nature, and how his mission will be accomplished, as revealed to various figures claiming major *Christian* status: John, Peter, Mary, Thomas, Mark, James, Matthew, and others. I suppose that if Gnosticism were primarily Jewish, much more attention would have been devoted to Old Testament matters and many of the manuscripts would have been attributed to various prophets. Of course, Pearson was careful to say only that Gnosticism was of Jewish *origins.* This leaves room for its Jewish authors to have been Christian converts. In that case, all Pearson really said is that Gnosticism originated with Jewish Christians. But so did Christianity! If one can spot Jewish elements in Gnostic writings, so what? The gospels contain at least as much Judaism! And for all the concern over the anti-Jewish passages of the New Testament,[55] they are mild and infrequent compared with many Gnostic gospels.

For all these reasons, a reaction has been building up against the notion that Gnosticism is Jewish rather than Christian. The celebrated French historian Simone Pétrement delivered a major blow to that notion in 1990, with the publication of her book *A Separate God: The Christian Origins of Gnosticism.* This is just the sort of never-ending dispute that is suitable for a quantitative approach to early church history. Let's use the data to test the following:

HYPOTHESIS 6-3: *Heretical schools did not cluster in cities having large Diasporan Jewish communities.*

This hypothesis is very strongly supported: there is *no* significant correlation between the Diaspora and Gnostic schools (Table 6-3). Of course, this does not prove that Gnosticism wasn't mainly a Jewish enterprise, but it would seem to make it rather less probable: if the Gnostics were intellectual Jewish rebels, they must have left home.

Churches and Schools

Finally, there is no particular reason to suppose that Gnostic schools were more apt to be established in cities that were in the forefront of Christianization. For one thing, the presence of vigorous local Christian groups may have been a deterrent when heretical teachers were deciding where to set up a school. Such teachers may have considered it far more important to locate in a community where religious novelty and diversity thrived.

And that leads to an additional consideration, one that mostly has been ignored by recent participants in this dispute concerning the origins of Gnosticism. Fully in accord with von Harnack's claim that Gnosticism was "the acute secularizing or hellenising of Christianity,"[56] a strong case can be made that paganism and Greek philosophy played an even more important role in Gnosticism than did either Judaism or Christianity—in other words, that many Gnostic works were pagan adaptations of the rapidly expanding Christian and Jewish monotheism. As noted in Chapter 5, many elements found in *Genesis* and in the Christ story were familiar pagan doctrines well before the birth of Jesus. In addition, the idea of a remote supreme God and a lesser divinity called the Demiurge does not derive from either Judaism or Christianity, but was prevalent in classical philosophy. (As noted earlier, Plato probably originated the Demiurge thesis.) In addition to these correspondences, consider how much more like paganism than either Judaism or Christianity is the relentlessly 'mythical' and ahistorical character of the Gnostic materials. A serious examination of the pagan roots of Gnosticism will be undertaken in the next chapter. Here it is sufficient to hypothesize that:

HYPOTHESIS 6-4: *Heretical schools did not cluster in cities having an early Christian congregation.*

The data confirm that, as hypothesized, Christianization is not significantly related to heretical schools (Table 6-4).

To sum up: in founding their schools, heretical teachers did not favor port cities, nor did they seek places abundant in either Jews or Christians. What they did was gravitate to the cultural centers which were, for the most part, the larger cities.

Major Heretical Movements

We now shift our attention from manuscripts and schools to more significant undertakings. Whatever can be deduced about the intentions of those who wrote the texts buried at Nag Hammadi, the leaders of major heretical movements aimed to supplant the conventional Christian church. As we characterize and analyze these movements, it will be useful to keep in mind just how tiny they must have been. Consider that during the first half of the second century, when "Marcionites could be found all over the empire,"[57] there probably were no more than twenty to thirty thousand Christians of all varieties. How many of these were Marcionites is impossible to say, although many historians believe that they made up a very significant minority.[58] Even if this is so, there never were all that many people involved in the movement—surely not more than ten thousand, and probably many fewer—although their numbers may have increased by the third century (given that Marcionite congregations still existed as late as the fifth century). In any event, Marcion was regarded as "the most formidable heretic of the second century CE."[59] His was also the earliest of the major heretical movements.

Marcionism

Marcion probably was born late in the first century in Sinope, a Black Sea port in Asia Minor; his father may have been the bishop of Sinope. There is some reason to believe that Marcion made a huge fortune in the shipping industry, but beyond that very little is known of his life and career. Some historians assume he must have become a bishop at some point before going to Rome, since no layman would have been permitted to debate theology with the church presbyters.[60] The only date of probable reliability is that he was excommunicated in Rome in 144 CE. What is certain is that "Marcion was apparently the first Christian ever to set forth a 'New Testament'—that is, a closed collection of Christian Scriptures."[61] His consisted *only* of Luke's gospel (somewhat edited), ten letters of Paul (not including the Pastoral Epistles and *Hebrews*) and his own *Antitheses,* which has not survived but which was an elaborate statement of what Marcion believed to be the many contradictions between the Old Testament and what Jesus taught. Therefore, Marcion argued, if one were to fully embrace Christ, one must expel the Judaizers from Christianity—he included Peter, James, and John among those who had "diluted and distorted the true teaching of Jesus"[62] to accommodate the Old Testament. Many historians of the early church agree that in defining his testament, Marcion made it necessary for the church fathers to be specific about what was and was not part of their official canon, thus creating the New Testament pretty much as we know it.

On purely theological grounds, Marcion's position might have had considerable appeal. Clearly there was conflict between Jewish and Gentile Christians, and there always have been difficulties in harmonizing the New and Old Testaments. But Marcion was not content to promote a purely Pauline brand of Christianity. He demanded total celibacy, charging that the directive to be fruitful and multiply came from the God of the Jews. He also preached other forms of abstinence, declaring that it was sinful to enjoy food or drink; he even substituted water for wine in liturgical use. Consequently, what Marcion founded was not so much a mass movement as an ascetic 'order' for the laity.

There is some disagreement among scholars as to whether Marcion should be identified as a Gnostic. He was bitterly opposed to Judaism and dismissed the Jewish God as inferior and unjust, thereby seeming to echo the essential Gnostic idea of the evil Demiurge. But, as Hans Jonas explained, he did not pursue this point to the Gnostic conclusion: "[H]owever unsympathetically depicted, he [the Jewish God] is not the Prince of Darkness."[63] Nor did Marcion spin out a new *Genesis:* "[H]is teaching is entirely free of the mythological fantasy in which gnostic thought reveled: he does not speculate about the first beginnings; he does not multiply divine and semi-divine figures."[64] Instead, Marcion was content to catalogue the contradictions between Christianity, as he understood it, and the Old Testament. Moreover, within his limits he was an orthodox Christian who fully accepted Luke's gospel and Paul's teachings, without adding any esoteric touches. As von Harnack put it, Marcion "unequivocally confessed a Pauline Christianity."[65] Consequently, Marcion seems to have been somewhat optimistic about his chances when he took his proposals for a 'purified' Christianity to leaders of the Christian church in Rome. It was only after they rejected him, and excommunicated him when he refused to recant, that Marcion became a rebel—although he probably had attracted followers and founded congregations prior to visiting Rome.

Perhaps quantitative analysis can shed light on some of these matters.

Let's look at Map 6-2, which draws primarily on von Harnack's extensive study of Marcionism,[66] supplemented by others.[67] We see on the map that 13 of the 31 cities in the data set were determined to have harbored a Marcionite congregation.

First to be addressed is the question of whether Marcion was a Gnostic. On the basis of his teachings, there is no reason to suspect that Marcion was especially influenced by any of the heretical schools discussed above. Hence:

HYPOTHESIS 6-5: *Marcionite congregations were not more common in cities having heretical schools.*

The data reveal no significant difference between cities with a heretical school and those without as to having had a Marcionite congregation; thus the hypothesis is confirmed (Table 6-5). This finding supports those who contend that Marcion was not a Gnostic.

What seems far more important, however, is Marcion's anti-Judaism. There are substantial grounds for assuming that this was not a purely intellectual matter, but that it reflected real antagonism between Jewish and Gentile Christians. In this regard, the *Gospel of John,* which is taken to be the latest of the four synoptic gospels and which probably was written not long before Marcion began his career, is notably more antagonistic toward Judaism than are the other three gospels. Unlike Marcion, John clearly accepts that the God of the Jews is the Father of Christ, but he quotes Jesus "time and again, that the Jews *do not know God.*"[68]

This was symptomatic of a worsening in relations between the two faiths, which by Marcion's time was exacerbated by the Bar-Kokhba Revolt (132–135) in Palestine against the Romans—a revolt that Christians disavowed. But it seems probable that Jewish-Gentile conflicts *within* the Christian community played an even more important role. First of all, that Marcion could so easily be anathematized suggests that the fledgling church still was greatly influenced by Jewish Christians—the success Marcion had in recruiting followers suggests that his proposal to dismiss the Jewish heritage was popular among Gentile Christians. Indeed, the proposal to dispense with the Old Testament has been favorably reinterpreted by a series of modern scholars who hail Marcion as the first Protestant, "harking back to the pure message of Jesus and his Father."[69] Second, despite Paul's ruling against Jewish Christians continuing to observe the Law, many clearly did continue to observe it, and it seems likely that they regarded Gentile Christians as somewhat inferior. In fact, there was a heretical form of Jewish Christianity whose members "wished to maintain their Jewish observances (circumcision, food laws, the Sabbath, etc.). Moreover, many of them, even though they venerated Christ, did not consider him absolutely divine or consubstantially united to the one God."[70]

One can plausibly hypothesize, therefore, that the anti-Judaism of many early heresies was, as Pheme Perkins suggested, "formed by people who lived in close proximity to Judaism and in reaction against it."[71] That is, these attitudes were aroused by close contact and conflict, not by separation and unfamiliarity. Hence:

HYPOTHESIS 6-6: *Marcionite congregations were more likely to arise in cities having large Diasporan Jewish communities than in those without.*

This hypothesis is very strongly confirmed. Marcion gathered congregations more successfully in cities with large Jewish populations (89 percent)—cities where conflicts between Jews and

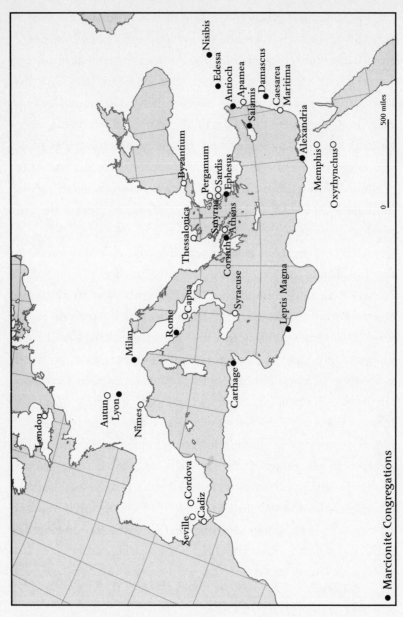

MAP 6-2. Marcionite Congregations

Christians, and especially between Jewish and Gentile Christians, would have been maximized—in contrast with cities lacking Diasporan communities, only 27 percent of which had a Marcion congregation (Table 6-6). Indeed, the growth of Marcionism and the severe official church response to its teachings can be taken as additional evidence that Jewish conversion to Christianity, and hence Jewish influence within Christianity, lasted rather longer than has been recognized (see Chapter 5).

In addition, Marcionism proved not to be significantly related to Christianization, ports, or city-size (tables not shown).

Valentinianism

All historians classify Valentinus, unlike Marcion, as a 'Gnostic'—indeed, perhaps the prototype thereof. They take the same view of the Valentinians, the heretical religious movement launched by his successors. Map 6-3 locates Valentinian congregations.[72]

In keeping with the traditional view of the Valentinians as Gnostics, it follows:

HYPOTHESIS 6-7: *Valentinian congregations were more common in cities having heretical schools than in cities having none.*

Seven out of eight cities with a heretical school had a Valentinian congregation, while only two of twenty-three cities without a school had a Valentinian congregation (Table 6-7). The correlations are huge and significant. This not only demonstrates that the Valentinians were in some sense Gnostics but also reinforces the finding that the Marcionists weren't.

Not surprisingly, there was no significant correlation between Valentinianism and Marcionism, nor was Valentinianism correlated with Diasporan communities, Christianization, or ports. What about city-size?

HYPOTHESIS 6-8: *Valentinian congregations were more common in larger cities than in smaller ones.*

True! Seventy-five percent of the larger cities had a Valentinian congregation, compared with 13 percent of the smaller cities (Table 6-8).

Using regression analysis to inspect the impact of both city-size and heretical schools on Valentinianism (Regression 6-1), we discover that both factors matter, but heretical schools matter much more. This indicates, in part, what it was about big cities that attracted the Valentinians: they were intellectual and cultural centers conducive to nonconformity, in addition to being large enough that the nucleus of members needed to form a local congregation could be found.

Montanism

Had they appeared in modern times, the followers of Montanus would probably have been designated as a "doomsday cult." Their two primary tenets were that Montanus and his two female associates, Priscilla and Maximilia, had the gift of prophecy (achieved during states of ecstasy), and that their most important prophecy was that the end was very near. "After me there will no longer be a prophet, but the end,"[73] was how Maximilia put it. It also has long been assumed (based on writings by Eusebius and by Tertullian) that the Montanists were eager for martyrdom, but they probably were "not substantially different from" other Christians in that regard.[74]

Fundamentally, the heresy of the Montanists lay in their claim to have gained authentic new revelations and in their method for gaining revelations, rather than the *content* of these revelations. To condone continuing revelations puts all religious organizations at serious risk of constant doctrinal upheavals; thus most religious

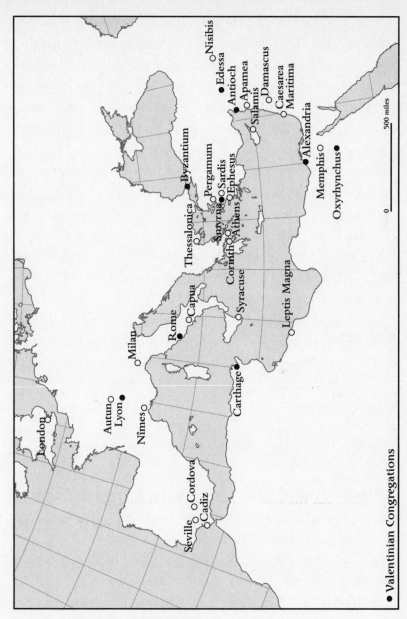

MAP 6-3. Valentinian Congregations

groups, after the founders are gone, prohibit or monopolize revelations.[75] Moreover, in this particular circumstance, condoning revelations gained during ecstatic states came far too close to embracing pagan oracles.[76] As for doctrinal matters, even late in the second century, when Montanus first began to preach and prophesy, many church fathers still accepted that the Day of Judgment was near. Nor did the rest of the Montanist teachings and practices differ in other than minor ways from that of the conventional church; "prophecy was the primary point of contention."[77]

Consequently, historians agree that the Montanists were *not* Gnostics, but merely heretics—the words *Montanus* and *Montanism* do not even appear in the indexes of most of the leading books on Gnosticism. Thus, Montanism provides a useful basis for comparison with other movements.

See Map 6-4, which identifies the twenty-two cities with Montanist congregations.[78] You will note that there is less of an eastern tilt to this map than to many of the other maps.

Since historians do not consider the Montanists Gnostics, it follows that:

HYPOTHESIS 6-9: *Montanist congregations were not more common in cities having heretical schools.*

The data revealed no significant difference between cities with and without heretical schools as to the presence of Montanist congregations (Table 6-9). The hypothesis is confirmed.

While the Montanists seem not to have been Gnostics, they were condemned as heretics. That being the case, on the basis of Fischer's subcultural theory: Montanists ought to have been more successful in the larger cities:

HYPOTHESIS 6-10: *Montanist congregations were more common in larger cities than in smaller ones.*

All of the larger cities had Montanist congregations, compared with 61 percent of the smaller cities (Table 6-10). The difference is significant, and the hypothesis is confirmed.

Montanism was not significantly correlated with Christianization or with the Diaspora, however.

Manichaeism

The 'prophet' Mani managed to be declared a heretic in both the East (by the Zoroastrian state church in Persia) and the West. Born in 216 CE in Mesopotamia, he was related to the local nobility through his mother and was enrolled in a "Judeo-Christian baptismal sect with gnostic and ascetic features"[79] by his father at age four. He began receiving revelations at age twelve, and at twenty-four received one in which he was ordered by an angel to begin his ministry.

Unfortunately, because he was a Persian and missionized quite successfully in the East, several generations of scholars, especially in Germany, erroneously dismissed Manichaeism as a Persian religion. Their error repeated one made in 279 CE by Emperor Diocletian, who issued an edict against the Manichaeians as "Persians who are our enemies."[80] This was nonsense. As Peter Brown put it, the "Manichees entered the Roman Empire not as . . . [an] Iranian religion . . . but at the behest of a man who claimed to be an 'Apostle of Jesus Christ': they intended to supersede Christianity, not spread a [Persian faith.]"[81] Manichaeism was, in the words of Christoph Markschies, "the culmination and conclusion of 'Gnosis.'"[82]

As to what Mani taught, it was the well-worn Gnostic account of an evil creator and an evil world, with some especially scandalous details. It was not Adam but an evil archon who had sex with Eve and fathered Cain. Then Cain had sex with his mother and fathered Abel. Later Eve managed to arouse the ascetic Adam

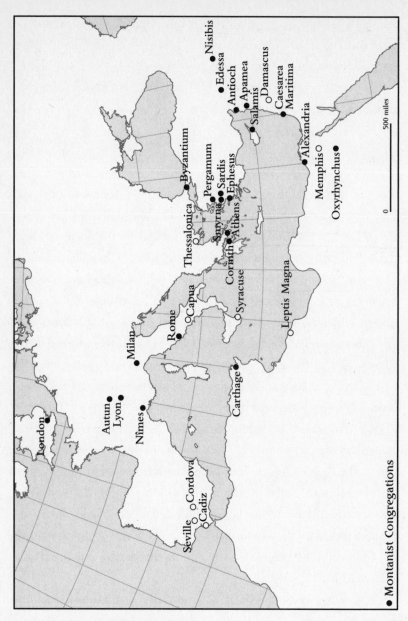

MAP 6-4. Montanist Congregations

to father Seth, thus beginning a race of beings who are noble in spirit but "entrapped in innately evil material bodies."[83]

Mani created two levels of membership: the Auditors and the Elect. The former 'heard' the word but did not live a life that could qualify for admission to the Kingdom of Light upon their death. Rather, they could hope only to be reborn as vegetables and then to be eaten by the Elect and "belched" to freedom from the evil archons and sent on their way to the Kingdom of Light. As for the Elect, they were bound by extraordinary restrictions: no sex, no alcohol, no meat, no baths, and virtually no physical activity of any kind. They could meet these requirements only if Auditors waited on them hand and foot.

The Manichaeians enjoyed some success. They missionized far eastward (into China), making converts even among the nobility, as well as far westward—the young St. Augustine was a Manichaean for a few years (but only as an Auditor and without giving up his mistress). The favorable response to Manichaeism can be seen in Map 6-5.[84]

If, as Pheme Perkins put it, "Manichaeism [was] the last powerful manifestation of Gnostic spirituality in the ancient world,"[85] it follows that:

HYPOTHESIS 6-11: *Manichaeist congregations were more common in cities having heretical schools than in cities without.*

This hypothesis is very strongly supported. Like Valentinianism, Manichaeism did better where there were heretical schools (Table 6-11).

Since the Manichaeists also were heretics, it follows that:

HYPOTHESIS 6-12: *Manichaeist congregations were more common in larger cities than in smaller ones.*

Seventy-five percent of the large cities had Manichaeist congregations, compared with 17 percent of the smaller cities (Table 6-12).

This, then, is another confirmation of Fischer's subcultural theory of urbanism.

Manichaeism was not significantly correlated with Christianization or with the Diaspora.

The Demiurgists: 'Gnosticism' Reconceived

Probably the primary flaw in the immense literature on Gnosticism has been a lack of discrimination. If the early church fathers condemned any work as heresy, it was likely to be treated as an instance of Gnosticism. If manuscripts were found stuffed in the same big earthen pot, that was prima facie evidence that each was a Gnostic work (aside from some obvious exceptions, such as a portion of Plato's *Republic*). But, despite all the variations that have invalidated the term *Gnostic* as an analytic category, clearly there is *something* here—a subset of manuscripts, schools, and movements that share a particularly outlandish heresy: that there are two gods and that the one who created and controls the world is utterly evil and inferior to the supreme God, who is good but remote.

In the conclusion of his book on the inadequacies of Gnosticism as a historical concept, Michael Williams proposed that his colleagues narrow their scope to this subgroup of heresies and dispense with the label Gnosticism as hopelessly compromised. He suggested that this subgroup be named "biblical demiurgical" and that "it would include all sources that made a distinction between the creator(s) and controllers of the material world and the most transcendent divine being, and that in so doing made use of Jewish or Christian scriptural traditions."[86] For ease of expression, it would seem adequate to refer to these sources as the *Demiurgists,* who embraced *Demiurgism,* with the understanding that the term is limited to those *within the Judeo-Christian tradition.*

The bases for this new concept, and for treating these instances as members of a single class, have been evident in some of the

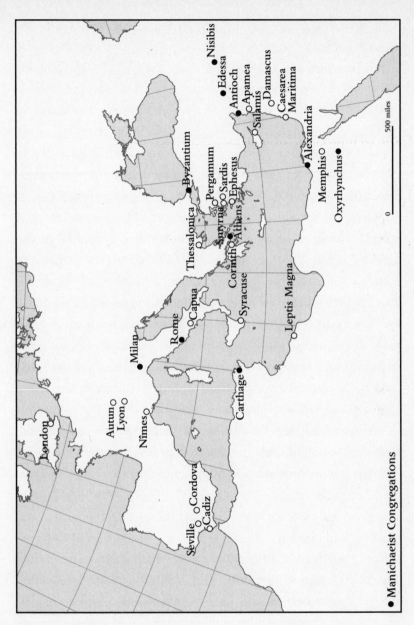

MAP 6-5. Manichaeist Congregations

analyses pursued above. It will be useful to bring these results into focus by examining how these movements are correlated with heretical schools. Theologically, both the Valentinians and the Manichaeists were Demiurgists, and so were the major heretical schools. These three measures are very highly intercorrelated, as should be the case with members of a common class. Moreover, the Marcionists and Montanists are not statistically part of this Demiurgical cluster, just as would be predicted from their doctrines (Correlations 6-1).

When one has identified several measures of the 'same' thing, it often is useful to combine them into a single measure—in this case, by adding the three measures of Demiurgism together into what we might call the index of Demiurgism. Previous results involving the individual measures of Demiurgism indicated that it was not an aspect of the sociocultural 'set' that has been the primary focus of this study. In support of this view, the index of Demiurgism is unrelated to Christianization, the Diaspora, Hellenism, or ports. However, the Demiurgical heresies were very highly correlated with city-size (Correlations 6-2). Just as in modern America one does not seek exotic cults in Peoria or Fargo, but in New York and Los Angeles, so too in ancient times one found them in Rome, Alexandria, Antioch, and the other major centers.

Conclusion

In some sense it is true that there were 'many' Christianities during the first several centuries. But, contrary to the wild claims made by members of the Jesus Seminar and by other media-consecrated experts concerning the lack of an early Christian consensus, the dissidents were mostly gadflies—even Marcion was easily turned away. As often is the case with gadflies, some were sufficiently annoying as to provoke significant responses: Marcion did prompt the early church to create a scriptural canon, for example. But the more overwhelming fact is that these heretics did not pose any real threat to the Christian church, if for no other reason than that their doctrines were so bizarre and the religious practices advocated by most of them (including non-Demiurgists) were so extreme as to appeal only to the few. As doctrines define behavioral prohibitions, they can matter a lot! Even if their friends and relatives do join, most people will not readily embrace a life of austere denial—a loveless, sexless, childless, meatless, bathless existence—especially if it offers no greater or more plausible posthumous rewards (the long shot chance to become an Elect belch, for example) than does a faith that is far less restrictive. For most Greco-Romans, it was far more attractive to be a conventional Christian or indeed to remain a pagan.

MITHRAEUM. The pagan cult of Mithraism met in underground caverns like this one excavated beneath the Church of San Clemente in Rome. Dozens of Mithraea have been found, and since all of them were as small as this one, the congregations could not have numbered more than fifty men. (Women were not allowed.)

—◈—

Chapter Seven

The Last Days of Paganism

AT THE DAWN of the fourth century, pagan gods still dominated life in the empire as Christians reeled under the vicious
persecution of Diocletian. At the close of that century, Christianity was the official religion and in some places the gods had become
virtual fugitives, lurking at the edges of society and sequestered in
underground grottoes. How was this possible?

As explained by Edward Gibbon near the end of the eighteenth
century, and then embraced by generations of equally anti-Catholic
scholars, the Christian victory was produced by "intolerant zeal,"[1]
aided and abetted by Constantine after he took the throne in 312.
It is claimed that, having empowered the Christians, Constantine
connived at their brutal persecution of paganism. Worse yet, the

pagans were unable to survive this onslaught because they were, in Gibbon's oft-quoted phrase, imbued with "the mild spirit of antiquity."[2]

For several centuries this summed up the historical consensus: as recently as 1990 a distinguished historian could write, "Polytheism is by definition tolerant and accommodating."[3] Of course, the mere existence of a long roster of Christian martyrs might have suggested that the truth is far more complex, although Voltaire went so far as to deny that the persecutions amounted to much.[4] So did Gibbon, who charged that Christian "writers of the fourth and fifth centuries" exaggerated the extent of the persecutions because they "ascribed to the magistrates of Rome the same degree of implacable and unrelenting zeal which filled their own breasts against heretics." In truth, Gibbon continued, the Roman magistrates "behaved like men of polished manners . . . [and] respected the rules of justice."[5] However, during the past generation the most distinguished historians of the early church have reaffirmed the reality of the pagan persecutions of Christians and have greatly qualified and amended claims concerning the Christian coercion of paganism—as will be seen. Still, paganism did succumb. This last chapter will examine how that happened.

The chapter begins by tracing the career of the last creative outburst of paganism: the cult of Mithras, also known as Mithra. We will examine appropriate data to show why Mithras was not a challenge to Christianity. Then we will turn to the period of relative tolerance and tranquillity that prevailed between Christians and pagans during Constantine's reign. The Christians were, of course, growing rapidly in this era, but without substantial recourse to coercive methods. Enter Julian the Apostate. An examination of Emperor Julian's anti-Christian efforts reveals how it fully rekindled Christian fears of renewed persecutions and thereby empowered the most militant elements in the early church. Even so, post-Julian efforts by this Christian faction to settle 'old scores' with pagans resulted in only sporadic efforts at coercion and reprisal—far less extensive and severe than had been thought.

Consequently, and contrary to the prevailing historical view that was begun by fifth-century Christian writers, paganism didn't "one day just topple over dead."[6] Instead, it slowly seeped away. The obdurately pagan Academy, founded by Plato at Athens, did not close until 529, and "even in most Christian Edessa ... organized communities of pagans were still sacrificing to Zeus-Hadad in the last quarter of the sixth century."[7] Earlier, and for a considerable time, the prevailing religious perspectives and practices consisted of a remarkable amalgam of paganism and Christianity. Moreover, a very major factor in the decline of paganism was opportunism—people professed Christianity or were discreet about their paganism, not to escape penalties, but in order to gain social and political advantages.

Not only did paganism die out slowly, but it persisted far longer in some places than in others. Consequently, after we have constructed a measure of pagan vitality during the fifth century, we will test hypotheses concerning pagan persistence and Christian heresies.

Mithraism: An 'Underground' Faith

Too often confused with the ancient Persian god Mitra,[8] Mithras was a new god, so closely associated with the sun that he sometimes was called "Mithras, the Invincible Sun." Mithraic worship took the form of a mystery cult that began in the city of Rome.[9] There is no record of its gradual development; evidence of the cult's existence suddenly appears in the historical record dating from about 90 CE. This has led scholars to agree with Martin Nilsson that Mithraism was created all at once by some "unknown religious genius."[10] Although some scholars continue to trace Mithraism to

Iran in the sixth century BCE, it "was an independent creation with its own unique value within a given historical, specifically Roman, context."[11] Some of the confusion over the cult's origins was caused by the fact that Mithraism represented itself as based on the wisdom of Zoroaster and of Persian origins. But this seems to have been a bogus attempt to gain credibility and prestige,[12] very similar to claims by modern groups to be descended from the Druids or various other ancient groups—in fact, someone recently founded a Church of Mithra in Illinois.

Because it was a mystery cult, only initiated members were informed of the key elements of the Mithraic faith or allowed to know and take part in its secret rituals, and each member was sworn to secrecy. That fact has inspired an immense amount of nonsense by writers who believe they have decoded the "Mithraic mysteries."[13] But the fact remains that we know very little about Mithraic doctrines, Mithraic mysteries, or what went on at the secret meetings. What we do know is based largely on archaeology. Scores of Mithraic sites have been discovered and studied, including a large number of Mithraea—the man-made caverns within which the groups met. These are remarkably uniform, the average Mithraeum being from 16 to 22 feet long and 9 to 12 feet wide—dimensions that mean, of course, that the average congregation could hardly have numbered fifty people.[14] Since these underground grottoes had no windows, everything was done by the light of oil lamps or torches, creating a darkened room with flickering lights and shadows that heightened the mysterious effect of the rituals. Access to a Mithraeum was through a maze of subterranean passages that seem to have played a role in the initiation ceremonies.[15]

Several years ago archaeologists found the top of a human skull buried beneath the altar in a Mithraeum excavated in Germany.[16] Combined with the report from the fourth century that human skulls were found when a Mithraeum in Alexandria was being cleansed for Christian use,[17] this suggests that human sacrifice may sometimes have entered into Mithraic practices, perhaps to punish those who failed to observe their vows of silence.

As with all initiation cults, Mithraism had a series of ranks, or levels of initiation. Each of the seven ranks was associated with a planet, because astrology played a crucial role in the group's doctrines. In fact, several leading scholars have proposed that the image of Mithras slaying the bull, which dominated the front of each Mithraeum, actually was a star map.[18] In any event, from lowest to highest, the ranks of Mithraism were Raven, Bride, Soldier, Lion, Persian, Heliodromos, and Father.[19] The cult excluded women from membership and seems to have relied entirely on a volunteer clergy.

Since a key aspect of Mithraic belief involved the god Mithras sacrificing a bull by leaping onto its back and severing the carotid artery, some scholars believe that (echoing Cybelene faith) a bull sacrifice was a part of the inner mysteries practiced at the secret ceremonies. Others doubt this, especially in light of the smallness of the sanctuary, and believe that the bull sacrifice took place only in a symbolic form. What is well known is that each Mithraeum was also a dining hall and that a sacred meal was served at each gathering. This meal was reported to be remarkably similar to the Christian Eucharist. Bread and wine were shared in the belief that members were thereby reborn, and perhaps the words consecrating the 'meal' were quite similar to those used by Christians. (Given when the cult began, this sacrament easily could have been copied from Christianity.) Justin Martyr, who seems to have had firsthand knowledge of Mithraism dating from his pre-Christian days, was so concerned about the similarities between the two rites that he attributed it to the work of evil demons.[20] Tertullian offered a similar explanation.

Perhaps because these two distinguished early Christians paid attention to parallels with Mithraism, many modern scholars have concluded that this pagan faith was the primary competitor of the early church. The famous nineteenth-century French historian Ernest Renan wrote, "If Christianity had been arrested in its growth by some fatal malady, the world would have become Mithraist."[21] This has often been repeated: "In the 2nd and 3rd centuries this mystery cult competed with its slightly older rival, Christianity."[22] "The cult of Mithras was indeed one of Christianity's chief competitors."[23] It was "a religion which very nearly became the foundation of our modern world."[24] "Mithraism was in fact Christianity's most serious competitor during the critical years of the third century."[25]

But it's not so, and a glance at any map of known Mithraic sites reveals why.[26] The dots locating individual sites provide a very good outline of the borders of the Roman Empire! Why? Because, first and last, Mithraism was an army cult. Most of the sites have been found in old legionary camps and fortresses, which were, of course, mainly along the frontiers. By the time in question, the Roman army was not composed of citizens-in-arms, but was primarily a professional force. It was not representative of the population and was quite deficient in social ties to civilians. Given those limitations, a cult that grew up within the army had little chance of becoming a popular movement—especially an army cult that excluded the more religious portion of the population: women.[27] If further evidence is required, the data show that Mithraism is not significantly correlated with *any* of the measures examined in this study (Table 7-1: Correlations).

Clearly, Mithraism was not just another pagan faith, but a very special case unto itself. Moreover, aside from the few upper-class Roman men who commanded troops, especially along the Danube, the Roman elite was conspicuous by its absence from Mithraism— as demonstrated by dedications and inscriptions.[28] These same inscriptions reveal that Mithraism primarily recruited soldiers of lower ranks, and "members of the imperial administration in clerical and subclerical grades."[29]

Events proved that this was a very undependable membership base. "When Constantine lent his support to Christianity, the Mithras initiates, who were frequently imperial employees and soldiers, apparently abandoned their cult with almost no opposition."[30] There is no evidence that any Mithraeum held services later than the fourth century CE. As Manfred Clauss summed up: "The cult of Mithras disappeared earlier than that of Isis, for example, and, unlike her, almost without trace. Isis survived in legend, and was still known in the Middle Ages as a pagan deity, whereas Mithras was already forgotten by late antiquity."[31] Indeed, anyone reading this book is likely to know that when Constantine expanded his hold on the empire to include the East, he marched under the banner of Christ. But only a few specialists know that his eastern opponent, Licinius, marched under the banner of Mithras.

Constantine's Reign: Pluralism and Amalgamation

Constantine was not responsible for the triumph of Christianity. By the time he gained the throne, Christian growth already had become a tidal wave of exponential increase (see Chapter 3). If anything, Christianity played a leading role in the triumph of Constantine, providing him with substantial and well-organized urban support. And, although historians long reported bitter outcries by pagans against Constantine's support of Christianity, the best recent scholars now agree that there is no evidence of such protests[32] and propose that even those pagans most directly involved regarded the emperor's favors to the Christian church as a "bearable evil."[33] Well they might have, for Constantine neither outlawed paganism nor condoned persecution of non-Christians. In fact, although Constantine subsidized and gave official standing to the Christian church, he continued some funding of pagan temples.[34] As for charges that he encouraged Christian mobs to destroy pagan temples—a claim that originated with Eusebius, who used it to show how "the whole rotten edifice of paganism" rapidly came crashing down as part of God's plan—"it is very likely that Eusebius report[ed] everything he knew of temple destruction," yet he could offer only four instances,[35] and only one of these seems a legitimate case. The other three involved temples of Aphrodite, which featured ritual prostitution.

More significant even than his tolerance of pagan temples, Constantine continued to appoint pagans to the very highest positions, including those of consul and prefect, especially if we may assume that most whose religious affiliation is unknown were, in fact, pagans (see opposite). In addition, pagan philosophers played a prominent role in his court[36] and depictions of the sun god appeared on his coins. Indeed, "Constantine directed his most ferocious rhetoric" not against pagans, but against Christian heretics: Valentinians, Marcionites, and the Gnostic schools.[37] Partly for these reasons, ever since Gibbon's time, leading historians have dismissed Constantine's conversion as an insincere political gambit. But the most recent historians now regard Constantine's conversion as genuine and cite the persistence of pagan elements in his reign as examples of his commitment to religious harmony.[38]

Amazingly, Gibbon and subsequent historians who dismissed Constantine's conversion as insincere all claimed that he was utterly sincere in brutally suppressing paganism, although it clearly was not in his best political interests to do so. These historians have offered no credible reason for this remarkable inconsistency, while ignoring the fact that Constantine not only failed to suppress paganism, but repeatedly reasoned and commanded against all such

Religious Affiliations of Men Appointed as Consuls and Prefects, 317–455

Reign	Christians	Pagans	Unknown	Number
Constantine (317–337)*	56%	18%	26%	55
Constantinus & Constans (337–350)*	26%	46%	28%	43
Constantius (351–361)*	63%	22%	15%	27
Julian (361–363)**	18%	82%	0%	17
Valentinian (364–375)**	31%	38%	31%	32
Valens (364–378)**	39%	25%	36%	36
Gratian (375–383)**	50%	11%	39%	44
Valentinian II (383–392)**	32%	32%	36%	19
Theodosius (379–395)**	27%	19%	54%	83
Arcadius & Honorius (395–423)**	34%	12%	54%	161
Theodosius II & Valentinian III (408–455)**	48%	4%	48%	157

*Computed from Barnes, 1995.

**Computed from van Haehling (1978) in Barnes, 1995.

efforts. Of critical importance are two edicts issued by Constantine soon after he defeated Licinius to reunite the empire. Both stressed peaceful pluralism.

The *Edict to the Palestinians* is notable for the pluralism of its language. In it, Constantine repeatedly referred to God but never mentioned Christ, using "phrases common to Christians and pagans alike[, which] is consistent with the search for a common denominator that was the hallmark of his religious policy."[39] But it is the *Edict to the Eastern Provincials* that fully expressed Constantine's commitment to accommodation and his rejection of coercive forms of conversion. He began with a prayer invoking "the most mighty God" on behalf of "the common benefit of the world and all mankind," saying, "I long for your people to be at peace and to remain free from strife." He went on: "Let those who delight in error alike with those who believe partake of the advantages of peace and quiet. . . . Let no one disturb another, let each man hold fast to that which his soul wishes, let him make full use of this." He continued, "What each man has adopted as his persuasion, let him do no harm with this to another. . . . For it is one thing to undertake the contest for immortality voluntarily, another to compel it with punishment." Finally, Constantine condemned "the violent opposition to wicked error . . . immoderately embedded in some souls, to the detriment to our common salvation."[40]

In both word and deed Constantine supported religious pluralism, even while making his own commitment to Christianity explicit. Thus, during Constantine's reign, "friendships between Christian bishops and pagan grandees" were well-known, and the many examples of the "peaceful intermingling of pagan and Christian thought may . . . be thought of as proof of the success of [Constantine's] . . . policy" of consensus and pluralism.[41] This policy was continued by "the refusal of his successors for almost fifty years to take any but token steps against pagan practices."[42] And a public culture emerged that mixed Christian and pagan elements in ways that seem remarkable, given the traditional accounts of unrelenting repression.

A newly famous example of that blending of religious elements is a calendar prepared in 354 for an upper-class Roman.[43] The calendar was created by a prominent artist who later fulfilled commissions for Pope Damasus I, and it is likely that many similar calendars were circulated. As with Catholic calendars ever after, this one noted all of the festivals of the church and commemorated the burial dates of important popes. But it also included illustrated sections consisting of "representations of those rites of the Roman public cult associated with each month." Careful examination of the calendar confirms that the Christian and pagan elements are not discordant, but rather, as Peter Brown put it, "form a coherent whole; they sidle up to each other."[44] Indeed, a sort of Christo-paganism was prevalent well into the fifth century and probably later. In Ravenna during the 440s, the bishop expressed his dismay that "the new birth of the year is blessed by outworn sacrilege" in reaction to the participation of "the most Catholic princes" of the city in pagan rites involving their dressing as "the gods of Rome" and comporting themselves before a huge audience in the Hippo-drome.[45] In similar fashion, not even St. Augustine could convince his flock in Hippo that such matters as bountiful crops and good health were not, in effect, subcontracted to pagan gods by the One True God;[46] Christians in Hippo continued to regard the performing of pagan rites as both legitimate and valuable. In many parts of Europe, the use of paganism as magic has continued into the modern era.[47]

Unfortunately, the era of toleration that existed under Constantine was misrepresented by early Christian writers, particularly Eusebius, who wanted to show that the emperor was the chosen instrument to achieve God's will that all traces of paganism be quickly stamped out and the One True Faith established as the Church Triumphant. It may have been an effective polemic, but it was spurious history, and worst of all, it was avidly seized upon by eighteenth- and nineteenth-century historians who were eager to place the church in the worst possible light. In truth it was not Constantine who reinstituted religious persecution, but the last pagan emperor.

Julian's Folly

Flavius Claudius Julianus, now known as Julian the Apostate, had only a brief (361–363) and quite disastrous rule as emperor. Despite that, he has become a virtual saint among anti-Catholic and anti-Christian intellectuals. Edward Gibbon complained[48] that Julian's many virtues have been "clouded" by the "irreconcilable hostility" of his Christian enemies, who despised him for his "devout and sincere attachments to the gods of Athens and Rome."[49] Two centuries later, Gore Vidal turned Julian's life into a heroic novel. Throughout, the central theme in popular thought has been that while Julian did seek to revive the vigor of paganism, he did so in a tolerant spirit. The truth is quite different.

Julian was ostensibly raised as a Christian, but some of his prominent tutors were pagans and they steeped him in the Greek classics.[50] Under their tutelage, Julian became a puritanical,[51] ascetic, and fanatical[52] pagan, who had been initiated into several of the mystery cults, including the Eleusinian mysteries[53] and probably Mithraism[54] as well. Julian was careful to comport "himself publicly as a Christian while worshipping the pagan gods"[55] until he took the throne. Once installed as emperor, Julian loudly revealed his contempt for those he reviled as "Galileans," whose "haughty ministers," according to Gibbon, "neither understood nor believed their religion,"[56] and he at once set about trying to restore paganism as the state-supported, dominant faith.

Not wanting to create new martyrs, Julian did not initiate the bloody persecution of Christians à la Nero or Diocletian, but he did condone the torture of several bishops, exiled others, and ignored the "summary executions that seem to have taken place in large numbers in central and southern Syria during [his] reign."[57] Thus, there was no imperial response when the "holy virgins [in Heliopolis] were rent limb from limb and their remains thrown to the pigs."[58] When knowledge that a pagan emperor now ruled prompted pagans in Alexandria to torture the city's Christian bishop, to tear him limb from limb, and to then crucify "many Christians," Julian's main concern was to obtain the dead bishop's library for himself.[59]

In a gesture that H. A. Drake compared to "a schoolboy thumbing his nose at his teachers," Julian revived the widespread celebration of blood sacrifices, sometimes involving a hundred cattle at a time, a practice that had long been outlawed in response to Christian influence.[60] In addition, Julian cut off state funding of the churches and subsidized the pagan temples. He replaced Christians with pagans in high imperial offices. He unsuccessfully urged pagan priests to initiate extensive charity programs (see Chapter 2). In an action that was far more significant than it might appear to modern readers, Julian made it illegal for Christians to teach the classics. This meant that upper-class parents had to choose between sending their offspring to be instructed by pagans or denying them the opportunity to acquire "the language, the looks, the innumerable coded signals that were absorbed unconsciously with classical *paideia* [or education, without which] Christian children would not have been able to compete in the elite culture of classical antiquity, as Julian knew full well."[61]

But, as Drake noted, the deepest of all the "wounds [Julian] was able to inflict, despite a relatively short tenure," was to revive Christian anxieties that another era of vicious persecution lay ahead. "Christians at the time . . . had no assurance that another Julian was not in the offing, and they could plausibly fear that worse was yet to come."[62] Consequently, "Julian was a blessing" for those Christians who opposed pluralism. As Drake summed up: "The effect of Julian's efforts was to polarize Christians and pagans, to remove the middle ground that traditional culture had previously provided, while at the same time lending credence to militant fears of a revival of persecution."[63] Julian's friend and admirer Liabius agreed that Julian "refused the use of force, but still the threat of fear hung over [the Christians], for they expected to be blinded or beheaded: rivers of blood would flow in massacres, they thought, and the new master would devise new-fangled tortures, the fire, sword, drowning, burial alive, hacking and mutilation seemed child's play. Such had been the behaviour of his predecessors and they expected his measures to be more severe still."[64]

Persecution and Persistence

Although he ruled for only eighteen months and was killed during battle in a foolish campaign against the Persians, Julian's name still terrorized Christians a generation later.[65] He was not replaced by another pagan emperor, although his favorite, Procopius, tried to take the throne, naming himself emperor at Constantinople late in 365. However, Procopius was deserted by the army and executed as a rebel, so it was Jovian who managed to take the throne. Jovian was a Christian who undid some of Julian's anti-Christian actions, but he ruled for only a year before being succeeded by Valentinian in the West and by his brother Valens, who ruled in the East. Although Valentinian was a devoted Christian, he also was quite tolerant[66] and continued to appoint many pagans to high office. Valens was a rather fanatical Arian Christian who persecuted non-Arian Christians from time to time, but he also appointed many pagans.

Nevertheless, in the wake of Julian's campaign for paganism, the Christian church was able to obtain statutes forbidding certain pagan activities. In three edicts issued during 391–392, Theodosius I banned public and private sacrifices to the gods—not only blood sacrifices, but also "such pagan devotions as sprinkling incense on altars, hanging sacred fillets on trees and raising turf altars."[67] However, these prohibitions were so widely ignored that each of the next two emperors, Arcadius and Justinian, reasserted the ban. Pagans obeyed to the extent of no longer conducting massive public animal slaughters, but commitment to paganism remained open and widespread.[68]

It is important to recognize that paganism was not merely a set of superficial practices and half-believed myths—or, as Lactantius put it, "no more than worship by the fingertips."[69] In past work I have been as guilty as most early church historians of underestimating the depth of paganism. Indeed, pagans of the late fourth and the fifth centuries often are portrayed as little more than "nostalgic antiquarians." But in fact theirs was an active faith "premised upon the conviction that the world was filled with the divine, and that proper sacrifice brought the human into intimate communion with the divine."[70] Although the rapid and extensive Christianization of the empire showed that pagans were very susceptible to conversion by their friends and relatives, the relative failure of legal prohibitions to dent paganism demonstrated that coercion was of no greater deterrent to commitment to the gods than it had been when used against commitment to the One True God. Moreover, imperial efforts to actually suppress paganism by force were far less sustained and far less vigorous than has long been claimed.

Consider that well into the fifth century, men who were openly pagans were still being appointed as consuls and prefects, as were many more who kept their religious preference obscure—something Christians had no reason to do. As late as the sixth century, temples remained open in many parts of the empire.[71]

In the post-Julian era, the public persistence of paganism did not reflect imperial tolerance so much as imperial pragmatism. Emperors often complained that their edicts against paganism were ignored, and it seems revealing that there is "no record of anyone in the fourth century having been prosecuted" for sacrificing to the gods.[72] One imperial letter complained that "[p]rovincial governors set aside imperial commands for the sake of private favors, and they openly allow the [Christian] religion which we [emperors] properly venerate to be openly disturbed, perhaps because they themselves are negligent."[73] Emperor Honorius complained that laws against paganism went unenforced because of the "sloth of the governors . . . [and] the connivance of their office staffs."[74] However, the emperors carefully did not crack down on those provincial governors who justified their inaction on grounds that enforcement of edicts against paganism would create levels of public discontent that "would seriously disrupt the collection of taxes in the province."[75] Hence, in 400 CE Emperor Arcadius rejected a proposal to destroy the temples in Gaza, remarking, "I know that the city is full of idols, but it shows [devotion] in paying its taxes. . . . If we suddenly terrorize these people, they will run away and we will lose considerable revenues."[76] Roger Brown proposed that persistent paganism served the emperor especially well, as cities would "have been all the more punctual in paying their taxes, if they needed to preserve . . . their ancestral religious practices" from imperial intervention.[77]

It even is questionable whether most emperors expected their various edicts involving Christianity and paganism to be fully ob-

Dr Slyke!

served. For example, when urged to do so by the bishops, Constantine outlawed gladiatorial combats. But when some Umbrian towns petitioned him for permission to celebrate the Imperial Cult with a festival that would include gladiatorial combats, Constantine granted their request. In similar fashion, Constantius issued an edict to close all pagan temples immediately. Then, in virtually the same breath, he advised the prefect of Rome to care for and sustain the temples around the city. During a subsequent visit to Rome, Constantius toured these temples and expressed his admiration for them.[78] For the fact was that even well into the fifth century "a considerable section of the population of the Roman empire, at all social levels, remained unaffected" by Christianity. "They [remained] impenitently polytheistic, in that the religious common sense of their age, as of all previous centuries, led them to assume a spiritual landscape rustling with invisible presences—with countless divine beings and their ethereal ministers."[79]

In the end, of course, the pagan temples did close and Christianity became, for many centuries, the only licit faith. But early Christian and later anti-religious historians to the contrary, it didn't happen suddenly, nor did it involve substantial bloodshed. The latter was limited mainly to conflicts *among* Christians, which sometimes resulted in military action against various heretical movements.[80]

The Decline of Paganism

Gibbon dates the "final destruction of Paganism" to the reign of Theodosius (379–395), noting that this "is perhaps the only example of the total extirpation of any ancient and popular superstition; and may therefore deserve to be considered, as a singular event in the history of the human mind." And, of course, this extirpation occurred because "Rome submitted to the yoke of the Gospel."[81] But, as with so much reported by Gibbon, it simply wasn't so. Consider one fact alone: Theodosius, the emperor who, according to Gibbon, extirpated paganism, appointed nearly as many men who were openly pagans as he did Christians to the positions of consuls and prefects.

These data have been referred to earlier in the chapter, but here is the appropriate place to consider them in detail. The initial coding was done by Raban von Haehling in 1978. Subsequently, T. D. Barnes corrected von Haehling's statistics through the reign of Constantius to eliminate some duplications (i.e., when the same man was appointed several times). Although Barnes's figures are undoubtedly more accurate, they resulted in no fundamental reinterpretations and there are no grounds not to use von Haehling's original findings for the reign of Julian and later.

Reading across the table, there seem to be three major patterns. First, except narrowly during the reign of Constantine and by a greater margin under Constantius, men known to be Christians were not in the majority, and this held for the first half of the fifth century as well. Second, Julian did discriminate against Christians, although not entirely. Third, if it can be assumed that men whose religious affiliation is unknown were unlikely to have been Christians, then the decline of pagan influence and power was very slow indeed.

Many have argued that paganism held its own far longer among the upper classes and the educated than among persons of lesser rank.[82] But that is inferred primarily from the known paganism of many persons of rank and the 'assumption' that Christianity's primary appeal was to the lower classes. However, since it is now recognized that Christianity had as much or more appeal to the upper classes as to the lower, that inference is unjustified. Rather, data on appointments more likely demonstrate is that paganism per se died slowly in all classes.

The data shown below might seem to challenge this claim. They show that in three areas, pagan inscriptions on gravestones suddenly ceased at the start of the fourth century. Notice, however, that Christian inscriptions did not become abundant at that time, but only slowly increased in number over the next several centuries, never becoming as frequent as had pagan inscriptions at their peak. This might be interpreted in favor of the sudden death of paganism, but that would put it in opposition to an abundance of contrary evidence. A better interpretation is that since inscribed gravestones mark upper-class burials, early in Constantine's reign the upper classes became increasingly discreet about their religious

**The Shifting Frequency of Pagan and Christian
Inscriptions on Gravestones: 100–650**

	Location					
	Carthage		North Africa		Spain	
Years	Pagan	Christian	Pagan	Christian	Pagan	Christian
100–150	273	0	121	0	139	0
150–200	306	0	189	0	181	0
200–250	183	0	196	0	121	0
250–300	70	0	92	3	52	1
300–350	0	0	1	14	9	10
350–400	0	54	0	23	0	23
400–450	0	75	0	20	0	42
450–500	0	97	1	24	0	58
500–550	0	42	0	75	0	86
550–600	0	115	0	147	0	59
600–650	0	77	0	59	—	—

SOURCE: Galvao-Sobrinho, 1995; actual frequencies provided to the author by Professor Galvao-Sobrinho.

identity. Seeking to maintain their positions and their access to imperial favor, many families ceased to identify themselves as pagans in such public ways as gravestone inscriptions—a caution that would seem to be reflected in the large number of appointees whose religious preferences are unknown. By the same token, most Christians were reluctant to display their family faith on gravestones until it clearly had become safe to so—that is, after 350 CE.

And that brings into view a major factor in the final Christianization of the empire: opportunism. From the time of Constantine, with the very brief exception of Julian's reign, the imperial throne was in Christian hands and very likely to remain there. Although some identifiable pagans continued to be appointed to high political offices, their prospects were on the downward trend. In addition, the many powerful and increasingly lucrative positions in the church were closed to them. Understandably, many ambitious individuals and families chose to convert. As Roger Brown put it, "A groundswell of confidence that Christians enjoyed access to the powerful spelled the end of polytheism far more effectively than did any imperial law or the closing of any temple."[83] Even many pagan philosophers broke ranks, some of them becoming leading bishops of the church.[84]

Patterns of Decline

Another factor also may be reflected in data above. These graveyards are all in the western empire, two of them in North Africa. Paganism seems to have declined more rapidly in these areas than farther east. This can be seen quite clearly in Map 7-1, where cities having a substantial level of pagan persistence in the fifth century are indicated, having been identified from the fine study by Pierre Chuvin and other sources.[85] As can be seen, except for Rome there was no city with much paganism west of Greece.

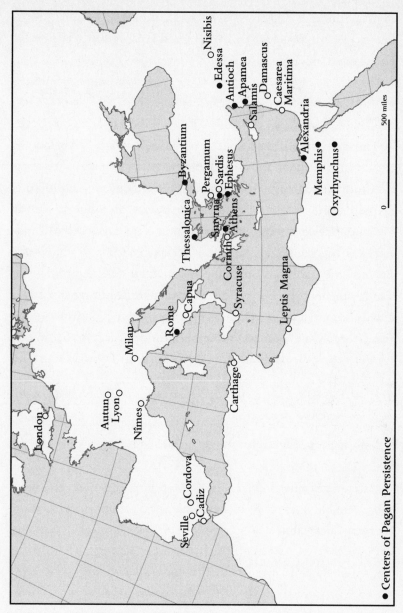

MAP 7-1. Centers of Pagan Persistence

What the map reflects is, of course, not the spread of paganism, but its persistence—where it managed to hold on longer than elsewhere. Consequently:

HYPOTHESIS 7-1: *Port cities were no more likely than inland cities to have a substantial amount of paganism.*

The hypothesis is confirmed. The differences are well below the level of statistical significance (Table 7-2).

Although paganism had long been the conventional religion of the empire, it can be argued that by the fifth century it had become a deviant faith and hence should be covered by Claude Fischer's theory of city-size and deviant subcultures. However, Fischer's mechanism is lacking—pagans did not persist by *recruiting* a sustaining nucleus, but by *retaining* one. On the other hand, larger cities also provide greater shelter for deviant subcultures because of a generally higher level of tolerance for diversity and because of greater anonymity. Hence:

HYPOTHESIS 7-2: *Larger cities were more likely than smaller cities to have substantial paganism.*

This hypothesis is supported: paganism did persist longer in the larger cities (Table 7-3).

As can easily be inferred from Map 7-1, paganism remained more durable in cities having a Hellenic culture than in the more Roman cities. Hence:

HYPOTHESIS 7-3: *Hellenic cities were more likely than more Roman cities to have substantial paganism.*

Again the hypothesis is supported. Paganism was persistent in more than half of the Hellenized cities and in only 8 percent of the less Hellenized cities (Table 7-4).

It might be supposed that paganism would be negatively related to Christianization—in other words, that where Christianity was stronger, paganism was weaker. That is not the case. There is a weak, positive correlation between Christianization and pagan persistence. However, this is due to the fact that both are correlated with Hellenism; with that factor controlled by regression, the correlation between Christianization and paganism disappears (Regression 7-1). There is no significant correlation between pagan persistence and the Diaspora.

Pagans and Gnostics

Many have noted the pagan aspects of the Gnostic scriptures, especially those writings associated with Demiurgism. Kurt Rudolph has suggested that the involvement of Greek philosophers in Gnosticism was stimulated "by the disintegration of the ancient religion," which also served as "a decisive prerequisite for the genesis of Gnosis." Rudolph traced the interpenetration of paganism and Gnosticism to Alexandria and to the Gnostic schools, where men trained in Greek philosophy and religious ideas generated Christian heresies. He pointed out that "the vocabulary of most gnostic systems . . . derived from the conceptual language of Greek philosophy; without it Gnosis, as indicated by the very word, is unthinkable."[86] Some might wish to dispute this linkage based on the celebrated attack on the Gnostics by Plotinus, the third-century founder of Neoplatonism. But, as Joseph Katz demonstrated, this seems to have been mainly a battle over intellectual priority, since differences between Plotinus's own writings and those he attacks are very slight and, indeed, confirm the link between a developing Neoplatonism and Demiurgism.[87]

This discussion leads us to our next hypothesis:

HYPOTHESIS 7-4: *Paganism was more persistent in cities having heretical schools than in cities having none.*

This hypothesis is very strongly supported (Table 7-5). Not only did paganism and Gnosticism cluster in Alexandria, but more generally heretical schools are linked to the persistence of paganism across the empire.

An even more important test of this clustering involves the use of the index of Demiurgism developed in the previous chapter:

HYPOTHESIS 7-5: *Paganism was more persistent in cities that scored high on the index of Demiurgism than in those that scored low.*

Once again the hypothesis is strongly supported (Table 7-6). Paganism was persistent in 86 percent of the cities high on Demiurgism and in only 17 percent of those low on that index. Clearly, then, persistent paganism and Demiurgism coexisted, thus confirming geographically what seems likely on the basis of textual analysis and interpersonal relations.

The possibility exists, however, that the real basis of these correlations is simply city-size—that all varieties of religious nonconformity sheltered in the big cities—which leads us to:

HYPOTHESIS 7-6: *With city-size controlled, the correlation between Demiurgism and paganism will disappear.*

This hypothesis is rejected! It is not city-size that matters, but the presence of a substantial amount of heretical local culture (Regression 7-2). That is, the effects of Demiurgism remain very strong, while the effects of city-size disappear.

Thus, it does appear that Demiurgism arose as an amalgamation of Greek philosophy and paganism in reaction to conventional Christianity. But there is a final, truly compelling basis for linking Demiurgism and paganism. As Kurt Rudolph noted, the "Gnostic sects" enjoyed "complete immunity" from the Roman persecutions of Christians. Clearly, the Romans did not regard them as

Christians even though their teachings included some Christian elements. The crucial aspect probably was that, like Basilides and his disciples, these heretics were willing to eat meat that had been sacrificed to pagan gods, and "consented to take part in pagan religious ceremonies on demand."[88] They were not Christians with some pagan leanings; they were pagans attempting to incorporate Christianity.

These connections make a mockery of revisionist claims that Gnosticism was the true Christianity, long suppressed by despotic bishops. In truth, both paganism, with its stress on sacred mysteries for the initiated, and Demiurgism failed, not primarily because of suppression, but for lack of general appeal: "[F]or this they were too narrow-mindedly esoteric and, above all, too hostile to the world."[89] When confronted with the option of embracing One True God of unlimited scope and benevolence, or the many small and often fickle gods of antiquity, or the evil Demiurge, most people made the reasonable choice.

Conclusion

For the past twenty-five years or so, there has been an increasingly concerted attack on monotheism, not only from ditzy New Agers and self-identified witches, but from more serious intellectuals and even a few respected historians, many of whom express nostalgia for paganism. Some have taken this so far that they can best be classified as neo-pagans. Consider Jonathan Kirsch. Having begun his recent book, *God Against the Gods,* with a brief catalogue of lurid episodes of religious intolerance, Kirsch proceeded to regret that Emperor Julian was unable to undo Constantine's boost of Christianity and restore the empire to paganism: "[I]t is tantalizing to consider how close he [Julian] came to bringing the spirit of respect and tolerance back into Roman government and thus back into the roots of Western civilization, and even more tantalizing to consider how different our benighted world might have been if he had succeeded."[90]

Remarkably, these attacks on monotheistic intolerance (many with colorful evocations of recent Muslim terrorism) fail to acknowledge the bloody pagan persecutions of Jews and Christians, as well as of various eastern and Egyptian 'cults,' to say nothing of death sentences imposed on philosophers for 'atheism.' It was, after all, the 'enlightened' Athenian pagans who forced Socrates to suicide and prosecuted many other philosophers, including Anaxagoras and Protagoras, for impiety.[91] In fact, as has been seen, it was Julian's efforts to reverse the rise of Christianity that poisoned what had been a relatively amicable relationship between pagans and Christians during Constantine's reign and provoked much of the conflict that ensued.

What is even more important is that behind all this newfound enthusiasm for 'tolerant' pagan religion lurks an objection to *effective* religion, to any God worthy of the name. Rather, these are praises sung to *ineffective* religion, to unimportant gods of small scope, limited power, and moral ambiguity precisely because such religion can't really matter. Far better, these neo-pagans believe, to have a religion that has no effects than to have one with a significant capacity to motivate human action. Can that capacity of monotheism result in tragedy? Of course. So isn't polytheism safer? Perhaps in terms of holy wars, but not when it comes to sustaining moral behavior or many attractive forms of humanitarianism.[92] More important, the choice between monotheism and polytheism does not present itself. Julian's effort to restore the temples was a fool's errand that achieved nothing because when monotheism and polytheism collide, monotheism always wins. Easily. It does so precisely because it offers far more, and does so with far greater credibility, making it the choice of philosophers as well as of the people.

Why Historians Ought to Count

I N 1962, Arthur Schlesinger Jr.—on leave from the Harvard history department to serve as a White House intellectual for John F. Kennedy—told an assembled audience of American scholars that "almost all important [historical] questions are important precisely because they are *not* susceptible to quantitative answers."[1] Such arrogance thrilled many of his listeners, as clever nonsense so often does. For others it prompted reflections on how someone so poorly trained had risen so high in the profession of history. In truth, many of the really significant historical questions *demand* quantitative answers. They do so because they involve statements of proportion: they turn on words such as *none, few, some, many, most, all,* along with *never, rarely, seldom, often, usually, always,* and so on.

To say that in the year 325 Emperor Constantine appointed the Christian Publilius Optatianus Porfyrius to be Proconsul of Achaea is to assert a *simple* fact.[2] It is adequately verified by reference to reliable surviving sources. But to say that, following the abortive reign of Julian the Apostate, Roman emperors rarely appointed a pagan as a consul or prefect, giving nearly all of those positions to Christians, is to assert a *proportional* fact. The second statement is far more significant than the first, and it is far more difficult to verify. To do so requires information on the religious identity of *all* men appointed to those positions during the relevant period. As we have seen, when these data finally were assembled, the claim turned out to be absolutely *false*. During the time in question, *every* emperor appointed *many* pagans to these positions, and under only one of them (Gratian) did Christians receive even as many as half of these appointments!

Frequently, it may not be possible for a historian to obtain the appropriate numbers needed to justify proportional statements, but there is no altering the fact that all such statements presume a numerical state of affairs. It is precisely in that sense that I mean the title of this conclusion: "Why Historians Ought to Count."

To proceed, let us turn back to Arthur Schlesinger and the book that made his reputation: *The Age of Jackson*. For decades before Schlesinger wrote, the central question posed about "Jacksonian democracy" was how Old Hickory had managed to motivate millions more Americans to vote in his presidential elections than ever had done so before. All the stars of American historiography had addressed the matter, including Charles and Mary Beard, Richard Hofstadter, and John Bach McMasters. A remarkable jumble of explanations had been offered, but everyone agreed with the Beards that Jackson was swept into office by "the roaring flood of the new democracy."[3] Thus, Schlesinger launched his career by attempting to explain the "immense popular vote" received by Jackson in 1828 when he was elected by a "mighty democratic uprising."[4] Notice that Schlesinger was not content simply to assert that Jackson was elected. He stressed the proportion of the victory—it was "immense" and "mighty." His book was awarded the Pulitzer Prize in 1946 because reviewers found Schlesinger's explanation of Jackson's huge appeal to the 'common man' so convincing.

But trouble soon arose. In 1960, two years *before* Schlesinger's expressions of contempt for quantification, Richard P. McCormick bothered to count the votes. He demonstrated conclusively that what was notable about the Jacksonian elections was *low* voter turnout! There was no "mighty" or "immense" outpouring. More votes had been cast in many previous elections. What seems to have so misled historians for so long was that these were apparently the first presidential elections in which attention was paid to the total popular vote, as opposed to merely reporting the results of the electoral college. Confronted with large numbers of votes, no one bothered to calculate whether these were many more or fewer than usual. As a result, generations of historical analysis was patent nonsense, having been devoted to explaining something that hadn't happened!

Some of those in the audience that night, upon hearing Schlesinger blithely ignore the fact that his famous work was in shambles due to his innumeracy, must have been reminded of children trying very hard to whistle as they walk past the graveyard in the dark. But, in fact, although McCormick's exposé was published in *The American Historical Review,* the most distinguished journal in the field, it was generally ignored, and many textbooks continued for several more decades to discuss Jackson's immense appeal. To the best of my knowledge, Schlesinger never recanted.

It remains a sad fact that many historians still delight in claims that quantification not only is often impossible, but is of no particular value. For example, Pierre Chuvin, the distinguished French historian, recently seemed quite happy to claim that "ancient history remains wholly refractory to quantitative evaluations."[5] I am not sure what he would make of the fact that, in Chapter 7, I quantified the strength of fifth-century paganism primarily by assembling fugitive facts dug out of his fine *Chronicle of the Last Pagans*. Thus does a major issue come into view: great benefits would be realized if historians could be persuaded to count.

To write a book such as this one requires an author to sift through a mountain of highly specialized studies. Because life is far too short, no author of a general work can master the original sources upon which the specialists thrive. I could not have quantified the rise of Christianity had von Harnack not provided me with the information that he gleaned bit by bit from the many years he devoted to the study of ancient sources. Nor could I have quantified the strength of paganism except as I was able to filter the information out of publications by Chuvin and others. Unfortunately, *filter* is the proper verb, because of the many authors I consulted, only von Harnack seemed to understand the need for providing complete coverage and offering it in an orderly fashion. All the many other scholars I have drawn upon for other measures offered the critical information as scattered asides and comments, and it often was necessary to build up the measure from many different authors. Had these scholars been sensitive to the possibilities of the quantitative uses of their work, they could have provided it as von Harnack did; and consequently I probably could have achieved greater precision (far more easily).

I am content that the variables used in previous chapters are reasonably well measured. But I am equally sure that Peter Brown,[6] for example, could have quickly produced more accurate data on the cities having groups of Manichaeists than I was able to dig out of his fine paper, even as augmented by Samuel Lieu's[7] extended work. Likewise, Lynn Roller[8] could have produced better data on cities with Cybelene temples than I could glean from her book. Of course, none of these authors expected anyone to try to quantify their work. But that's the whole point! Why didn't they? The unfortunate answer is: *because nobody does this sort of thing.*

Many historians, especially those devoted to ancient history, will receive this book with the deepest of suspicions; and others of them, with enthusiastic contempt. Of course, I didn't write it for them. I wrote it for the general reader, for numerate scholars, and especially for graduate students in history, to tempt the latter to pursue more disciplined and sophisticated undertakings. For not only could the experts mentioned above have surpassed me in quantifying many variables used in this study, only specialists can quantify many additional variables that require use of the original sources. As an example, and to express a wish list, consider the potential contained in the huge collections of inscriptions (including graffiti) that have been assembled by ancient historians.

Over the past two centuries an enormous number of ancient inscriptions have been discovered, carved in stone (especially on tombstones and monuments), painted on walls, impressed in clay blocks and bricks, scratched on lead sheets, and written on parchment or papyrus. There are huge collections of inscriptions in Sumerian, Egyptian, Persian, Hebrew, and other ancient languages. But even leaving these aside, there are hundreds of thousands of inscriptions in Greek and Latin (and various other languages spoken within the Roman Empire) that have been collected and published, with frequent supplements.[9] In recent years some of these collections have been digitized, and more such projects are under way or scheduled. Most of the collections have been organized by various topics, although some of the organizational schemes are unfortunate. I suppose that when digitization is complete, students of history will be able to search collections electronically and organize them to suit any particular research agenda.

Although historians often quote a few inscriptions to illustrate various assertions, only very rarely have they used them in a quantitative way. And even these instances usually have been limited to constructing very simple descriptions, such as Ramsay MacMullen's chart of the popularity of various pagan gods.[10] But these huge collections of inscriptions easily could be made to yield remarkably sensitive quantitative measures of significant variables.

To be more specific, consider measures of religious contexts. MacMullen demonstrated that the popularity of various pagan gods differed across four major regions of the Roman Empire. He warned, however, that in some areas the inscriptions were concentrated in a few places and that this might distort the overall regional picture. This problem could be greatly eliminated by breaking down the inscriptions into sets for each of the thirty-one cities; then, if too few inscriptions survived for some cities to justify coding, they could be omitted. MacMullen's data also are very difficult to compare across regions, because he reported only frequencies, not taking into account that there were many more inscriptions for some regions than others. Thus, for example, computing the percentage of inscriptions devoted to, say, Diana within each region would have yielded meaningful regional comparisons, whereas such comparisons are difficult to make using raw frequencies.

Assuming that persons able to read and comprehend these inscriptions were inclined to quantify, what measures might they code? They could start with the following (knowing some measures might turn out to be impossible and some might have no effects):

1. What is the percentage of inscriptions that have a significant religious content?

Many such inscriptions will be dedications to the donor or donors who built, refurbished, or otherwise made a substantial contribution to a particular temple or shrine. For example, a surviving inscribed block reports that M. Valerius Messalla Corvinus was the

Patron and benefactor of the temple of Artemis in the city of Ephesus.[11]

Many other inscriptions thank a particular god or goddess for some blessing; some offer detailed instructions for conducting a specific ritual; others list the rights and duties of priests. Expressed as a percentage of all surviving inscriptions in order to allow for variations in the total number that have survived from various cities, such a measure might well provide an overall estimate of the general religiousness of each community. Perhaps anti-religious sentiments should be excluded and placed in other measures (see 11 below).

2. Were inscriptions scattered rather evenly across many gods, of did one or two dominate? A very simple measure could consist of the total number of different gods mentioned for each city.

Such a measure might offer an opportunity to test the notion that traditional Roman religion eventually was weakened by offering too many gods—"a bewildering mass of alternatives," as E. R. Dodds put it (see Chapter 2). Did new faiths from the East, including Christianity, succeed sooner in cities with a greater diversity of gods?

3. What variations exist as to the deity most often mentioned, the top five, and the least popular?

Were cities more devoted to Jupiter different from those where Diana was number one? In MacMullen's data, Diana was second only to Mithras in the "north-central provinces," but she was little mentioned in North Africa. Was Mars more popular in frontier cities threatened by invaders? An intriguing item is found in MacMullen's data: the popularity of Mercury was in direct proportion to the distance of an area from Rome. Was this about speeding messages on their way if they had a long way to go?

4. What is the gender mix of gods vis-à-vis their popularity? What is the ratio of inscriptions to gods versus goddesses?

Are goddesses relatively more popular some places than others? For example, are Hellenic cities more receptive to goddesses? MacMullen found that Venus was far more popular in North Africa than in Gaul. Do gods cluster by gender? That is, are all goddesses relatively more popular in some cities than in others?

5. What is the proportion of religious inscriptions devoted to various 'oriental' religions, such as the worship of Cybele and Isis? For example, from Pompeii:

Numerius Popidius Celsinus, son of Numerius, restored the temple of Isis from its foundation at his own expense, after it had collapsed in an earthquake.[12]

Such a measure based on inscriptions could augment those based on temples or congregations as a way of tracking the spread of new faiths from the East.

6. What are the proportions of inscriptions associated with Judaism and with Christianity? (There are separate collections of inscriptions devoted to each.)

A Christian tomb inscription from Rome:

May he who wishes to violate this tomb, incur the fate of Judas.[13]

Another from Como:

*All you Christians, keep this tomb safe to the end of the world, so
that I may return to life without impediment, when He who comes
will judge the living and the dead.*[14]

Turning now to persons who originated the inscriptions, in
many cases the gender, social status, and ethnicity of the *author* of
the inscription can be determined. Here is an example found on a
marble plaque in Smyrna dating from about the second century CE:

*Rufina Ioudaia, head of the synagogue, built this tomb for her freed
slaves and the slaves raised in her house.*[15]

The donor was a wealthy Jewish female slave-owner; and from
this and a number of similar inscriptions, it now is recognized that
among Jews in the Diaspora, women often held religious leadership roles.[16] Nor was this peculiar to the Jews. Clearly there were
Christian women who held prominent positions in the early
church.[17] In fact, inscriptions reveal that Greek and Roman women
played a far more important role in civic affairs than is suggested
by legal documents, ancient historians, or even dramatists. For example, an inscription from the first century BCE discovered in
Priene, a small city in Asia Minor (where Alexander the Great
dedicated a large temple to Athena),[18] acknowledges that a woman
"paid for the city's aqueduct and reservoir" and served as one of
the magistrates.[19]

Nevertheless, given the dependent status of women in classical
societies, no doubt men were more likely than women to have left
inscriptions. But does that vary across cities? Thus we ask:

7. What is the overall sex ratio of those initiating or being the
subject of an inscription? Moreover, in all known societies women
are more religious than men. Does that show up here? Thus:

8. Compared with inscriptions in general, did women devote a higher percentage of their inscriptions to religion? Does this vary across cities?

9. What is the gender mix of religious inscriptions according to the particular deity or faith?

MacMullen reported that twenty-four of forty-four dedications to Cybele in northwestern Italy were by women. Not surprisingly, only one of eighty-one made to Mithras was by a woman.[20]

10. What is the status mix of those initiating religious inscriptions?

Way back in 1913 Dwight Nelson Robinson analyzed 1,149 inscriptions to "oriental cults" to identify whether the "devotee" was an official, priest, private citizen, soldier, trader, freedman, or a slave.[21] He divided his results into eight regions and found considerable variation. For example, in the Danube provinces, of 199 inscriptions to Mithras, 22 were by freedmen and 23 were by slaves, while of 31 such inscriptions in the "Germanies" none was by a freedman and only 1 was by a slave. In contrast, MacMullen reported that in Rome, "three-fifths" of the "inscriptions to Isis" were by slaves or freedmen.[22]

11. What percentage of all inscriptions, and also of all religious inscriptions specifically, were by ethnic minorities?

Many have claimed that 'oriental' religions, as they spread across the empire, failed to attract local devotees but were sustained by 'outsiders' from the East.[23] The cited quantitative basis for this conclusion is very thin. In any event, this measure might nicely augment the one based on port cities, since it might help us identify which minorities were present and compute their relative sizes.

Turning to another aspect of the religious context, consider the sacrilegious graffiti that some researchers have catalogued. For example, the walls of Pompeii "display dozens of blasphemous graffiti, insults to Venus (patron deity of the town), or, in a tavern, an obscene painting at Isis' expense."[24] Another famous graffiti, this one from a wall in Rome and dating from about 200 CE, shows a man in front of an ass-headed figure on the cross and reads:

Alexamenos worships his god.[25]

Sacrilegious graffiti testify to two different matters: irreligious (or anti-religious) sentiments and religious conflict. The blasphemies on the walls of Pompeii probably reflect the former—being the equivalent of "God is dead" scrawled in alleys. The depiction of Christ with the head of an ass might be irreligious, or it might be specifically anti-Christian. Pagan curse tablets have been found in Britain directed against Christians.[26] In any event:

12. What percentage of all inscriptions, and also of all religious inscriptions specifically, are sacrilegious? Can distinctions be made between blasphemy and conflict?

I suppose that blasphemy and religious conflict would both reflect a changing and competitive religious situation. Are these measures correlated with the influx of faiths from the East?

In addition to religious conflicts, many (most?) Greco-Roman cities suffered from intense ethnic hatreds that often broke out into bloody riots. Consequently, we might ask:

13. What proportion of inscriptions include ethnic slurs?

14. How much variety is there in the groups attacked by such slurs? Is it a one-sided, two-sided, or many-sided phenomenon?

15. What group(s) was (were) the primary target(s)?

Finally, Greco-Roman cities also suffered from political conflicts and rebellions. Hence:

16. What is the prevalence of inscriptions involving political protest? Toward whom are such inscriptions directed? How do they correlate with religion variables?

The preceding list is merely illustrative of some of the things that specialists could do to transform the study of religion in the ancient world. One could easily create many similar lists for other primary topics—social class, family life, and slavery, to name but a few. I find the prospects truly glittering, but having only little-remembered schoolboy Latin and no Greek, I can only hope that someday someone else will code some of these measures. For now it is appropriate to review what my present efforts at quantitative analysis may have added to the understanding of early church history.

First of all, the statistics inspire confidence because they are so stable and consistent. A second very encouraging result is that, as mentioned along the way, the data strongly confirm so many things that everyone agrees are true. Christianity did spread from east to west, gaining its earliest congregations in cities that were closer to Jerusalem. It did find a warmer reception in the Hellenic cities. It did reach the port cities sooner than those inland. Had the data not strongly supported these expectations, I would have called off the project. But because of these expected results, the less-expected findings take on considerable weight.

Moreover, although some findings may be somewhat unex-pected, it also is very encouraging that there were no truly 'novel' or implausible findings—results no one ever would have antici-pated. It did not turn out that the Gnostic schools lurked prima-rily in the small inland cities or in those visited by Paul. Nor was Mithraism found to be a big-city movement. Instead, *all* of the re-sults that might be regarded as unexpected had been anticipated by at least a few prior writers and thus are not without pedigree or plausibility.

Consider Paul's missions. The data show that Paul's visits had no independent impact on the speed of Christianization, once ac-count is taken of the existence of Diasporan Jewish communities.

Although this is contrary to the tradition that Paul's mission was to the Gentiles, a careful reading of *Acts* reveals that he focused his attention on witnessing to the Jews. It wasn't Gentiles who whipped him eight different times and repeatedly drove him out of synagogues. Indeed, it seems likely that when Paul taught that converts to Christianity need not observe the Law, the greatest initial appeal might have been not to Gentiles but to the not-very-observant Hellenized Jews of the Diaspora. This, then, is not an instance where a quantitative finding is at utter variance with other evidence.

By the same token, the findings relative to Cybele and Isis encourage us to recognize the extent to which Christianity also was an 'oriental' faith, appealing to the emotions, the conscience, and the intellect, just as Cumont argued vis-à-vis the other new religions from the East. This recognition encourages us to examine more closely how similarities between Isis worship and Christianity may have made the latter more appealing and plausible to pagans. Because this too has been suggested by several respectable scholars,[27] the quantitative result is not novel, but confirms and thereby advances a less popular position.

Nor did the data on the Gnostics come as a sudden shock. Good historians had already argued that the standard bundle of doctrines and movements was an illogical assortment, leading Michael Williams to conclude that substituting a subset of Demiurgist groups makes far more sense. What the correlations add to this discussion is a convincing display that Williams is correct. Now, in addition to qualitative arguments, there are quantitative data showing the strength of the connections within the subset and the lack of connections of this subset to other measures too often lumped with them.

Finally, the data strongly support the notion that Demiurgism originated neither as a Jewish nor as a Christian heresy, but as a pagan creation, just as Kurt Rudolph argued so vigorously.

In the end, what quantification mainly contributes to historical discussions and disputes is discipline. To work with quantitative data, one must make systematic arguments and draw clear conclusions—no dancing about and having it both ways. Then one must deal with concrete evidence for or against. Of course, even when historians are careful to consult quantitative data, they will still sometimes get it wrong. But not nearly as often. And that leads to the fundamental insight that prompted this entire project: when it comes to proportional statements, the opinions of those who wouldn't count, shouldn't count.

Acknowledgments

—m—

THIS BOOK would not have been written were it not for
Robert Wortham. It happened this way. In 1991 I published a
paper based on twenty-two Greco-Roman cities in which I applied quantitative methods to several questions concerning the
Christianization of the urban empire.* I had begun it partly as a
lark, and I was amazed at how well the data behaved statistically
and how much light the results seemed to shed on significant is-
sues. Even so, that effort was quite crude compared with the present study. Moreover, at the time I had no credentials as any sort of
historian, let alone one who studied early Christian history. So in
the article I invited specialists in the area to join the enterprise by
adding significant variables to the data set. Several years later, Tim
Hegedus, a graduate student at the University of Toronto, added a
variable consisting of the location of temples of Isis with results
that complemented mine, and eventually his paper was published.[1]
But that was it.

---

* Stark, 1991, and republished as ch. 6 in Stark, 1996.

I was very surprised when, in August 2003, I discovered that Robert Wortham had taken up my invitation and submitted a paper for the next annual meeting of the Society for the Scientific Study of Religion (SSSR), convening in Norfolk, Virginia, that October. I wrote him asking for an advance copy of the paper and was impressed with his innovations, especially in creating a variable reflecting which of the cities had been missionized by Paul. I had breakfast with Robert and his wife, Carol, at the SSSR meetings, and his interest in my old project motivated me to do more with it, especially since I had learned a great deal more about the history of the early church in the intervening twelve years.[2] Subsequently, Robert brought it to my attention that new studies of the population of Greco-Roman cities had appeared since I had selected the twenty-two having at least 30,000 residents. These new sources indicated that nine more cities within the Roman Empire as of 100 CE had populations at least that large. This substantial increase in the number of cases has, of course, enhanced the statistical stability of the results. Robert has generously offered insightful comments on draft chapters and continues his own interesting work in the area. Thank you, Robert.

I also had the benefit of careful readings of various portions of the book by several distinguished scholars, including Daniel Williams, Michael Allen Williams, and Magnus Zetterholm.

Statistical Appendix

—ɯ—

O N CORRELATIONS: If a correlation were perfect—for example, if all port cities had Christian congregations before any inland city did—then the correlation between these two variables would be 1.0. If there were no correlation between the two—that is, if they varied randomly with respect to one another—then the correlation would be 0.0. Hence, the closer to 1.0, the stronger the correlation. However, in the real world, correlations of 1.0 are rare. When working with data such as these, a correlation of 0.4 is quite respectable.

Table 3-1: Travel and Christianization

	Port cities	Inland cities
Had a church by 100 CE	64%	24%
Had a church by 180 CE	22%	41%
No church by 180 CE	14%	35%
	100%	100%
$n =$	(14)	(17)

$r = .430^{**}$ $V = .413^{*}$ $\gamma = .598^{**}$

By comparing across the first row of the table we can see that most port cities (64 percent) had a church by the end of the first century, while few inland cities (24 percent) had a church that soon. Or, reading across the bottom row, we see that only 14 percent of port cities still lacked a church in 180, while many inland cities (35 percent) still were without a church by that year. These are very substantial differences.

Now look at the correlation coefficients, shown at the bottom of the table. There are many ways to calculate correlations, and specialists disagree as to which is best for what sort of data. To forestall such concerns, the three most appropriate measures are reported here. The first, known as Pearson's product-moment correlation (r), is an extremely robust but conservative measure. The second is Cramer's V. Many experts recommend V because it does not assume the data are ordinal—in other words, that the cases can be ordered on each variable. The variables used in this book meet minimum standards of ordinality (some cities were Christianized *sooner* than others, for example, while ports had *more travelers* than did inland cities). But, rather than endlessly pursue the matter, it is sufficient to provide the coefficients for V, *except* when the analysis involves 2 × 2 tables, one in which each of two variables has two values. In such cases r and V produce precisely the same value. The third measure is gamma (γ). It is a less conservative measure than either r or V, but it has valuable properties when data have limited variability—that is, when they take only a few values. Gamma tends to yield coefficients that are far higher than either r or V, and on 2 × 2 tables it will go to unity (1.000) whenever there is one empty cell.

As shown below the table, all three of these correlations strongly support the hypothesis. Port cities did tend to be Christianized sooner than inland cities. Notice that the correlation as measured by r (.430) and the correlation as measured by γ (.598) both carry two asterisks, while the correlation as measured by V carries only one. The asterisks indicate *statistical significance:* the odds that a correlation this large, and based on this number of cases, could *not* have occurred by random chance. One asterisk means the odds against a chance finding are at least 20 to 1, known as the .05 level of significance. Two asterisks means the odds are at least 100 to 1, or the .01 level of significance. It is not possible, even when analyzing the same set of data, to determine a threshold of significance from one table to the next. Thus, for example, a *V* of .413 is significant in the table above but would not be significant on some others—since significance has to do with the distribution of cases as well as the value of a correlation. It also is the case that gamma tends to require a much higher coefficient in order to achieve significance.

There is a technical dispute among statisticians as to whether significance is meaningful when the data are not based on random samples. These 31 cities were not selected randomly from among all Greco-Roman cities; rather, the set consists of all cities above 30,000 population. Even so, an excellent case has been made for using significance as a guide to whether or not a correlation is sufficiently large to be meaningful, and that is how significance is to be interpreted here.[1] Correlations falling short of the .05 standard (one asterisk) will be dismissed as trivial.

Table 3-2: Distance and Christianization

	Within 1,000 miles of Jerusalem	*More than 1,000 miles from Jerusalem*
Had a church by 100 CE	71%	7%
Had a church by 180 CE	29%	36%
No church by 180 CE	0%	57%
	100%	100%
n =	(17)	(14)

$r = .744^{**}$ $V = .744^{**}$ $\gamma = .950^{**}$

Table 3-3: Hellenism and Christianization

	Very Hellenic cities	Less Hellenic cities
Had a church by 100 CE	63%	8%
Had a church by 180 CE	37%	25%
No church by 180 CE	0%	67%
	100%	100%
n =	(19)	(12)

$r = .733$** $V = .767$** $\gamma = .928$**

Table 3-4: City-Size and Christianization

	Larger cities	Smaller cities
Had a church by 100 CE	75%	30%
Had a church by 180 CE	25%	35%
No church by 180 CE	0%	35%
	100%	100%
n =	(8)	(23)

$r = .430$* $V = .431$* $\gamma = .778$**

Regression 3-1: Hellenism, City-Size, and Christianization

Dependent variable: Christianization
N: 31 Missing: 0
Multiple R-Square = 0.635 Y-Intercept = 0.319
Standard error of the estimate = 0.513
LISTWISE deletion (1-tailed test) Significance levels: **=.01 *=.05

Source	Sum of squares	DF	Mean square	F	Prob.
Regression	12.832	2	6.416	24.403	0.000
Residual	7.362	28	0.263		
Total	20.194	30			

	Unstandardized beta	Standardized beta	Standard error beta	t
Hellenism	1.128	0.681	0.192	5.881**
City-size	0.585	0.317	0.213	2.741*

There are only a few numbers of interest in a regression analysis; the others are there for concerned specialists. Among these are the standardized betas. These are somewhat like correlations, except they reflect the effect of each variable *independent* of the other. That is, .681 represents the impact of Hellenism on Christianization with the effect of city-size removed, and .317 shows the impact of city-size on Christianization with the effect of Hellenism removed. While Hellenism has the greater effect, both variables have a significant independent effect. To see if a particular beta is significant, look to see if the *t* value is marked by asterisks. The other number of importance is the Multiple R-Square. This is the *joint* effect of Hellenism and city-size on Christianization: their combined effect. In this example, there is a very large effect (.635), and together these two variables account for 40 percent of the variation in Christianization (.635 × .635 = .403).

Some might suggest the use of dummy variables here on grounds that city-size and Hellenism are not ordinal variables. But surely city-size *is* ordinal, even if it takes only two values (larger and smaller). Hellenism too is a matter of degree: there was a significant amount of Hellenic influence in all Greco-Roman cities, but some had much more than others. Given the small number of cases (thirty-one) involved here, I usually limit use of regression analysis to three variables; in several instances I use four variables, but only with extreme care and caution. For those readers with specialized statistical concerns, be assured that use of logistic regression did not alter any outcomes.

Table 4-1: Ports and Cybelene Temples

	Port cities	Inland cities
Had a Cybelene temple	57%	12%
No Cybelene temple	43%	88%
	100%	100%
n =	(14)	(17)

$r = .483^{**}$ $\gamma = .818^{**}$

Table 4-2: City-Size and Cybelene Temples

	Larger cities	Smaller cities
Had a Cybelene temple	63%	22%
No Cybelene temple	37%	78%
	100%	100%
n =	(8)	(23)

$r = .382^{*}$ $\gamma = .714$

Regression 4-1: Ports, City-Size, and Cybelene Temples

Dependent variable: Cybelene temples
N: 31   Missing: 0
Multiple R–Square = 0.317   Y-Intercept = 0.062
Standard error of the estimate = 0.407
LISTWISE deletion (1-tailed test)   Significance levels: **=.01   *=.05

Source	Sum of squares	DF	Mean square	F	Prob.
Regression	2.144	2	1.072	6.485	0.005
Residual	4.630	28	0.165		
Total	6.774	30			

	Unstandardized beta	Standardized beta	Standard error beta	t
City-size	0.315	0.295	0.171	1.846
Ports	0.397	0.423	0.150	2.647*

Table 4-3: Cybelene Temples and Christianization

	Cybelene temple	No Cybelene temple
Had a church by 100 CE	80%	24%
Had a church by 180 CE	20%	38%
No church by 180 CE	0%	38%
	100%	100%
n =	(10)	(21)

$r = .546^{**}$ $V = .556^{**}$ $\gamma = .875^{**}$

Regression 4-2: Ports, Cybelene Temples, and Christianization

Dependent variable: Christianization
N: 31   Missing: 0
Multiple R-Square = 0.316   Y-Intercept = 0.786
Standard error of the estimate = 0.702
LISTWISE deletion (1-tailed test)   Significance levels: **=.01   *=.05

Source	Sum of squares	DF	Mean square	F	Prob.
Regression	6.383	2	3.191	6.470	0.005
Residual	13.811	28	0.493		
Total	20.194	30			

	Unstandardized beta	Standardized beta	Standard error beta	t
Ports	0.248	0.153	0.289	0.855
Cybelene temples	0.816	0.472	0.308	2.646*

Table 4-4: Hellenism and Isiac Temples

	Very Hellenic cities	Less Hellenic cities
Had an Isiac temple by 100 CE	74%	25%
No Isiac temple by 100 CE	26%	75%
	100%	100%
n =	(19)	(12)

$r = .477$** $\gamma = .787$**

Table 4-5: Ports and Isiac Temples

	Port cities	Inland cities
Had an Isiac temple by 100 CE	93%	24%
No Isiac temple by 100 CE	7%	76%
	100%	100%
$n =$	(14)	(17)

$r = .693^{**}$ $\gamma = .954^{**}$

Regression 4-3: Ports, Hellenism, and Isiacism

Dependent variable: Isiacism
$N:$ 31   Missing: 0
Multiple R-Square = 0.604   Y-Intercept = 0.041
Standard error of the estimate = 0.329
LISTWISE deletion (1-tailed test)   Significance levels: **=.01 *=.05

Source	Sum of squares	DF	Mean square	F	Prob.
Regression	4.641	2	2.320	21.395	0.000
Residual	3.037	28	0.108		
Total	7.677	30			

	Unstandardized beta	Standardized beta	Standard error beta	t
Ports	0.626	0.626	0.121	5.169^{**}
Hellenism	0.366	0.358	0.124	2.961^{**}

Table 4-6: City-Size and Isiac Temples

	Larger cities	Smaller cities
Had an Isiac temple by 100 CE	75%	48%
No Isiac temple by 100 CE	25%	52%
	100%	100%
$n =$ (8)	(23)

$r = .239$ $\gamma = .532$

Table 4-7: Isiac Temples and Christianization

	Had an Isiac temple by 100 CE	No Isiac temple by 100 CE
Had a church by 100 CE	65%	14%
Had a church by 180 CE	29%	36%
No church by 180 CE	6%	50%
	100%	100%
$n =$ (17)	(14)

$r = .583^{**}$ $V = .583^{**}$ $\gamma = .815^{**}$

Table 4-8: Temples to Cybele and Isis

	Had a temple to Cybele	No temple to Cybele
Had an Isiac temple by 100 CE	90%	38%
No Isiac temple by 100 CE	10%	62%
	100%	100%
$n =$ (21)	(10)

$r = .488^{**}$ $\gamma = .872^{**}$

Regression 4-4: Cybelene Temples, Isiacism, and Christianization

Dependent variable: Christianization
N: 31   Missing: 0
Multiple R-Square = 0.430   Y-Intercept = 0.600
Standard error of the estimate = 0.641
LISTWISE deletion (1-tailed test)   Significance levels: **=.01   *=.05

Source	Sum of squares	DF	Mean square	F	Prob.
Regression	8.678	2	4.339	10.551	0.000
Residual	11.515	28	0.411		
Total	20.194	30			

	Unstandardized beta	Standardized beta	Standard error beta	t
Isiac temples	0.674	0.415	0.265	2.542*
Cybelene temples	0.593	0.344	0.282	2.102*

Table 5-1: Distance and the Diaspora

	Within 1,000 miles of Jerusalem	More than 1,000 miles from Jerusalem
Had a significant Jewish community	47%	7%
No significant Jewish community	53%	93%
	100%	100%
n =	(17)	(14)

$r = .438$** $\gamma = .841$**

Table 5-2: Ports and the Diaspora

	Port cities	Inland cities
Had a significant Jewish community	50%	12%
No significant Jewish community	50%	88%
	100%	100%
$n =$	(14)	(17)

$r = .419^{**}$ $\gamma = .765^{**}$

Regression 5-1: Ports, Closeness to Jerusalem, and the Diaspora

Dependent variable: Diaspora
N: 31   Missing: 0
Multiple R-Square = 0.352   Y-Intercept = −0.086
Standard error of the estimate = 0.384
LISTWISE deletion (1-tailed test)   Significance levels: $^{**}=.01$ $^{*}=.05$

Source	Sum of squares	DF	Mean square	F	Prob.
Regression	2.251	2	1.126	7.620	0.002
Residual	4.136	28	0.148		
Total	6.387	30			

	Unstandardized beta	Standardized beta	Standard error beta	t
Ports	0.366	0.402	0.139	2.638^{*}
Closeness to Jerusalem	0.384	0.421	0.139	2.764^{**}

Table 5-3: City-Size and Diasporan Jewish Communities

	Larger cities	Smaller cities
Had a significant Jewish community	50%	22%
No significant Jewish community	50%	78%
	100%	100%
n =	(8)	(23)

$r = .272$ $\gamma = .565$

Table 5-4: Hellenism and Paul's Visits

	Very Hellenic cities	Less Hellenic cities
Missionized by Paul	42%	0%
Not missionized by Paul	58%	100%
	100%	100%
n =	(19)	(12)

$r = .469^{**}$ $\gamma = 1.000^{**}$

Table 5-5: Ports and Paul's Missions

	Port cities	Inland cities
Missionized by Paul	43%	12%
Not missionized by Paul	57%	88%
	100%	100%
n =	(14)	(17)

$r = .354^{*}$ $\gamma = .678^{*}$

Table 5-6: The Diaspora and Paul's Missions

	Had a significant Jewish community	No significant Jewish community
Missionized by Paul	67%	9%
Not missionized by Paul	33%	91%
	100%	100%
	n = (9)	(22)

$r = .597^{**}$ $\gamma = .905^{**}$

Table 5-7: Paul and Christianization

	Missionized by Paul	Not missionized by Paul
Had a church by 100 CE	100%	23%
Had a church by 180 CE	0%	41%
No church by 180 CE	0%	36%
	100%	100%
	n = (9)	(22)

$r = 577^{**}$ $V = .614^{**}$ $\gamma = .933^{**}$

Table 5-8: The Diaspora and Christianization

	Had a significant Jewish community	Had no significant Jewish community
Had a church by 100 CE	100%	18%
Had a church by 180 CE	0%	46%
No church by 180 CE	0%	36%
	100%	100%
	n = (9)	(22)

$r = .665^{**}$ $V = .753^{**}$ $\gamma = 1.000^{**}$

Regression 5-2: The Diaspora, Paul's Missionizing, and Christianization

Dependent variable: Christianization
N: 31   Missing: 0
Multiple R–Square = 0.514   Y–Intercept = 0.762
Standard error of the estimate = 0.592
LISTWISE deletion (1-tailed test)   Significance levels: **=.01   *=.05

Source	Sum of squares	DF	Mean square	F	Prob.
Regression	10.384	2	5.192	14.820	0.000
Residual	9.810	28	0.350		
Total	20.194	30			

	Unstandardized beta	Standardized beta	Standard error beta	t
Diaspora	0.825	0.464	0.292	2.827**
Paul's missionizing	0.619	0.336	0.303	2.044

Regression 5-3: The Diaspora, Hellenism, and Christianization

Dependent variable: Christianization
N: 31   Missing: 0
Multiple R–Square = 0.721   Y–Intercept = 0.349
Standard error of the estimate = 0.449
LISTWISE deletion (1-tailed test)   Significance levels: **=.01   *=.05

Source	Sum of squares	DF	Mean square	F	Prob.
Regression	14.556	2	7.278	36.144	0.000
Residual	5.638	28	0.201		
Total	20.194	30			

	Unstandardized beta	Standardized beta	Standard error beta	t
Diaspora	0.817	0.459	0.191	4.287**
Hellenism	0.939	0.567	0.178	5.290**

Regression 5-4: Paul, Hellenism, Diaspora, and Christianization

Dependent variable: Christianization
N: 31   Missing: 0
Multiple R-Square = 0.730   Y-Intercept = 0.358
Standard error of the estimate = 0.449
LISTWISE deletion (1-tailed test)   Significance levels: **=.01   *=.05

Source	Sum of squares	DF	Mean square	F	Prob.
Regression	14.744	3	4.915	24.350	0.000
Residual	5.450	27	0.202		
Total	20.194	30			

	Unstandardized beta	Standardized beta	Standard error beta	t
Diaspora	0.705	0.396	0.223	3.158**
Hellenism	0.878	0.530	0.189	4.648**
Paul's missionizing	0.236	0.128	0.244	0.966

Regression 5-5: Diaspora, Isiacism, and Christianization

Dependent variable: Christianization
N: 31   Missing: 0
Multiple R-Square = 0.547   Y-Intercept = 0.579
Standard error of the estimate = 0.571
LISTWISE deletion (1-tailed test)   Significance levels: **=.01   *=.05

Source	Sum of squares	DF	Mean square	F	Prob.
Regression	11.051	2	5.526	16.923	0.000
Residual	9.142	28			
Total	20.194	30			

	Unstandardized beta	Standardized beta	Standard error beta	t
Diaspora	0.901	0.507	0.251	3.582**
Isiacism	0.586	0.361	0.229	2.554*

Regression 5-6: Diaspora, Cybelene Temples, and Christianization

Dependent variable: Christianization
N: 31   Missing: 0
Multiple R-Square = 0.566   Y-Intercept = 0.672
Standard error of the estimate = 0.559
LISTWISE deletion (1-tailed test)   Significance levels: **=.01   *=.05

Source	Sum of squares	DF	Mean square	F	Prob.
Regression	11.432	2	5.716	18.266	0.000
Residual	8.762	28	0.313		
Total	20.194	30			

	Unstandardized beta	Standardized beta	Standard error beta	t
Diaspora	0.971	0.546	0.234	4.158*
Cybelene temples	0.642	0.372	0.227	2.833**

Table 6-1: Ports and Heretical Schools

	Port cities	Inland cities
Had a heretical school	29%	24%
No heretical school	71%	76%
	100%	100%
n =	(14)	(17)

$r = .057$ $\gamma = .130$

Table 6-2: City-Size and Heretical Schools

	Larger cities	Smaller cities
Had a heretical school	63%	13%
No heretical school	37%	87%
	100%	100%
n =	(8)	(23)

$r = .495$** $\gamma = .835$**

Table 6-3: Diasporan Communities and Heretical Schools

	Significant Jewish community	No significant Jewish community
Had a heretical school	33%	23%
No heretical school	67%	77%
	100%	100%
n =	(9)	(22)

$r = .110$ $\gamma = .259$

Table 6-4: Christianization and Heretical Schools

	Had a church by 100 CE	Had a church by 180 CE	No church by 180 CE
Had a heretical school	23%	50%	0%
No heretical school	77%	50%	100%
	100%	100%	100%
n =	(13)	(10)	(8)

$r = .156$ $V = .436$ $\gamma = .225$

Table 6-5: Heretical Schools and Marcionite Congregations

	Had a heretical school	No heretical school
Had a Marcionite congregation	62%	38%
No Marcionite congregation	38%	62%
	100%	100%
$n =$	(8)	(23)

$r = .205$ $\gamma = .443$

Table 6-6: Diasporan Communities and Marcionism

	Had a significant Jewish community	No significant Jewish community
Had a Marcionite congregation	89%	27%
No Marcionite congregation	11%	73%
	100%	100%
$n =$	(9)	(22)

$r = .562^{**}$ $\gamma = .910^{**}$

Table 6-7: Heretical Schools and Valentinian Congregations

	Had a heretical school	No heretical school
Had a Valentinian congregation	88%	9%
No Valentinian congregation	12%	91%
	100%	100%
$n =$	(8)	(23)

$r = .760^{**}$ $\gamma = .973^{**}$

Table 6-8: City-Size and Valentinian Congregations

	Larger cities	*Smaller cities*
Had a Valentinian congregation	75%	13%
No Valentinian congregation	25%	87%
	100%	100%
$n =$	(8)	(23)

$r = .597^{**}$ $\gamma = .905^{**}$

Regression 6-1: City-Size, Heretical Schools, and Valentinianism

Dependent variable: Valentinian congregations
$N:$ 31   Missing: 0
Multiple R-Square = 0.642   Y-Intercept = 0.047
Standard error of the estimate = 0.286
LISTWISE deletion (1-tailed test)   Significance levels: **=.01 *=.05

Source	Sum of squares	DF	Mean square	F	Prob.
Regression	4.101	2	2.051	25.115	0.000
Residual	2.286	28	0.082		
Total	6.387	30			

	Unstandardized beta	Standardized beta	Standard error beta	t
Heretical schools	0.638	0.615	0.135	4.725^{**}
City-size	0.304	0.293	0.135	2.255^{*}

Table 6-9: Heretical Schools and Montanist Congregations

	Had a heretical school	No heretical school
Had a Montanist congregation	88%	65 %
No Montanist congregation	12%	35%
	100%	100%
n =	(8)	(23)

$r = .215$ $\gamma = .577$

Table 6-10: City-Size and Montanist Congregations

	Larger cities	Smaller cities
Had a Montanist congregation	100%	61%
No Montanist congregation	0%	39%
	100%	100%
n =	(8)	(23)

$r = .377^*$ $\gamma = 1.000^{**}$

Table 6-11: Heretical Schools and Manichaeist Congregations

	Had a heretical school	No heretical school
Had a Manichaeist congregation	88%	13%
No Manichaeist congregation	12%	87%
	100%	100%
n =	(8)	(23)

$r = .697^{**}$ $\gamma = .958^{**}$

Table 6-12: City-Size and Manichaeist Congregations

	Larger cities	Smaller cities
Had a Manichaeist congregation	75%	17%
No Manichaeist congregation	25%	83%
	100%	100%
$n =$	(8)	(23)

$r = .539^{**}$ $\gamma = .869^{**}$

Correlations 6-1

	Heretical schools (r)
Valentinians	.760**
Manichaeism	.697**
Montanism	.215
Marcionism	.205

Correlations 6-2

	Demiurgism (r)
Christianization	.186
Diaspora	.127
Hellenism	.134
Ports	.097
City-size	.611**

Table 7-1: Correlations*

	Mithraism (r)
City-size	.019
Ports	.029
Christians	.046
Hellenized	-.158
Diaspora	-.193
Isiac temples	.230
Cybelene temples	.022
Heretical schools	.167
Marcionism	-.100
Valentinianism	.092
Montanism	-.092
Manichaeism	.160
Demiurgism	.156

*The presence of Mithraism in a city is based on the work of Manfred Clauss (2000).

Table 7-2: Ports and Paganism

	Port cities	Inland cities
Substantial paganism	50%	29%
Little paganism	50%	71%
	100%	100%
n =	(14)	(17)

$r = .210$ $\gamma = .412$

Table 7-3: City-Size and Paganism

	Larger cities	Smaller cities
Substantial paganism	75%	26%
Little paganism	25%	74%
	100%	100%
$n =$	(8)	(23)

$r = .439^*$ $\gamma = .789^*$

Table 7-4: Hellenism and Paganism

	Very Hellenic cities	Less Hellenic cities
Substantial paganism	58%	8%
Little paganism	42%	92%
	100%	100%
$n =$	(19)	(12)

$r = .496^{**}$ $\gamma = .876^{**}$

Regression 7-1: Paganism, Hellenism, and Christianity

Dependent variable: Christianization
N: 31   Missing: 0
Multiple R–Square = 0.541   Y-Intercept = 0.407
Standard error of the estimate = 0.575
LISTWISE deletion (1-tailed test)   Significance levels: **=.01   *=.05

Source	Sum of squares	DF	Mean square	F	Prob.
Regression	10.929	2	5.464	16.514	0.000
Residual	9.265	28	0.331		
Total	20.194	30			

	Unstandardized beta	Standardized beta	Standard error beta	t
Hellenic	1.158	0.699	0.244	4.742**
Pagan	0.115	0.069	0.244	0.469

Table 7-6: Heretical Schools and Paganism

	Had a heretical school	No heretical school
Substantial paganism	88%	22%
Little paganism	12%	78%
	100%	100%
n =	(8)	(23)

$r = .591**$ $\gamma = .924**$

Table 7-6: Demiurgism and Paganism

Demiurgism:	High	Medium	None
Substantial paganism	86%	50%	17%
Little paganism	14%	50%	83%
	100%	100%	100%
$n =$	(7)	(6)	(18)

$r = .583$** $\gamma = .821$**

Regression 7-2: City-Size, Demiurgism, and Paganism

Dependent variable: paganism
N: 31   Missing: 0
Multiple R-Square = 0.345   Y-Intercept = 0.175
Standard error of the estimate = 0.415
LISTWISE deletion (1-tailed test)   Significance levels: **=.01   *=.05

Source	Sum of squares	DF	Mean square	F	Prob.
Regression	2.536	2	1.268	7.366	0.003
Residual	4.819	28	0.172		
Total	7.355	30			

	Unstandardized beta	Standardized beta	Standard error beta	t
City-size	0.155	0.139	0.215	0.720
Demiurgist index	0.198	0.492	0.078	2.546*

Notes

—m—

Chapter One: Missions and Methods

1. As Ramsay MacMullen put it: "Of any organized or conscious evangelizing in paganism there are very few signs indeed[;] ...of any god whose cult required or had anything ordinarily to say about evangelizing, there is no sign at all." 1981:98–99.
2. Nock, 1933:12.
3. See MacMullen, 1984:5; Stark, 2001.
4. Stark, 1999; Stark and Finke, 2000.
5. Aldred, 1988; Redford, 1984; Stark, 2001.
6. See Cohen, 1992; Goodman, 1994.
7. See Feldman, 1992; for an extensive summary see Stark, 2001:52.
8. Moore, 1927, 1:324.
9. In Berger, 1979:107.
10. Unless otherwise noted, all biblical quotations are from the Revised Standard Version.
11. In Grant, 1973:61.
12. In Bamberger, 1939:153.
13. *Against Apion,* 2.40.
14. *On the Life of Moses,* 1.27.247.
15. Moore, 1927, 1:324.
16. Frend, 1965:133; Meeks, 1983.
17. von Harnack, 1904, 1:10–11.
18. *The Jewish War,* 7.44.
19. *Acts* 16:13–15; Freed, 1986:302.
20. *Acts* 13:16.
21. *Acts* 13:26.
22. *Acts* 10:22.
23. Mitchell, 1999; Reynolds and Tannenbaum, 1987; Zetterholm, 2003a.
24. *Matthew* 28:18–20.

25. *Romans* 3:29.
26. Engels, [1894] 1967:316.
27. *Mark* 10:31.
28. Judge, 1960:60.
29. Malherbe, 1977:29–59.
30. Theissen, 1982:97.
31. For a summary see Stark, 1996.
32. Lofland and Stark, 1965.
33. Nock, 1938:60.
34. Jenkins, 2001:75.
35. Stark and Bainbridge, 1985.
36. Kox, Meeus, and t'Hart, 1991; Stark and Finke, 2000.
37. Koester, 1982b, esp. p. 108.
38. Koester 1982b; Nock, 1937.
39. Bauckham, 1990.
40. von Harnack, 1904, 1:1.
41. Beard, North, and Price, 1998:276.
42. Beard, North, and Price, 1998:276.
43. See Freke and Gandy, 2001; Price, 2000; and *Journal of Higher Criticism*.
44. Gasque, 1989; Richardson, 1964.
45. Conzelmann, 1987; Gasque, 1989:249; Hanson, 1968.
46. Hanson, 1968; White, 2001.
47. White, 2001.
48. Elliott, 1993.
49. Niebuhr, 1929; Stark and Bainbridge, 1985; Stark and Finke, 2000.
50. Finke and Stark, 1992.
51. Merton, 1957.
52. Stark, 2003.
53. Delumeau, 1977; Stark, 2004:164.
54. von Harnack, 1904–1905, vol. 2.
55. Stark, 2003.

Chapter Two: The Urban Empire

 1. Fletcher, 1997:16.
 2. Stambaugh, 1988; MacMullen, 1974.
 3. Carcopino, 1940:45–46.
 4. Finley, 1977:222.
 5. Carcopino, 1940:33.
 6. Carcopino, 1940:36.
 7. Carcopino, 1940:42.
 8. White, 1984:168.
 9. Stambaugh, 1988:137.
10. Bagnall, 1993:187.
11. Carcopino, 1940:47.
12. Brown, 1978:2.
13. Brown, 1978:6.
14. Johnson, 1976:75.
15. In Ayerst and Fisher, 1971:179–181.
16. Quoted in Grant, 1986:45.
17. MacMullen, 1981:7.

18. Brown, 1995:3–4.
19. Herodotus, [ca. 450 BCE] 1987:152–153.
20. MacMullen, 1981:112.
21. Dodds, 1970:133.
22. Iannaccone, 1995.
23. MacMullen, 1981:109.
24. MacMullen, 1981:100.
25. See Stark and Finke, 2000.
26. Brown, 1978:28.
27. Rostovtzeff, 1926.
28. For a summary, see Brown, 1978, ch. 2, nn. 10–14.
29. Brown, 1978:29.
30. Modern demographers will not identify a place as urban unless it has 2,500 residents, and they set the minimum size for city classification at 50,000.
31. Parkin, 1992; Russell, 1958.
32. Crossan and Reed, 2001.
33. Jeffers, 1999; Longenecker, 1985.
34. Chandler, 1987.
35. *Encyclopaedia Britannica,* 1981, "Pergamum"; Chandler, 1987.
36. Chandler, 1987; Chandler and Fox, 1974; Crossan and Reed, 2001; Gates, 2003; Harrison, 1985; Russell, 1958; Yamauchi, 1980.
37. Holum, 2004:42; Smith, 1878:1; Spencer, 1985.
38. Livingston, 1985:105.
39. Finley, 1977:222.
40. Levick, 1967:46.
41. Zetterholm, 2003b:31.
42. Downey, 1963.
43. Josephus, *Antiquities of the Jews,* bk. 14, ch. 3.
44. Smith, 1878, 1:152.
45. *The Catholic Encyclopedia of 1914.*
46. Smith, 1878, 2:440.
47. Mellink, 1962:734.
48. Yamauchi, 1980:36.
49. Ramsay, [1893] 1979:294.
50. DeVries, LaMoine F. 1997:373.
51. Yamauchi, 1980:107.
52. In Jones, 1978:30.
53. Frank, 1988:231; Nock, 1938:132–133.
54. *The Catholic Encyclopedia of 1914.*
55. Yamauchi, 1980:87–107.
56. Young, 1972.
57. Smith, 1878, 2:906.
58. Godwin, 1981:20, 111.
59. Yamauchi, 1980:57.
60. Smith, 1878, 1:658.
61. Moo, 1985:3.
62. Moo, 1985:5.
63. Smith, 1878, 2:324–325.
64. Pagels, 2003.
65. Smith, 1878, 2:507–508.
66. Finley, 1977; Smith, 1878, 2:162–163.

67. Frank, 1988:228.
68. *Acts* 17:23.
69. See *1 Corinthians* 1:22–25.
70. Frank, 1988:229.
71. Smith, 1878, 1:678.
72. Lane, 1985:94.
73. Judge, 1960:52.
74. Furnish, 1988:20.
75. Theissen, 1982:97.
76. For a summary see Stark, 1996.
77. Donaldson, 1985:261.
78. Frank, 1988:228.
79. Some writers attribute 2 Thessalonians not to Paul, but to a member of his 'school.' Whatever the case, both letters are accepted as among the earliest writings included in the New Testament. See Meeks, 1972; Robinson, 1976.
80. Nock, 1938:160–161.
81. Twenty-six individuals and two households are identified.
82. Nock, 1938:207.
83. Sordi, 1986:28.
84. *The Epistles of Ignatius of Antioch.*
85. Smith, 1878, 2:1056.
86. Smith, 1878, 2:1056–1057.
87. *The Catholic Encyclopedia of 1914.*
88. Smith, 1878, 1:401.
89. *The Catholic Encyclopedia of 1914.*
90. Gascon, 1981:216; Smith, 1878, 2:214.
91. Eusebius, [ca. 325 CE] 1927:139–149.
92. Smith, 1878, 1:923.
93. Smith, 1878, 1:924.
94. In Smith, 1878, 1:924.
95. Smith, 1878, vol. 1:1074.
96. Sjoberg, 1960.
97. Meeks, 1983:15.
98. MacMullen, 1974:27.
99. Five percent of 60 million.

Chapter Three: Christianization

1. von Harnack, 1905, 2:29; MacMullen, 1997:151.
2. Quoted in Gager, 1975:142.
3. *Ecclesiastical History,* 3.37.3.
4. von Harnack, 1905, 2:335n.
5. MacMullen, 1984:29.
6. During their early days in San Francisco the Unificationists encountered a young man who 'converted' within the first half hour of missionizing. Unfortunately for them, he turned out to be psychotic and caused them no end of difficulty before they managed to be free of him.
7. Lofland, 1977:817. Also see Bainbridge, 1978, and Barker, 1984.
8. In Jones, 1953:184.
9. Turner and Killian, 1987.
10. Bulliet, 1979; Stark, 2001:83–85.

11. *Against Celsus,* 3.10.
12. *1 Corinthians* 15:6.
13. For a more complete discussion see Stark, 1996.
14. Russell, 1958; MacMullen, 1984; Wilken, 1984.
15. Wilken, 1984:31.
16. Fox, 1987:317.
17. Goodenough, 1931; Grant, 1978; MacMullen, 1984.
18. See Stark, 1996:10–11.
19. Chuvin, 1990; MacMullen, 1997; McKechnie, 2001.
20. McKechnie, 2001:57.
21. (*r* = .86) Bagnall, 1982, 1987.
22. Galvao-Sobrinho, 1995.
23. von Harnack, 1905, 2:242–246.
24. Aharoni and Avi-Yonah, 1977; Barraclough, 1998; Chadwick and Evans, 1987.
25. *Inscriptiones Graecae ad Res Romanas Pertientes,* 4.841.
26. Meeks, 1983:17.
27. Lopez, 1976:8.
28. Leighton, 1972:59.
29. Lopez, 1976:8.
30. Leighton, 1972:74–75.
31. Casson, 1950; Witt, 1997.
32. MacMullen, 1981:113–114.
33. MacMullen, 1981:115.
34. Koester, 1982a:97.
35. Betz, 1992:130.
36. Batey, 1991.
37. Betz, 1992.
38. von Harnack, 1905, 2:380–381.
39. Riley, 1997.
40. Chadwick, 1966:6.
41. Chadwick, 1966:11.
42. Fischer, 1975:1328.

Chapter Four: Cybele and Isis: 'Oriental' Forerunners

1. Beard, North, and Price, 1998, maps 1 and 2.
2. Cumont, [1906] 1956:20–45.
3. Beard, North, and Price, 1998:287.
4. Cumont, [1906] 1956:28.
5. Burkert, 1985:109.
6. In Burkert, 1987:113.
7. Cumont, [1906] 1956:30.
8. Burkert, 1985:248.
9. Burkert, 1985:248.
10. Cumont, [1906] 1956:39.
11. Cumont, [1906] 1956:31.
12. Beard, North, and Price, 1998:284.
13. Cumont, [1906] 1956:44.
14. Cumont, [1906] 1956:43–44.
15. Roller, 1999.
16. Roller, 1999:108.

17. Roller, 1999:113.
18. Ferguson, 1970:27.
19. Cumont, [1906] 1956:52.
20. Cumont, [1906] 1956:53.
21. Beard, North, and Price, 1998:97.
22. Roller, 1999:317.
23. MacMullen, 1981:116.
24. Beard, North, and Price, 1998:284; Burkert, 1985:120.
25. Albright, 1957:265.
26. Efforts to show that Socrates wasn't guilty of atheism don't alter the fact that he was convicted of that 'crime.'
27. *Encyclopaedia Britannica,* 1981, "Xenophanes."
28. Gaskin, 1989:18.
29. Quoted in Gaskin, 1989:19.
30. Quoted in Gaskin, 1989:31.
31. Quoted in Gaskin, 1989:33–35.
32. Lindberg, 1992.
33. Such views remain largely irrelevant, as demonstrated by the rapid decline of those Protestant denominations that followed radical theologians such as Immanuel Kant or Paul Tillich in proclaiming inert conceptions of God. (See Finke and Stark, 1992; Stark, 2004.)
34. Witt, 1997:25.
35. Witt, 1997.
36. His history of Egypt was the first to present a scheme of the succeeding dynasties and is still in use.
37. Witt, 1997:52–55.
38. Bailey, 1932:258.
39. Bailey, 1932:258.
40. Grant, 1986:103.
41. Apuleius, *The Golden Ass,* 11.25.
42. Working from fragmentary census forms dating from the first several centuries CE, Hopkins (1980) found that from 15 to 21 percent of marriages were between brothers and sisters.
43. Beard, North, and Price, 1998, maps 1 and 2.
44. Witt, 1997:129.
45. Bailey, 1932:271.
46. Hurtado, 2003:266.
47. Barrett, 1996.
48. Irbie-Massie in Donalson, 2003:vii.
49. Donalson, 2003:11–13.
50. Ferguson, 1970:29.
51. For a summary, see Stark and Finke, 2000, ch. 1.
52. Preus, 1987:8.
53. See the snide attacks on Sir Idris Bell and on Ramsay MacMullen in Athanassiadi and Frede, 1999:4.
54. In Benin, 1993:68.
55. In Benin, 1993:52.
56. In Benin, 1993:183.
57. Calvin, [ca. 1555] 1980:52–53.
58. In Benin, 1993:173–174.
59. Bailey, 1932:270–271.

60. Hegedus, 1998; Donalson, 2003; Wild, 1981; Witt, 1997.
61. Kirsch, 2004:9.
62. MacMullen, 1997:2.
63. Bailey, 1932:186.
64. Grant, 1986:34.
65. Bailey, 1932:186.
66. Josephus, *Antiquities of the Jews,* bk. 18, chap. 3.
67. Bailey, 1932:186.
68. Donalson, 2003:132–133.
69. MacMullen, 1981:116.
70. Homans, 1974.
71. Chen, 1995.
72. Tamney and Hassan, 1987.
73. Stark, 2004, ch. 7.
74. For an extended account of these matters see Stark, 2001.

Chapter Five: Paul and the Mission to the Hellenized Jews

1. Meyers, 1988; Stark, 1996a; Weiss, [1937] 1959.
2. Bickerman, 1988:38.
3. Bickerman, 1988:37–38.
4. Zetterholm, 2003a:171.
5. For a summary see Stark, 2001.
6. Claussen, 2003:149.
7. MacLennan and Kraabel, 1986.
8. Barraclough, 1998; Gilbert, 1984; Grant, 1971.
9. Barclay, 1996; Feldman, 1993; Grant, 1973.
10. Barclay, 1996.
11. Tcherikover, [1959] 1999:346–347.
12. Tcherikover, [1959] 1999:353.
13. Barclay, 1996; Zetterholm, 2003b:176.
14. As numbered in the Torah. It is 28:28 in the Old Testament.
15. Roetzel, 1985:80.
16. Tcherikover, [1959] 1999:346.
17. Grant, 1986:45, 104.
18. *1 Corinthians* 10:14–21.
19. Tcherikover, 1958:81.
20. Stark, 1987, 1996a; Stark and Finke, 2000.
21. Leatham, 1997; Stark, 1996b; Stark and Bainbridge, 1985, 1997; Stark and Finke, 2000.
22. Collins, 1983:9.
23. Frend, 1984:35.
24. *Acts* 11:20–24.
25. Nock, 1938:90.
26. Malherbe, 2003:47. Also Judge, 1960–61.
27. Judge, 1960–61:134; Malherbe, 2003:47.
28. MacMullen, 1997:5.
29. Koester, 1982b:110.
30. Koester, 1982b:110.
31. *2 Corinthians* 11:24–25.
32. *1 Corinthians* 15:10.

33. *Against Heresies,* bk. 4, ch. 24.
34. Nock, 1938:121.
35. Ramsay, 1893:57.
36. Malherbe, 2003:65.
37. Meeks and Wilken, 1978:31.
38. Simon, 1964; Wilken, 1971.
39. Rutgers, 1992:115.
40. Baron, 1952; Stow, 1992.
41. Meyers, 1988:73–74.
42. Meyers, 1988:76.
43. Weiss, [1937] 1959:2:670.
44. Rutgers, 1992:118.

Chapter Six: Gnosticism and Heresy

1. Pétrement, 1990:24.
2. King, 2003a; Pagels, 2003.
3. Doresse, 1960; Ehrman, 2003.
4. Grant, 1981:214.
5. Perkins, 1990:371.
6. *Against Heresies,* bk. 1, ch. 2.; bk. 2, ch. 13.10.
7. Williams, 1996:40.
8. Williams, 1996:27.
9. Rudolph, 1992:1033.
10. Stark, 2004.
11. Jenkins, 2001:145.
12. Doresse, 1960:37.
13. Jenkins, 2001:29.
14. Meyer, 2005:2.
15. Quoted in Williams, 1996:8.
16. All quotes from the *The Secret Book According to John* are from Layton, 1987.
17. Williams, 1996:10.
18. Williams, 1996:11.
19. Williams, 1996:11.
20. Pearson, 1990.
21. Jonas, 1967:101.
22. Perkins, 1980:16.
23. *1 Corinthians* 7.
24. Remarkably, in celebrating the greater enlightenment of the Gnostics, Elaine Pagels and Karen King, fellow apologist for Gnosticism, avoid discussing sex. Indeed, in her 1979 book on the Gnostic gospels, Pagels's very brief mentions of sex are limited to conventional Christianity.
25. Douglas M. Parrott's translation.
26. In Williams, 1996:144.
27. Wesley Isenberg's translation.
28. Nock, 1933:252.
29. Grant, 1981:218.
30. *The Gnostics According to St. Epiphanius* (26.4.1–26.5.8) in Layton, 1987:206–208; also Perkins, 1990.
31. Pagels, 1979:xix.
32. Jenkins, 2001:103.

33. Perkins, 1980:10.
34. *Against Heresies,* bk. 1, ch. 18.1.
35. Pagels, 1979:19.
36. Wright, 2003:551.
37. For an extensive list see Williams, 1996.
38. Grant 1981:218.
39. Layton, 1987:360–361.
40. Layton, 1987:366.
41. All quotations from *The Gospel According to Thomas* are from Layton, 1987.
42. Layton, 1987:362–363.
43. Mirecki, 1992a.
44. Layton, 1987; Mirecki, 1992b.
45. Mirecki, 1992b:783.
46. Quotes from Layton, 1987:267, 273–274.
47. Mirecki, 1992b:784; also Rudolph, 1983:322–323.
48. Mirecki, 1992b:784.
49. Sites supported by Ferguson, 1990; Grant, 1981; Layton, 1987; Perkins, 1980; Rudolph, 1987; Williams, 1996.
50. Perkins, 1980:11.
51. Rudolph, 1987; Schmithals, 1971.
52. Grant, 1981:218.
53. Friedlander, 1898.
54. Pearson, 1973:35.
55. Glock and Stark, 1966.
56. von Harnack, 1905:227–228.
57. Clabeaux, 1992a:514.
58. Clabeaux, 1992a; Rudolph, 1987.
59. Clabeaux, 1992a:514.
60. See "Marcionites" in the 1914 *Catholic Encyclopedia*.
61. Williams, 1996:24.
62. Clabeaux, 1992a:514.
63. Jonas, 2001:138.
64. Jonas, 2001:137.
65. von Harnack, [1924] 1990:115.
66. von Harnack, [1924] 1990.
67. Clabeaux, 1992a; Pétrement, 1990; Rudolph, 1987.
68. Pétrement, 1990:35.
69. A. H. B. Logan, 1999, quoted in McKechnie, 2001:169.
70. Pétrement, 1990:36.
71. Perkins, 1980:16.
72. Based on Layton, 1987.
73. Heine, 1992:899.
74. Heine, 1992:899.
75. Stark, 1987, 2004.
76. Trevett, 1996.
77. Heine, 1992:900.
78. Based mainly on Tabbernee, 1997, plus Trevett, 1996.
79. Mirecki, 1992:503.
80. Clauss, 2000:7.
81. Brown, 1969:93.
82. Markschies, 2003:101.

83. Mirecki, 1992:507.
84. Based on Brown, 1969, and Lieu, 1999.
85. Perkins, 1980:3.
86. Williams, 1996:265.

Chapter Seven: The Last Days of Paganism

1. Gibbon, [1776] 1994, 1.15.447.
2. Gibbon, [1776] 1994, 1.2.57.
3. Bowersock, 1990:6.
4. In *Toleration and Other Essays*.
5. Gibbon, [1776] 1994, 1.16.539.
6. MacMullen, 1981:134.
7. Harl, 1990:14.
8. Cumont, 1903.
9. Clauss, 2000; Merkelbach, 1992.
10. M. P. Nilsson, 1974, quoted in Clauss, 2000:7.
11. Clauss, 2000:7.
12. Beard, North, and Price, 1998:280.
13. For example, Cooper, 1996.
14. Merkelbach, 1992:877.
15. Merkelbach, 1981:290.
16. Chuvin, 1990:41.
17. Chuvin, 1990:41.
18. Ulansky, 1989.
19. White, 1990:609.
20. *First Apology,* 66.
21. In Clauss, 2000:168.
22. Merkelbach, 1992:878.
23. White, 1990:609.
24. Cooper, 1996:ix.
25. Gager, 1975:133.
26. A superb example is included in Manfred Clauss's fine study, 2000:26–27.
27. Stark, 2004.
28. Clauss, 2000:33.
29. Clauss, 2000:33.
30. Merkelbach, 1992:878.
31. Clauss, 2000:171.
32. Even one of the strongest current proponents of the traditional view that Constantine quickly destroyed paganism has admitted that there is no evidence of pagan protests. "The opposition to Christianity can [only] be guessed rather than demonstrated . . ." Momigliano, 1963:94.
33. Winkelman, 1961, in Drake, 2000:246.
34. Geffcken, [1920] 1978:120.
35. Both quotes from Bradbury, 1994:123.
36. Drake, 2000:247.
37. Drake, 1996:29.
38. Brown, 1995; Drake, 2000.
39. Drake, 2000:244.
40. Quoted in Drake, 2000:244–287.
41. Drake, 2000:247.

42. Drake, 2000:249.
43. Salzman, 1990.
44. Both quotations from Brown, 1995:12.
45. Brown, 1995:15.
46. Brown, 1995:18.
47. For a summary see Stark, 2004, ch. 3.
48. Bowersock, 1978:18.
49. Gibbon, [1776] 1994, 2.23.864.
50. Levenson, 1990:510.
51. Bowersock, 1978:79–93.
52. Bowersock, 1978:16.
53. Geffcken, [1920] 1978:139.
54. Levenson, 1990:510.
55. Bowersock, 1978:18.
56. Gibbon, [1776] 1994, 2.23.866–867.
57. Chuvin, 1990:44.
58. Geffcken, [1920] 1978:144.
59. Athanassiadi, 1993:13.
60. Drake, 2000:434.
61. Drake, 2000:435.
62. Drake, 2000:434.
63. Drake, 2000:436.
64. *Oratio xviii,* quoted in Drake, 1996:34.
65. Wilken, 1983:128.
66. Bloch, 1963:195.
67. Harl, 1990:7.
68. Harl, 1990.
69. *Divine Institutes,* 5.23.
70. Harl, 1990:27.
71. Harl, 1990:14.
72. Bradbury, 1994:134.
73. In Bradbury, 1994:133.
74. Brown, 1992:23.
75. Bradbury, 1994:133.
76. In Brown, 1995:42.
77. Brown, 1995:42.
78. Bradbury, 1994:135–136.
79. Brown, 1998:632.
80. Brown, 1998:642.
81. Gibbon, [1776] 1994, 3.28.71, 77.
82. Beugnot, 1835; Bloch, 1963.
83. Brown, 1992:136.
84. For a summary see Brown, 1992.
85. Primarily Chuvin, 1990; Geffcken, [1920] 1978, Harl, 1990.
86. Rudolph, 1987:284.
87. Katz, 1954.
88. de Ste. Croix, 1963:29.
89. Rudolph, 1987:367.
90. Kirsch, 2004:18.
91. Garnsey, 1984:3.
92. See Stark, 1996, 2004.

Conclusion: Why Historians Ought to Count

1. Schlesinger, 1962.
2. Barnes, 1995:139.
3. Beard and Beard, 1933:550.
4. Schlesinger, 1945:36.
5. Chuvin, 1990:12.
6. Brown, 1969.
7. Lieu, 1999.
8. Roller, 1999.
9. Bodel, 2001.
10. MacMullen, 1981:6.
11. Gordon, Reynolds, Beard, and Roueche, 1997:216.
12. In Keppie, 1991:95.
13. In Keppie, 1991:122.
14. In Keppie, 1991:122.
15. *Corpus Inscriptionum Judaicarum,* 741.
16. Brooten, 1982; Trebilco, 1991.
17. Stark, 1996.
18. Cook, 1987:21.
19. Rives, 2001:136.
20. MacMullen, 1981:116.
21. Robinson, 1913.
22. MacMullen, 1981:114.
23. MacMullen, 1981:116.
24. MacMullen, 1981:63.
25. See Stark, 1996:146.
26. Reynolds, Beard, and Roueche, 1986:139.
27. Especially by Witt, 1997.

Acknowledgments

1. Hegedus, 1998.
2. As is too often the case, the article was written in 1989 but took two years to appear in print.

Statistical Appendix

1. Blalock, 1979:242; Stark and Roberts, 2002.

Bibliography

—∿—

Aldred, Cyril. 1988. *Akhenaten: King of Egypt*. London: Thames & Hudson.

Athanassiadi, Polymnia. 1993. "Persecution and Response in Late Paganism: The Evidence of Damascius." *The Journal of Hellenic Studies* 113:1–29.

Athanassiadi, Polymnia, and Michael Frede. 1999. Introduction to *Pagan Monotheism in Late Antiquity*, 1–20. Oxford: Clarendon Press.

Ayerst, David, and A. S. T. Fisher. 1971. *Records of Christianity*. Vol. 1. Oxford: Blackwell.

Bagnall, Roger S. 1993. *Egypt in Late Antiquity*. Princeton: University of Princeton Press.

———. 1987. "Conversion and Onomastics: A Reply." *Zeitschrift für Papyrologies und Epigraphik* 69:243–250.

———. 1982. "Religious Conversion and Onomastic Change in Early Byzantine Egypt." *Bulletin of the American Society of Papyrologists* 19:105–124.

Bailey, Cyril. 1932. *Phases in the Religion of Ancient Rome*. Berkeley: University of California Press.

Bainbridge, William Sims. 1978. *Satan's Power: A Deviant Psychotherapy Cult*. Berkeley: University of California Press.

Bamberger, Bernard J. 1939. *Proselytism in the Talmudic Period*. New York: Hebrew Union College Press.

Barclay, John M. 1996. *Jews in the Mediterranean Diaspora*. Berkeley: University of California Press.

Barker, Eileen. 1984. *The Making of a Moonie: Brainwashing or Choice?* Oxford: Blackwell.

Barnes, T. D. 1995. "Statistics and the Conversion of the Roman Aristocracy." *The Journal of Roman Studies* 85:135–147.

Baron, Salo Wittmayer. 1952. *A Social and Religious History of the Jews*. Vols. 1 and 2. New York: Columbia University Press.

Barraclough, Geoffrey, ed. 1998. *Atlas of World History*. New York: HarperCollins.

Barrett, Clive. 1996. *The Egyptian Gods and Goddesses*. London: Diamond Books.

Batey, Richard. 1991. *Jesus and the Forgotten City*. Grand Rapids, MI: Baker Book House.

Bauckham, Richard. 1990. *Jude and the Relatives of Jesus in the Early Church*. Edinburgh, U.K.: T & T Clark.

Beard, Charles A., and Mary R. Beard. 1933. *The Rise of American Civilization*. New ed. New York: Macmillan.

Beard, Mary, John North, and Simon Price. 1998. *Religions of Rome*. Vol. 1: *A History*. Cambridge: Cambridge University Press.

Beck, Roger. 1998. "The Mysteries of Mithras: A New Account of Their Genesis." *The Journal of Roman Studies* 88:115–128.

Berger, David, ed. 1979. *The Jewish-Christian Debate in the High Middle Ages*. Philadelphia: Jewish Publication Society.

Betz, Hans Dieter. 1992. "Hellenism." *Anchor Bible Dictionary* 3:127–135. New York: Doubleday.

Beugnot, Arthur Auguste. 1835. *Histoire de la destruction du paganisme en Occident*. 2 vols. Paris: Firmin Didot Freres.

Bickerman, Elias J. 1988. *The Jews in the Greek Age*. Cambridge: Harvard University Press.

Blalock, Hubert M., Jr. 1979. *Social Statistics*. New York: McGraw-Hill.

Bloch, Herbert. 1963. "The Pagan Revival in the West at the End of the Fourth Century." In *The Conflict Between Paganism and Christianity in the Fourth Century*, ed. Arnaldo Momigliano, 193–218. Oxford: Clarendon Press.

Bodel, John, ed. 2001. *Epigraphic Evidence*. New York: Routledge.

Bowersock, Glen W. 1990. *Hellenism in Late Antiquity*. Ann Arbor: University of Michigan Press.

———. 1978. *Julian the Apostate*. Cambridge: Harvard University Press.

Bradbury, Scott. 1994. "Constantine and the Problem of Anti-Pagan Legislation in the Fourth Century." *Classical Philology* 89:120–139.

Brooten, Bernadette. 1982. *Women Leaders in the Ancient Synagogue*. Chico, CA: Scholars Press.

Brown, Peter. 1998. "Christianization and Religious Conflict." *Cambridge Ancient History* 13:632–664.

———. 1995. *Authority and the Sacred: Aspects of the Christianization of the Roman World*. Cambridge: Cambridge University Press.

———. 1992. *Power and Persuasion in Late Antiquity: Towards a Christian Empire*. Madison: University of Wisconsin Press.

———. 1978. *The Making of Late Antiquity*. Cambridge: Harvard University Press.

———. 1969. "The Diffusion of Manichaeism in the Roman Empire." *The Journal of Roman Studies* 59:92–103.

———. 1963. "Religious Coercion in the Later Roman Empire: The Case of North Africa." *History* 48:282–305.

———. 1961. "Aspects of the Christianization of the Roman Aristocracy." *Journal of Roman Studies* 51:1–11.

Bulliet, Richard W. 1979. *Conversion to Islam in the Medieval Period*. Cambridge: Harvard University Press.

Bultmann, Rudolph. [1921] 1963. *History of the Synoptic Tradition*. Rev. ed. Trans. John Marsh. New York: Harper & Row.

Burkert, Walter. 1987. *Ancient Mystery Cults*. Cambridge: Harvard University Press.

———. 1985. *Greek Religion*. Cambridge: Harvard University Press.

Calvin, John, [ca.1555] 1980. *Sermons on the Ten Commandments*. Grand Rapids, MI: Baker Book House.

Chen, Hsinchih. 1995. *The Development of Chinese Folk Religion, 1683–1945*. Ph.D. dissertation. Seattle: University of Washington.

Carcopino, Jerome. 1940. *Daily Life in Ancient Rome*. New Haven: Yale University Press.

Casson, Lionel. 1950. "Isis and Her Voyage." *Transactions and Proceedings of the American Philological Association* 81:43–56.

Chadwick, Henry. 1966. *Early Christian Thought and the Classical Tradition*. Oxford: Clarendon Press.

Chadwick, Henry, and G. R. Evans. 1987. *Atlas of the Christian Church*. New York: Facts on File.

Chandler, Tertius. 1987. *Four Thousand Years of Urban Growth: An Historical Census*. 2nd ed. Lewiston, NY: Edwin Mellen Press.

Chandler, Tertius, and Gerald Fox. 1974. *Three Thousand Years of Urban Growth*. New York: Academic Press.

Chuvin, Pierre. 1990. *A Chronicle of the Last Pagans*. Cambridge: Harvard University Press.

Clabeaux, John J. 1992. "Marcion." In *The Anchor Bible Dictionary* (vol. 4), ed. David Noel Freedman. New York: Doubleday.

Clauss, Manfred. 2000. *The Roman Cult of Mithras*. New York: Routledge.

Claussen, Carsten. 2003. "Meeting, Community, Synagogue: Different Frameworks of Ancient Jewish Congregations in the Diaspora." In *The Ancient Synagogue from Its Origins until 200 C.E.*, ed. Birger Olsson and Magnus Zetterholm, 144–167. Stockholm: Almqvist & Wiksell.

Cohen, Shaye J. D. 1992. "Was Judaism in Antiquity a Missionary Religion?" In *Jewish Assimilation, Acculturation, and Accommodation*, ed. Menachem Mor, 14–23. Lanham, MD: University Press of America.

Collins, John J. 1983. *Between Athens and Jerusalem: Jewish Identity in the Hellenistic Diaspora*. New York: Crossroad.

Conzelmann, Hans. 1987. *Acts of the Apostles: A Commentary on the Acts of the Apostles*. Minneapolis: Augsburg Fortress Publishers.

Cook, B. F. 1987. *Greek Inscriptions*. Berkeley: University of California Press.

Cooper, D. Jason. 1996. *Mithras: Mysteries and Initiation Rediscovered*. York Beach, ME: Weiser Books.

Crossan, John Dominic, and Jonathan L. Reed. 2001. *Excavating Jesus*. San Francisco: HarperSanFrancisco.

Cumont, Franz. [1906] 1956. *Oriental Religions in Roman Paganism*. New York: Dover.

———. 1903. *The Mysteries of Mithra*. New York: Open Court.

Curran, John. 1996. "Constantine and the Ancient Cults of Rome: The Legal Evidence." *Greece & Rome* 43:68–80.

Delumeau, Jean. 1977. *Catholicism Between Luther and Voltaire*. London: Burns & Oats.

de Ste. Croix, G. E. M. 1963. "Why Were the Early Christians Persecuted?" *Past and Present* 26:6–38.

DeVries, LaMoine F. 1997. *Cities of the Biblical World: An Introduction to the Archaeology, Geography, and History of Biblical Sites*. Peabody, MA: Hendrickson.

Dodds, E. R. 1970. *Pagan and Christian in an Age of Anxiety*. New York: Norton.

Donalson, Malcolm Drew. 2003. *The Cult of Isis in the Roman Empire*. Lewiston, NY: Edwin Mellen Press.

Doresse, Jean. 1960. *The Secret Books of the Egyptian Gnostics*. New York: Viking Press.

Downey, Glanville. 1963. *Ancient Antioch*. Princeton: Princeton University Press.

———. 1957. "Education in the Christian Roman Empire: Christian and Pagan Theories Under Constantine and His Successors." *Speculum* 32:48–61.

Drake, H. A. 2000. *Constantine and the Bishops: The Politics of Intolerance*. Baltimore: Johns Hopkins University Press.

———. 1996. "Lambs into Lions: Explaining Early Christian Intolerance." *Past and Present* 153:3–36.

Ehrman, Bart D. 2003. *Lost Christianities: The Battles for Scripture and Faith We Never Knew*. Oxford: Oxford University Press.

Elliott, John H. 1993. *What Is Social-Scientific Criticism?* Minneapolis: Fortress Press.

Engels, Friedrich. [1894] 1964. "On the History of Early Christianity." In *On Religion,* by Karl Marx and Friedrich Engels, 316–347. Atlanta: Scholars Press.

Feldman, Louis H. 1993. *Jew and Gentile in the Ancient World.* Princeton: Princeton University Press.

———. 1992. "Was Judaism a Missionary Religion in Ancient Times?" In *Jewish Assimilation, Acculturation, and Accommodation,* ed. Menachem Mor, 23–37. Lanham, MD: University Press of America.

Ferguson, Everett, ed. 1990. *Encyclopedia of Early Christianity.* New York: Garland.

Ferguson, John. 1970. *The Religions of the Roman Empire.* Ithaca, NY: Cornell University Press.

Finke, Roger, and Rodney Stark. 1992. *The Churching of America, 1776–1990: Winners and Losers in Our Religious Economy.* New Brunswick: Rutgers University Press.

Finley, M. I. 1977. *Atlas of Classical Archaeology.* New York: McGraw-Hill.

Fischer, Claude S. 1975. "Toward a Subcultural Theory of Urbanism." *American Journal of Sociology* 80:1319–1341.

Fletcher, Richard. 1997. *The Barbarian Conversion: From Paganism to Christianity.* New York: Holt.

Fox, Robin Lane. 1987. *Pagans and Christians.* New York: Knopf.

Frank, Harry Thomas. 1988. *Discovering the Biblical World.* Rev. ed. Maplewood, NJ: Hammond.

Frede, Michael. 1999. "Monotheism and Pagan Philosophy in Later Antiquity." In *Pagan Monotheism in Late Antiquity,* ed. Polymnia Athanassiadi and Michael Frede, 41–67. Oxford: Clarendon Press.

Freed, Edwin D. 1986. *The New Testament: A Critical Introduction.* Belmont, CA: Wadsworth.

Freke, Timothy, and Peter Gandy. 2001. *The Jesus Mysteries: Was the "Original Jesus" a Pagan God?* New York: Three Rivers Press.

Frend, W. H. C. 1984. *The Rise of Christianity.* Philadelphia: Fortress Press.

———. 1965. *Martyrdom and Persecution in the Early Church.* Grand Rapids, MI: Baker Book House.

Gager, John G. 1975. *Kingdom and Community: The Social World of Early Christianity.* Englewood Cliffs, NJ: Prentice-Hall.

Galvao-Sobrinho, Carlos R. 1995. "Funerary Epigraphy and the Spread of Christianity in the West." *Athenaeum* 83:431–466.

Garnsey, Peter. 1984. "Religious Toleration in Classical Antiquity." In *Persecution and Tolerance,* ed. W. J. Sheils, 1–27. Oxford: Blackwell.

Gascon, Richard. 1981. "Lyon." *Encyclopaedia Britannica.* 15th ed. Chicago: University of Chicago Press.

Gaskin, J. C. A., ed. 1989. *Varieties of Unbelief: From Epicurus to Sartre.* New York: Macmillan.

Gasque, W. W. 1989. *A History of the Interpretation of the Acts of the Apostles.* Peabody, MA: Hendrickson.

Gates, Charles. 2003. *Ancient Cities: The Archaeology of Urban Life in the Ancient Near East and Egypt, Greece, and Rome.* London: Routledge.

Geffcken, Johannes. [1920] 1978. *The Last Days of Greco-Roman Paganism.* Amsterdam: North-Holland Publishing.

Gibbon, Edward. [1776] 1994. *The History of the Decline and Fall of the Roman Empire.* Vol. 1. London: Allen Lane/Penguin Press.

Gilbert, Martin. 1984. *Atlas of Jewish History.* 3rd ed. New York: Dorset Press.

Godwin, Joscelyn. 1981. *Mystery Religions in the Ancient World.* San Francisco: Harper & Row.

Goodenough, Erwin R. 1931. *The Church in the Roman Empire*. New York: Holt.

Goodman, Martin. 1994. *Mission and Conversion: Proselytizing in the Religious History of the Roman Empire*. Oxford: Clarendon Press.

Gordon, Richard, Joyce Reynolds, Mary Beard, and Charlotte Roueche. 1997. "Roman Inscriptions 1991–95." *The Journal of Roman Studies* 87:203–240.

Grant, Michael. 1978. *The History of Rome*. New York and London: Faber & Faber.

———. 1973. *The Jews in the Roman World*. New York: Scribner.

———. 1971. *Atlas of Ancient History, 1700 B.C. to 565 A.D.* New York: Dorset Press.

Grant, Robert M. 1986. *Gods and the One God*. Philadelphia: Westminster Press.

———. 1981. "Gnosticism." *Encyclopaedia Britannica*. 15th ed. Chicago: University of Chicago Press.

Harl, K. W. 1990. "Sacrifice and Pagan Belief in Fifth- and Sixth-Century Byzantium." *Past and Present* 128:7–27.

Hegedus, Tim. 1998. "The Urban Expansion of the Isis Cult: A Quantitative Approach." *Studies in Religion* 27:161–178.

Heine, Ronald E. 1992. "Montanus, Montanism." *Anchor Bible Dictionary* 4:898–902. New York: Doubleday.

Herodotus. [ca. 450 BCE] 1987. *The History*. Trans. David Grene. Chicago: University of Chicago Press.

Holum, Kenneth G. 2004. "Building Power: The Politics of Architecture." *Biblical Archaeology Review* 30:36–45, 57.

Homans, George C. 1974. *Social Behavior: Its Elementary Forms*. New York: Harcourt Brace Jovanovich.

Hopkins, Keith. 1980. "Brother-Sister Marriage in Roman Egypt." *Comparative Studies in Society and History* 22:303–354.

Hurtado, Larry W. 2003. *Lord Jesus Christ: Devotion to Jesus in Earliest Christianity*. Grand Rapids, MI: Eerdmans.

Iannaccone, Laurence R. 1995. "Risk, Rationality, and Religious Portfolios." *Economic Inquiry* 33:285–295.

Irbie-Massie, Georgia. 2003. Preface to *The Cult of Isis in the Roman Empire,* by Malcolm Drew Donalson, vii–viii. Lewiston, NY: Edwin Mellen Press.

Jaki, Stanley L. 1986. *Science and Creation*. Edinburgh, U.K.: Scottish Academic Press.

Jeffers, James S. 1999. *The Greco-Roman World of the New Testament Era*. Downers Grove, IL: InterVarsity Press.

Jenkins, Philip. 2001. *Hidden Gospels: How the Search for Jesus Lost Its Way*. Oxford: Oxford University Press.

Jonas, Hans. 2001. *The Gnostic Religion*. 3rd ed. Boston: Beacon Press.

———. 1967. "Delimitation of the Gnostic Phenomenon—Typological and Historical." In *Le origini dello Gnosticismo*, ed. U. Bianchi, 90–108. Leiden, Neth.: Brill.

Jones, Ernest. 1953. *Life and Works of Sigmund Freud*. Vol. 1. New York: Hogarth Press.

Judge, E. A. 1960–1961. "The Early Christians as a Scholastic Community." *Journal of Religious History* 1:125–141.

———. 1960. *The Social Pattern of Christian Groups in the First Century*. London: Tyndale.

Katz, Joseph. 1954. "Plotinus and the Gnostics." *Journal of the History of Ideas* 15: 289–298.

Keppie, Lawrence. 1991. *Understanding Roman Inscriptions*. Baltimore: Johns Hopkins University Press.

King, Karen L. 2003a. *The Gospel of Mary of Magdala: Jesus and the First Woman Apostle*. Santa Rosa, CA: Polebridge Press.

———. 2003b. *What Is Gnosticism?* Cambridge: Belknap Press.

Kirsch, Jonathan. 2004. *God Against the Gods*. New York: Viking.

Koester, Helmut. 1982a. *Introduction to the New Testament*. Vol. 1: *History, Culture, and Religion in the Hellenistic Age*. Philadelphia and Berlin: Fortress Press/Walter De Gruyter.

———. 1982b. *Introduction to the New Testament*. Vol. 2: *History and Literature of Early Christianity*. Philadelphia and Berlin: Fortress Press/Walter De Gruyter.

Kox, Willem, Wim Meeus, and Harm t'Hart. 1991. "Religious Conversion of Adolescents: Testing the Lofland and Stark Model of Religious Conversion." *Sociological Analysis* 52:227–240.

Kummel, Werner. 1972. *The New Testament: The History of the Investigation of Its Problems*. Nashville: Abingdon.

Lane, W. L. 1985. "Corinth." In *Major Cities of the Biblical World*, ed. R. K. Harrison, 83–95. Nashville: Thomas Nelson.

Layton, Bentley. 1987. *The Gnostic Scriptures*. Garden City, NY: Doubleday.

Leatham, Miguel C. 1997. "Rethinking Religious Decision-Making in Peasant Millenarianism: The Case of Nueva Jerusalem." *Journal of Contemporary Religion* 12: 295–309.

Leighton, Albert C. 1972. *Transportation and Communication in Early Medieval Europe, A.D. 500–1100*. Newton Abbot, U.K.: David and Charles.

Levenson, David. B. 1990. "Julian." In *Encyclopedia of Early Christianity*, ed. Everett Ferguson, 510–511. New York: Garland.

Levi, Peter. 1980. *Atlas of the Greek World*. New York: Facts on File.

Levick, Barbara. 1967. *Roman Colonies in Southern Asia Minor*. Oxford: Clarendon.

Lieu, Samuel N. C. 1999. *Manichaeism in Mesopotamia and the Roman East*. Leiden, Neth.: Brill.

Lindberg, David C. 1992. *The Beginnings of Western Science*. Chicago: University of Chicago Press.

Livingston, G. H. 1985. "Damascus." In *Major Cities of the Biblical World*, ed. R. K. Harrison, 96–106. Nashville: Thomas Nelson.

Lofland, John. 1977. "'Becoming a World-Saver' Revisited." *American Behavioral Scientist* 20:805–818.

Lofland, John, and Rodney Stark. 1965. "Becoming a World-Saver: A Theory of Conversion to a Deviant Perspective." *American Sociological Review* 30:862–875.

Longenecker, R. N. 1985. "Antioch of Syria." In *Major Cities of the Biblical World*, ed. R. K. Harrison, 8–21. Nashville: Thomas Nelson.

Lopez, Robert S. 1976. *The Commercial Revolution of the Middle Ages*. Cambridge: Cambridge University Press.

MacLennan, Robert S., and A. Thomas Kraabel. 1986. "The God-Fearers: A Literary and Theological Invention." *Biblical Archaeology Review* 12:47–53.

MacMullen, Ramsay. 1997. *Christianity and Paganism in the Fourth to Eighth Centuries*. New Haven: Yale University Press.

———. 1984. *Christianizing the Roman Empire (A.D. 100–400)*. New Haven: Yale University Press.

———. 1981. *Paganism in the Roman Empire*. New Haven: Yale University Press.

Malherbe, Abraham J. 2003. *Social Aspects of Early Christianity*. 2nd ed. Eugene, OR: Wipf & Stock.

Markschies, Christoph. 2003. *Gnosis: An Introduction*. London: T & T Clark.

McCormick, Richard P. 1960. "New Perspectives on Jacksonian Politics." *The American Historical Review* 65:288–301.

McKechnie, Paul. 2001. *The First Christian Centuries: Perspectives on the Early Church*. Downers Grove, IL: InterVarsity Press.

Meeks, Wayne. 1983. *The First Urban Christians*. New Haven: Yale University Press.

———. 1972. *The Writings of St. Paul*. New York: Norton.

Meeks, Wayne A., and Robert L. Wilken. 1978. *Jews and Christians in Antioch in the First Four Centuries of the Common Era*. Missoula, MT: Scholars Press.

Mellink, Machteld J. 1962. "Pergamum" ed. G. A. Buttrick, *The Interpreter's Dictionary of the Bible*, Vol. III. Nashville: Abingdon: 734.

Merkelbach, R. 1992. "Mithra, Mithraism." *Anchor Bible Dictionary* 4:877–878. New York: Doubleday.

———. 1981. "Mithraism." *Encyclopaedia Britannica.* 15th ed. Chicago: University of Chicago Press.

Merton, Robert K. 1957. *Social Theory and Social Structure.* Rev. ed. Glencoe, IL: Free Press.

Meyer, Marvin. 2005. *The Gnostic Discoveries: The Impact of the Nag Hammadi Library.* San Francisco: HarperSanFrancisco.

Meyers, Eric M. 1988. "Early Judaism and Christianity in the Light of Archaeology." *Biblical Archaeologist* 51:69–79.

Mirecki, Paul Allan. 1992a. "Basilides." *Anchor Bible Dictionary* 1:624–625. New York: Doubleday.

———. 1992b. "Manichaeans and Manichaeism." *Anchor Bible Dictionary* 4:502–511. New York: Doubleday.

———. 1992c. "Valentinus." *Anchor Bible Dictionary* 6:783–784. New York: Doubleday.

Mitchell, Stephen. 1999. "The Cult of Theos Hypsistos Between Oragans, Jews, and Christians." In *Pagan Monotheism in Late Antiquity,* ed. Polymnia Athanassiadi and Michael Frede, 81–148. Oxford: Clarendon Press.

Momigliano, Arnaldo, ed. 1963. *The Conflict Between Paganism and Christianity in the Fourth Century.* Oxford: Clarendon Press.

Moo, D. J. 1985. "Alexandria." In *Major Cities of the Biblical World,* ed. R. K. Harrison, 1–7. Nashville: Thomas Nelson.

Moore, George Foot. 1927. *Judaism in the First Centuries of the Christian Era.* Vol. 1. Cambridge: Harvard University Press.

Niebuhr, H. Richard. 1929. *The Social Sources of Denominationalism.* New York: Holt.

Nock, A. D. 1937. *St. Paul.* New York: Harper & Brothers.

———. 1933. *Conversion: The Old and the New in Religion from Alexander the Great to Augustine of Hippo.* Oxford: Clarendon Press.

Pagels, Elaine. 2003. *Beyond Belief: The Secret Gospel of Thomas.* New York: Random House.

———. 1979. *The Gnostic Gospels.* New York: Random House.

Parkin, Tim G. 1992. *Demography and Roman Society.* Baltimore: Johns Hopkins University Press.

Pearson, Birger A. 1990. *Gnosticism, Judaism, and Egyptian Christianity.* Minneapolis: Fortress Press.

Perkins, Pheme. 1990. "Gnosticism." In *Encyclopedia of Early Christianity,* ed. Everett Ferguson, 371–376. New York: Garland.

———. 1980. *The Gnostic Dialogue: The Early Church and the Crisis of Gnosticism.* New York: Paulist Press.

Pétrement, Simone. 1990. *A Separate God: The Christian Origins of Gnosticism.* San Francisco: HarperSanFrancisco.

Preus, J. Samuel. 1987. *Explaining Religion: Criticism and Theory from Bodin to Freud.* New Haven: Yale University Press.

Price, Robert M. 2000. *Deconstructing Jesus.* Amherst, NY: Prometheus Books.

Ramsay, W. M. [1893] 1979. *The Church in the Roman Empire Before A.D. 170.* New York: Putnam.

Redford, Donald B. 1984. *Akhenaten: The Heretic King.* Princeton: Princeton University Press.

Reynolds, Joyce, and Robert Tannenbaum. 1987. *Jews and God-Fearers at Aphrodisias.* Cambridge: Cambridge University Press.

Reynolds, Joyce, Mary Beard, and Charlotte Roueche. 1986. "Roman Inscriptions 1981–5." *The Journal of Roman Studies* 76:124–146.

Riley, Gregory J. 1997. *One Jesus, Many Christs*. San Francisco: HarperSanFrancisco.

Rives, James. 2001. "Civic and Religious Life." In *Epigraphic Evidence,* ed. John Bodel, 118–136. New York: Routledge.

———. 1995. *Religion and Authority in Roman Carthage from Augustus to Constantine*. New York: Oxford University Press.

Robinson, Dwight Nelson. 1913. "A Study of the Social Position of the Devotees of the Oriental Cults in the Western World, Based on Inscriptions." *Transactions and Proceedings of the American Philological Association* 44:151–161.

Robinson, John A. T. 1985. *The Priority of John*. Oak Park, IL: Meyer Stone Books.

———. 1976. *Redating the New Testament*. Philadelphia: Westminster Press.

Roetzel, Calvin J. 1985. *The World Shaped by the New Testament*. Atlanta: John Knox Press.

Roller, Lynn E. 1999. *In Search of God the Mother: The Cult of Anatolian Cybele*. Berkeley: University of California Press.

Rorty, Richard. 1998. "Pragmatism as Romantic Polytheism." In *The Revival of Pragmatism,* ed. Morris Dickstein, 21–36. Durham, NC: Duke University Press.

Rostovtzeff, Michael. 1926. *The Social and Economic History of the Roman Empire*. Oxford: Clarendon Press.

Rudolph, Kurt. 1992. "Gnosticism." *Anchor Bible Dictionary* 2:1033–1040. New York: Doubleday.

———. 1987. *Gnosis: The Nature and History of Gnosticism*. San Francisco: HarperSanFrancisco.

Russell, J. C. 1958. "Late Ancient and Medieval Population." *Transactions of the American Philosophical Society* 48:3.

Rutgers, Leonard Victor. 1992. "Archaeological Evidence for the Interaction of Jews and Non-Jews in Late Antiquity." *American Journal of Archaeology* 96:101–118.

Salzman, Michael. 1990. *On Roman Time: The Codex-Calendar of 354*. Berkeley: University of California Press.

Schlesinger, Arthur, Jr. 1962. "A Humanist Looks at Empirical Social Research." *American Sociological Review* 27:768–771.

———. 1945. *The Age of Jackson*. Boston: Little, Brown.

Schmithals, Walter. 1971. *Gnosticism in Corinth*. Nashville: Abingdon Press.

Sjoberg, Gideon. 1960. *The Preindustrial City*. New York: Free Press.

Smith, William, ed. 1878. *A Dictionary of Greek and Roman Geography*. London: John Walton.

Spencer, A. B. 1985. "Caesarea Maritima." In *Major Cities of the Biblical World,* ed. R. K. Harrison, 63–71. Nashville: Thomas Nelson.

Stambaugh, John E. 1988. *The Ancient Roman City*. Baltimore: Johns Hopkins University Press.

Stark, Rodney. 2004. *Exploring the Religious Life*. Baltimore: Johns Hopkins University Press.

———. 2003. *For the Glory of God: How Monotheism Led to Reformation, Science, Witch-Hunts, and the End of Slavery*. Princeton: Princeton University Press.

———. 2001. *One True God: Historical Consequences of Monotheism*. Princeton: Princeton University Press.

———. 1999. "Secularization, R.I.P." *Sociology of Religion* 60:249–273.

———. 1996a. *The Rise of Christianity: A Sociologist Reconsiders History*. Princeton: Princeton University Press.

———. 1996b. "Why Religious Movements Succeed or Fail: A Revised General Model." *Journal of Contemporary Religion* 11:133–146.

Stark, Rodney, and William Sims Bainbridge. 1997. *Religion, Deviance, and Social Control.* New York: Routledge.

————. 1985. *The Future of Religion: Secularization, Revival, and Cult Formation.* Berkeley: University of California Press.

Stark, Rodney, and Roger Finke. 2000. *Acts of Faith: Explaining the Human Side of Religion.* Berkeley: University of California Press.

Stark, Rodney, and Lynne Roberts. 2002. *Contemporary Social Research Methods.* Belmont, CA: Wadsworth.

Stow, Kenneth R. 1992. *Alienated Minority: The Jews of Medieval Latin Europe.* Cambridge: Harvard University Press.

Strauss, David Friedrich. [1840] 1972. *The Life of Jesus Critically Examined.* Philadelphia: Fortress Press.

Tabbernee, William. 1997. *Montanist Inscriptions and Testimonia: Epigraphic Sources Illustrating the History of Montanism.* Macon, GA: Mercer University Press.

Tamney, Joseph B., and Riaz Hassan. 1987. *Religious Switching in Singapore.* Flinders, Australia: Select Books.

Tcherikover, Victor. [1959] 1999. *Hellenistic Civilization and the Jews.* Peabody, MA: Hendrickson.

————. 1958. "The Ideology of the Letter of Aristeas." *Harvard Theological Review* 61:59–85.

Theissen, Gerd. 1992. *Social Reality and Early Christians.* Minneapolis: Fortress Press.

————. 1982. *The Social Setting of Pauline Christianity: Essays on Corinth.* Philadelphia: Fortress Press.

————. 1978. *Sociology of Early Palestinian Christianity.* Philadelphia: Fortress Press.

Trebilco, Paul. 1991. *Jewish Communities in Asia Minor.* Cambridge: Cambridge University Press.

Trevett, Christine. 1996. *Montanism: Gender, Authority and the New Prophecy.* Cambridge: Cambridge University Press.

Ulansky, David. 1989. *The Origins of the Mithraic Mysteries: Cosmology and Salvation in the Ancient World.* New York: Oxford University Press.

von Harnack, Adolf. [1924] 1990. *Marcion: The Gospel of the Alien God.* Durham, NC: Labyrinth Press.

————. 1905. *The History of Dogma.* Vol. 1. London: Williams & Norgate.

————. 1904–1905. *The Mission and Expansion of Christianity in the First Three Centuries.* 2 vols. New York: Putnam.

Weiss, Johannes. [1937] 1959. *Earliest Christianity: A History of the Period A.D. 30–150.* 2 vols. New York: Harper Torchbooks.

West, M. L. 1999. "Towards Monotheism." In *Pagan Monotheism in Late Antiquity,* ed. Polymnia Athanassiadi and Michael Frede, 21–40. Oxford: Clarendon Press.

White, Jefferson. 2001. *Evidence and Paul's Journeys.* Hilliard, OH: Parsagard Press.

White, K. D. 1984. *Greek and Roman Technology.* London: Thames & Hudson.

Wild, Robert A. 1981. *Water in the Cultic Worship of Isis and Sarapis.* Leiden, Neth.: E. J. Brill.

Williams, Michael Allen. 1996. *Rethinking "Gnosticism": An Argument for Dismantling a Dubious Category.* Princeton: Princeton University Press.

Wilken, Robert L. 1984. *The Christians as the Romans Saw Them.* New Haven: Yale University Press.

————. 1983. *John Chrysostom and the Jews: Rhetoric and Reality in the Late Fourth Century.* Berkeley: University of California Press.

Witt, R. E. 1997. *Isis in the Ancient World.* Baltimore: Johns Hopkins University Press.

Wright, N. T. 2003. *The Resurrection of the Son of God.* Minneapolis: Fortress Press.

Yamauchi, Edwin M. 1980. *The New Testament Cities in Western Asia.* Grand Rapids, MI: Baker Book House.

Young, W. J. 1972. "The Fabulous Gold of the Pactolus Valley." *Bulletin of the Museum of Fine Arts, Boston* 70:4–13.

Zetterholm, Magnus. 2003a. "The Covenant for Gentiles? Covenantal Nomism and the Incident at Antioch." In *The Ancient Synagogue from Its Origins until 200 C.E.*, ed. Birger Olsson and Magnus Zetterholm, 168–188. Stockholm: Almqvist & Wiksell.

Zetterholm, Magnus. 2003b. *The Formation of Christianity in Antioch*. London: Routledge.

Index